Letter Review

Letter Review

Say the name for each picture. (Circle) the letter that stands for its **beginning** sound. Write the lowercase letter on the double lines.

1. m
   p
   s

2. s
   w
   m

3. c
   n
   b

4. r
   p
   b

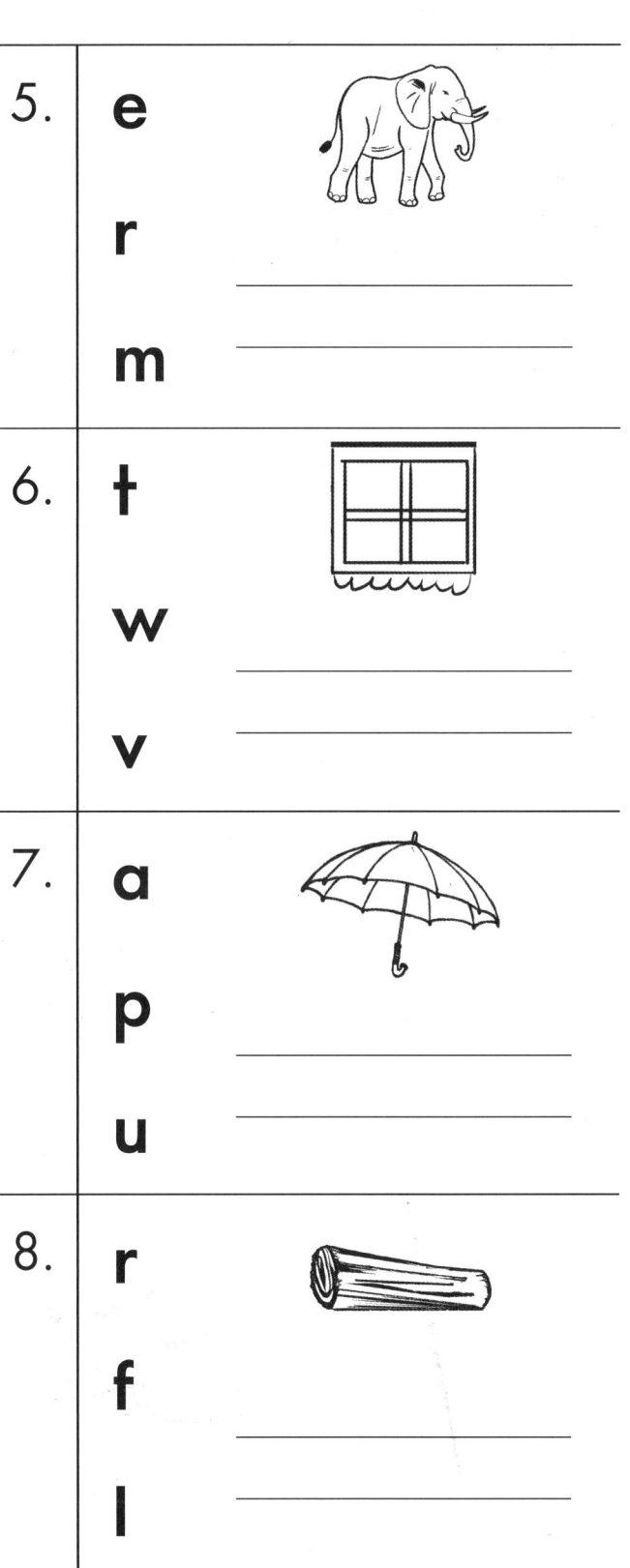

5. e
   r
   m

6. t
   w
   v

7. a
   p
   u

8. r
   f
   l

64 A–Z for Mat Man and Me: Practice for Developing Readers © 2022 Learning Without Tears

Letter Check 3

Letter Check 3, Part B

Say the name for each picture. Circle the letter that stands for its **beginning** sound. Write the lowercase letter on the double lines.

1.	x k a		5.	e r k
2.	s j t		6.	b n q
3.	k t f		7.	e g z
4.	y j s		8.	r w i

© 2022 Learning Without Tears

Letter Check 3

Letter Check 3, Part A

Say the name for each picture. Circle the letter that stands for its **beginning** sound. Write the lowercase letter on the double lines.

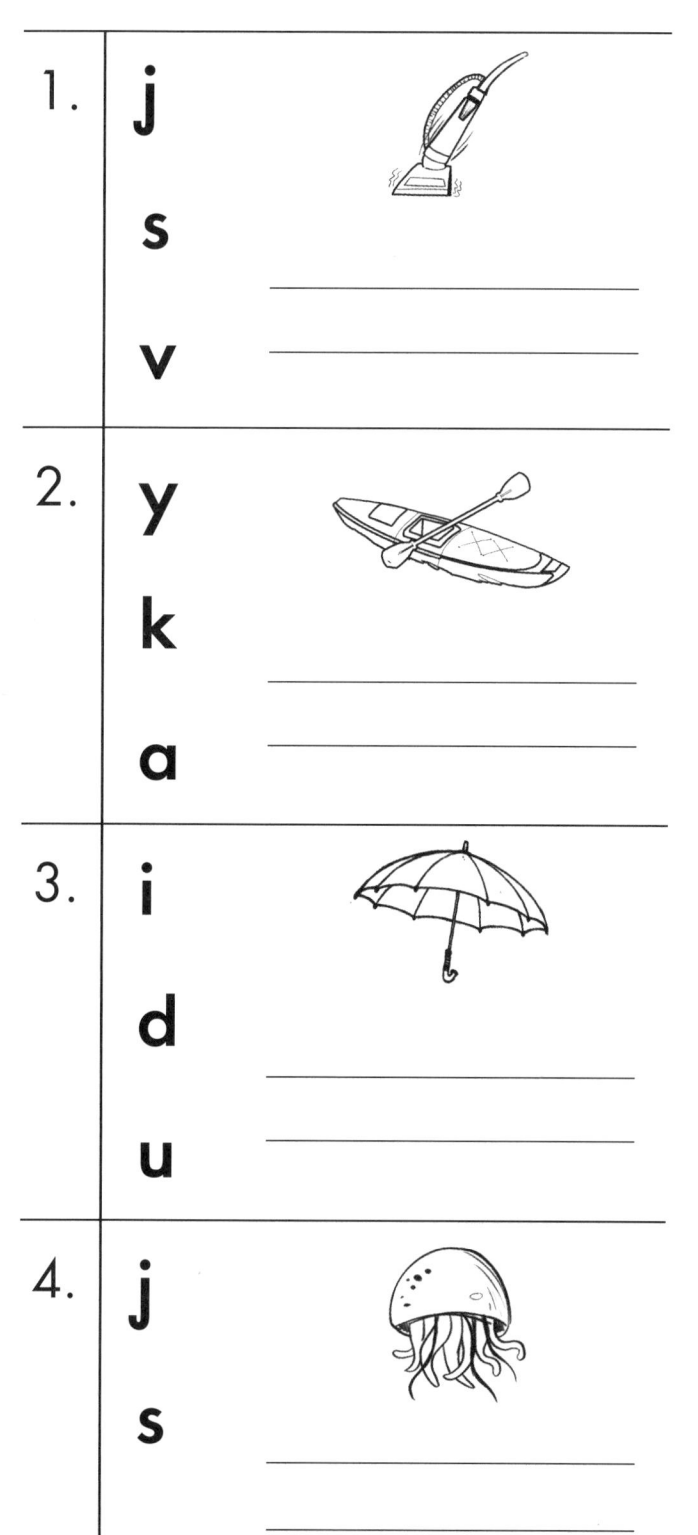

1.	j s v		5.	w f n	
2.	y k a		6.	d q e	
3.	i d u		7.	g p o	
4.	j s p		8.	q i l	?

Letter Check 2

Letter Check 2, Part B

Say the name for each picture. Circle the letter that stands for its **beginning** sound.
Write the lowercase letter on the double lines.

1. r l g

2. c p v

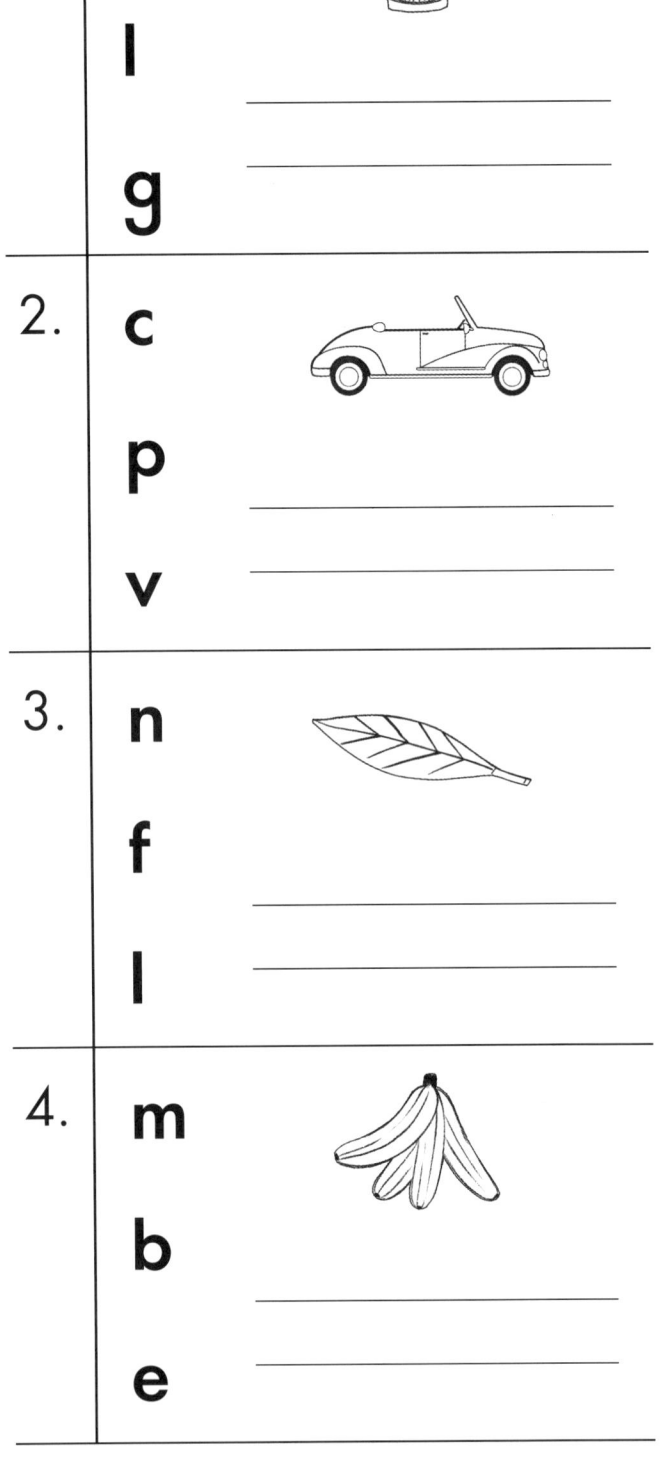

3. n f l

4. m b e

5. m d z

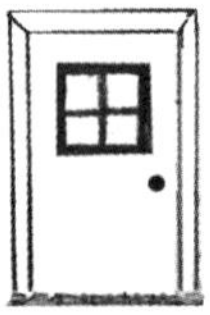

6. h l w

7. i d o

8. f g j

Letter Check 2, Part A

Say the name for each picture. Circle the letter that stands for its **beginning** sound.
Write the lowercase letter on the double lines.

1. l
   d
   k

2. p
   h
   b

3. g
   w
   s

4. z
   t
   l

5. f
   x
   i

6. b
   n
   h

7. n
   d
   c

8. o
   z
   r

Letter Check 1

Letter Check 1, Part B

Say the name for each picture. Circle the letter that stands for its **beginning** sound. Write the lowercase letter on the double lines.

1. s / r / l

2. i / y / p

3. p / n / g

4. k / s / r

5. a / v / m

6. b / v / a

7. t / n / r

8. t / q / p

© 2022 Learning Without Tears — A–Z for Mat Man® and Me: Practice for Developing Readers — 59

Letter Check 1

Letter Check 1, Part A

Say the name for each picture. Circle the letter that stands for its **beginning** sound. Write the lowercase letter on the double lines.

1. m
   p
   a

2. s
   p
   t

3. i
   n
   b

4. r
   d
   p

5. g
   r
   m

6. t
   s
   v

7. a
   b
   u

8. r
   o
   i

58 A–Z for Mat Man® and Me: Practice for Developing Readers

© 2022 Learning Without Tears

Zack and His Zipper — Zz

Understanding the Story: Characters

Think about what Zack does and how he feels. When does Zack feel mad? Draw and write about it.

When does Zack feel happy in the story? Draw and write.

© 2022 Learning Without Tears — A–Z for Mat Man® and Me: Practice for Developing Readers - **Meaning Making**

Zz Zack and His Zipper

Practice the Letter Zz

Say the letter name and the sound it stands for. Then, trace and write capital Z and lowercase z.

zipper

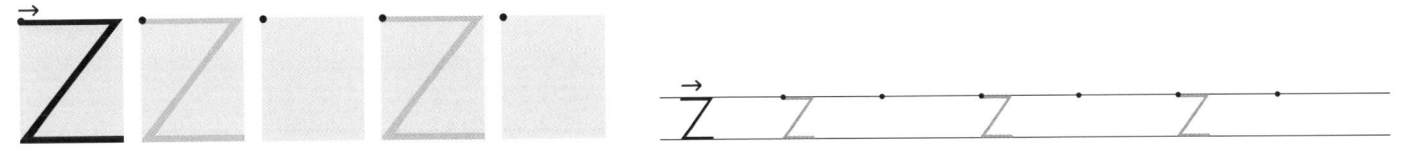

Read as much as you can. Then, circle every capital Z and lowercase z you see.

Liz zips up her coat.

It is a size too big.

It keeps out the breeze.

Liz and Zoe get to the zoo!

They look at a zebra.

Think of two things that start with the same beginning sound as **zipper**. Draw them.

Practice the Letter Yy — Yy

Understanding the Story: Events

Think about what happens in the story. The middle of the story is filled in. Now, draw and write about what happens in the beginning and end.

Beginning

Middle

Yaz does not trade back.

End

© 2022 Learning Without Tears — A–Z for Mat Man® and Me: Practice for Developing Readers - Meaning Making

Yy Practice the Letter Yy

yo-yo

Practice the Letter Yy

Say the letter name and the sound it stands for. Then, trace and write capital **Y** and lowercase **y**.

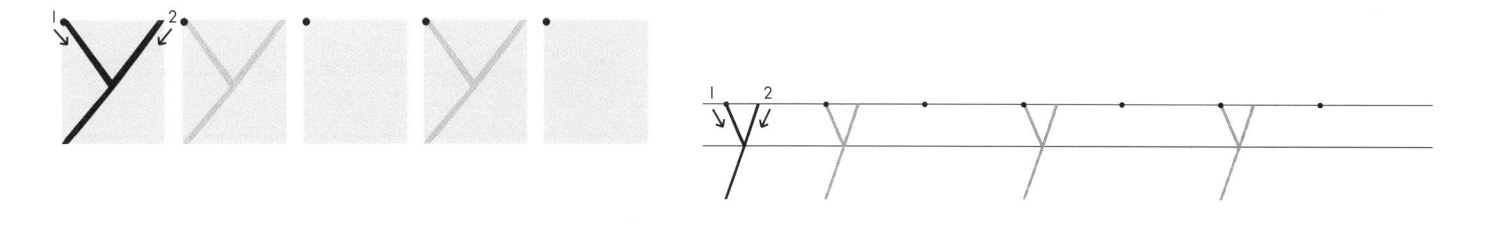

Read as much as you can. Then, circle every capital **Y** and lowercase **y** you see.

Yams are hot.

Yum! Cy says yes.

Cy gets a lot.

Jay says no.

Why yams? Yuck!

Jay gets a yogurt.

Think of two things that start with the same beginning sound as **yo-yo**. Draw them.

Xavier Gets an X-ray Xx

Understanding the Story: Setting

Where is Xavier in the story? Draw and write about three place where you see Xavier.

Xx Xavier Gets an X-ray

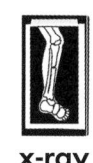

x-ray

Practice the Letter Xx

Say the letter name and the sound it stands for. Then, trace and write capital **X** and lowercase **x**.

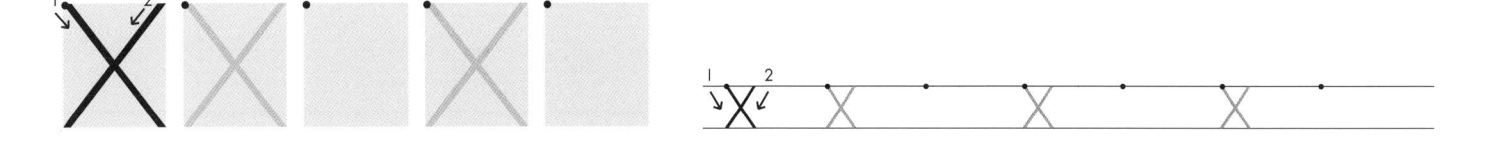

Say the name of each picture.
Write the letter that stands for the **ending** sound to complete the word.

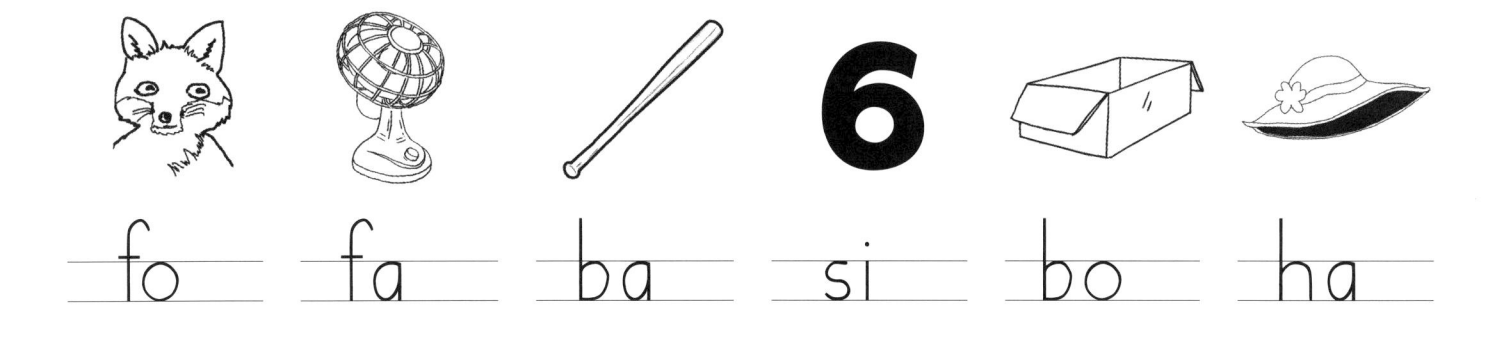

fo___   fa___   ba___   si___   bo___   ha___

Look around. Find names and words that have an **x** in them. Write the words.

_____
_____
_____
_____
_____
_____

52 A–Z for Mat Man® and Me: Practice for Developing Readers - Letter Learning © 2022 Learning Without Tears

Wes and the Watermelon — Ww

Understanding the Story: Setting

Circle the picture that shows where the story takes place.

Where is Wes in the story? Write about the place and draw a picture.

Ww   Wes and the Watermelon

watermelon

Practice the Letter Ww

Say the letter name and the sound it stands for. Then, trace and write capital **W** and lowercase **w**.

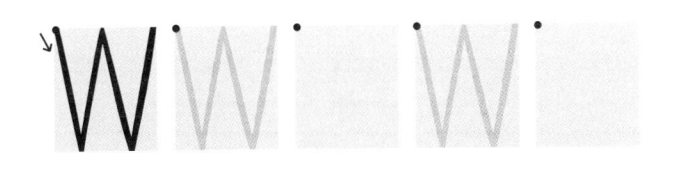

Read as much as you can. Then, circle every capital **W** and lowercase **w** you see.

Will has to win.

Wu has to win, too.

Who will win the swim race?

Will swims a lap.

Wu swims a lap.

They tap the wall. Tie!

Think of two things that start with the same beginning sound as **watermelon**. Draw them.

Vic, Val, and the Vacuum   Vv

Understanding the Story: Characters

Think about what Val does and how she feels. When does Val feel mad? Draw and write about it.

When does Val feel happy and thankful in the story? Draw and write.

© 2022 Learning Without Tears — A–Z for Mat Man® and Me: Practice for Developing Readers - **Meaning Making**   49

Vv Vic, Val, and the Vacuum

vacuum

Practice the Letter Vv

Say the letter name and the sound it stands for. Then, trace and write capital **V** and lowercase **v**.

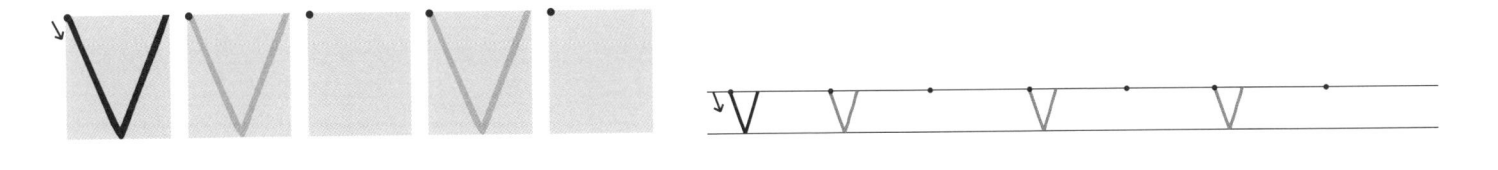

Say the name of each picture.
Write the letter that stands for the **beginning** sound to complete the word.

___ase   ___at   ___an   ___og   ___op   ___ug

Think of two things that start with the same beginning sound as **vacuum**. Draw them.

Umberto and the Umbrella   Uu

Understanding the Story: Events

What does Umberto do in the story? Draw three things Umberto uses to try to stay dry.

Uu — Umberto and the Umbrella

umbrella

Practice the Letter Uu

Say the letter name and the sound it stands for. Then, trace and write capital **U** and lowercase **u**.

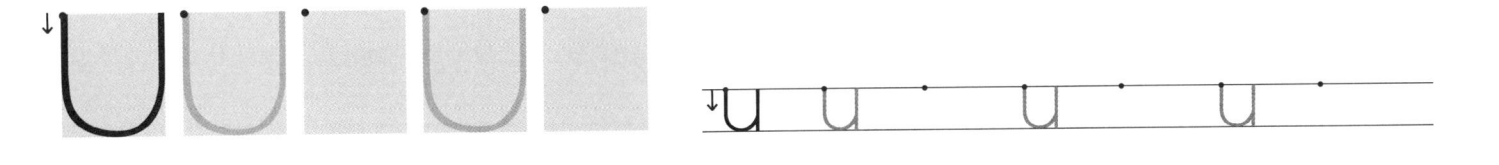

Say the name of each picture.
Write the letter that stands for the **middle** sound to complete the word.

r _ cks

b _ t

s _ n

d _ ck

n _ ts

b _ d

p _ g

b _ x

c _ p

r _ g

Tere and the Tomato Tt

Understanding the Story: Characters

Think about what Tere does and how she feels in the story. When does Tere feel worried? Draw and write about it.

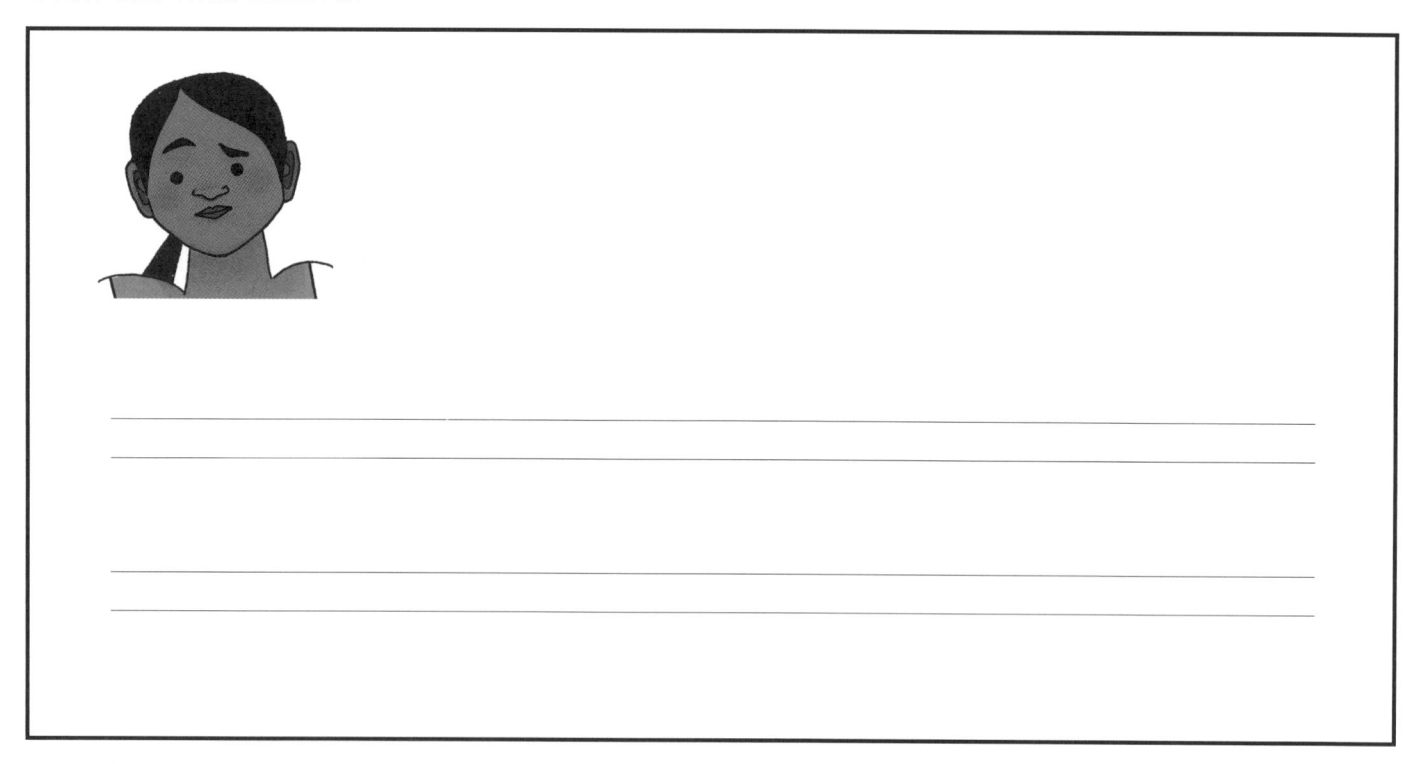

When does Tere feel happy in the story? Draw and write about it.

© 2022 Learning Without Tears · A–Z for Mat Man® and Me: Practice for Developing Readers - **Meaning Making** · **45**

Tt Tere and the Tomato

tomato

Practice the Letter Tt

Say the letter name and the sound it stands for. Then, trace and write capital **T** and lowercase **t**.

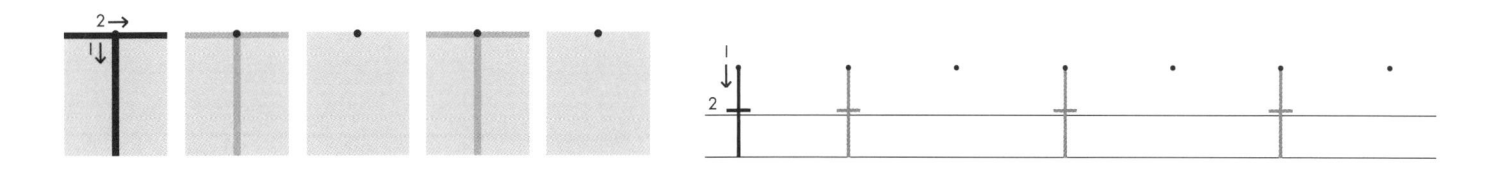

Say the name of each picture.
Write the letter that stands for the **beginning** sound to complete the word.

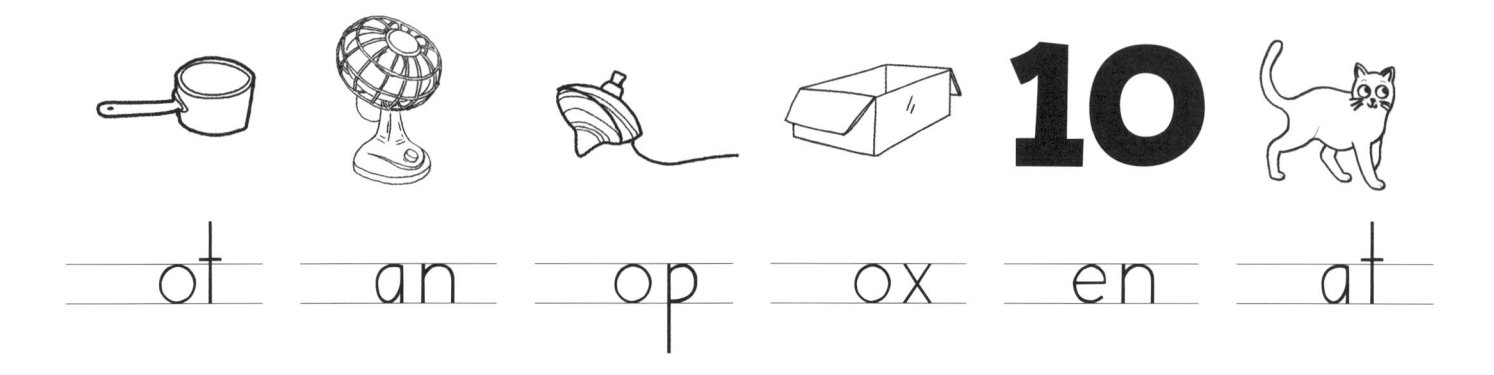

___ot   ___an   ___op   ___ox   ___en   ___at

Look around. Find names that start with capital **T** and things that start with lowercase **t**.
Write the words.

Sam in the Sun — Ss

Understanding the Story: Setting

Circle the picture that shows where the story takes place.

Where is Sam in the story? Write about the place and draw a picture.

Ss   Sam in the Sun

sun

Practice the Letter Ss

Say the letter name and the sound it stands for. Then, trace and write capital **S** and lowercase **s**.

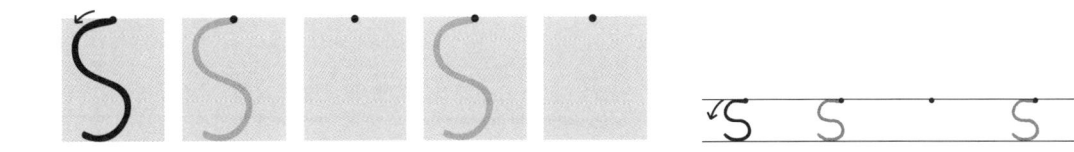

Say the name of each picture.
Write the letter that stands for the **beginning** sound to complete the word.

_at   _un   _ink   _og   _ix   _an

Think of two things that start with the same beginning sound as **sun**. Draw them.

42   A–Z for Mat Man® and Me: Practice for Developing Readers - Letter Learning   © 2022 Learning Without Tears

Rex and the Rake — Rr

Understanding the Story: Characters

Think about what Rex does and how he feels.
When does Rex feel confused about something in the story? Write and draw about it.

When does Rex feel upset and frustrated in the story? Write and draw about it.

© 2022 Learning Without Tears — A–Z for Mat Man® and Me: Practice for Developing Readers - Meaning Making   41

Rr Rex and the Rake

rake

Practice the Letter **Rr**

Say the letter name and the sound it stands for. Then, trace and write capital **R** and lowercase **r**.

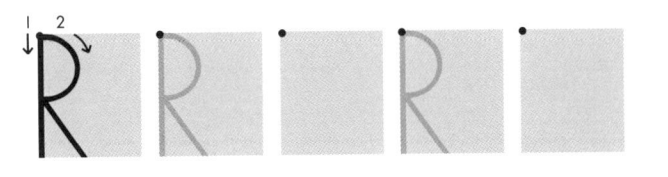

Say the name of each picture.
Write the letter that stands for the **beginning** sound to complete the word.

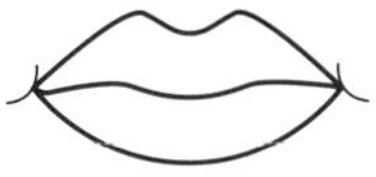

__oof   __an   __ocks   __un   __ug   __ips

Look around. Find names that start with capital **R** and things that start with lowercase **r**.
Write the words.

Quinn and the Quilt Qq

Understanding the Story: Events

Think about what happens in the story. The middle of the story is filled in. Now, draw and write about what happens in the beginning and end.

Beginning

Middle

The quilt gets wet.

End

© 2022 Learning Without Tears — A–Z for Mat Man® and Me: Practice for Developing Readers - **Meaning Making**

Qq Quinn and the Quilt

quilt

Practice the Letter Qq

Say the letter name and the sound it stands for. Then, trace and write capital **Q** and lowercase **q**.

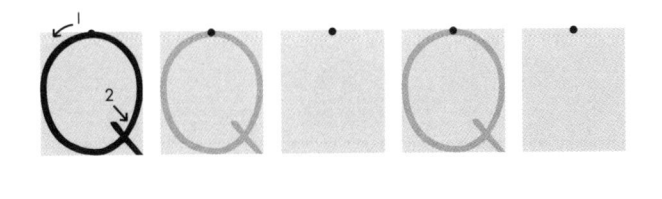

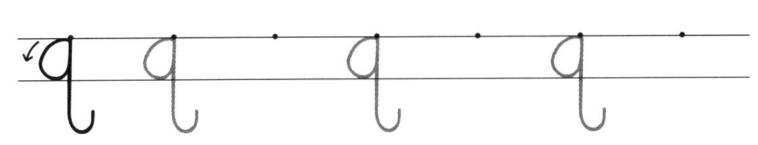

Read as much as you can. Then, circle every capital **Q** and lowercase **q** you see.

Monique has a duck.

Quack! Quack! Quack!

It is not quiet.

Raquan will get it.

Raquan can not.

The duck is quick!

Think of two things that start with the same beginning sound as **quilt**. Draw them.

Paco and the Piano — Pp

Understanding the Story: Setting

Circle the picture that shows where the story takes place.

Write and draw about where Paco goes in the story.

Pp Paco and the Piano

piano

Practice the Letter **Pp**

Say the letter name and the sound it stands for. Then, trace and write capital **P** and lowercase **p**.

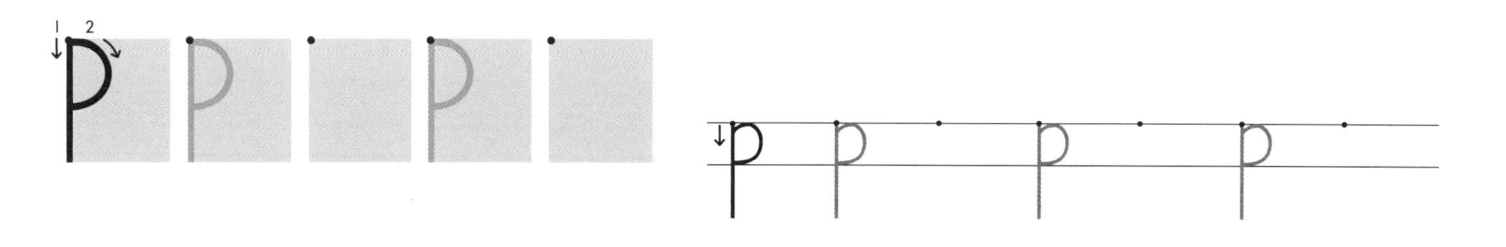

Say the name of each picture.
Write the letter that stands for the **beginning** sound to complete the word.

___ot   ___at   ___up   ___ig   ___ug   ___an

Look around. Find names that start with capital **P** and things that start with lowercase **p**.
Write the words.

Oz and the Octopus   Oo

Understanding the Story: Events

Think about what happens in the story. The middle of the story is filled in. Now, draw and write about what happens in the beginning and end.

Beginning

Middle

The octopus is
on the tank.

End

Oo Oz and the Octopus

octopus

Practice the Letter Oo

Say the letter name and the sound it stands for. Then, trace and write capital **O** and lowercase **o**.

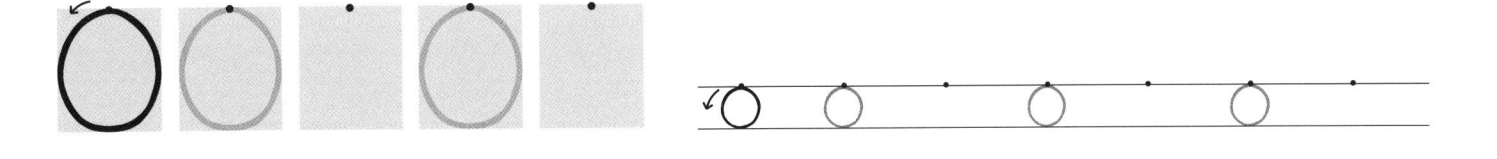

Say the name of each picture.
Write the letter that stands for the **middle** sound to complete the word.

f _ sh   m _ p

p _ t   l _ g

f _ n   d _ g

b _ d   c _ t

f _ x   b _ x

34 A–Z for Mat Man® and Me: Practice for Developing Readers - **Letter Learning**   © 2022 Learning Without Tears

Nell and the Nest — Nn

Understanding the Story: Setting

Circle the picture that shows where the story takes place.

Write and draw about the place where Nell is and why it is important to what happens in the story.

Nn Nell and the Nest

nest

Practice the Letter **Nn**

Say the letter name and the sound it stands for. Then, trace and write capital **N** and lowercase **n**.

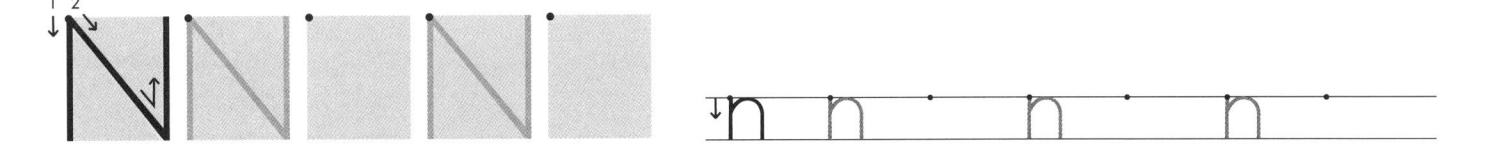

Say the name of each picture.
Write the letter that stands for the **beginning** sound to complete the word.

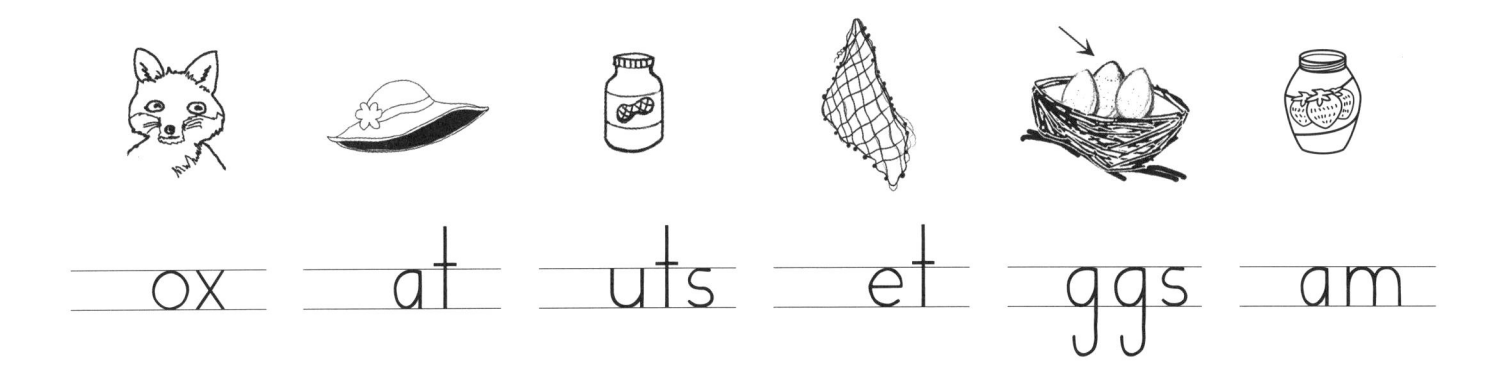

___ox ___at ___uts ___et ___ggs ___am

Think of two things that start with the same beginning sound as **nest**. Draw them.

32   A–Z for Mat Man® and Me: Practice for Developing Readers - **Letter Learning**   © 2022 Learning Without Tears

Mac and the Magnificent Masks — Mm

Understanding the Story: Events

Think about what happens in the story. The middle of the story is filled in. Now, draw and write about what happens in the beginning and end.

Beginning

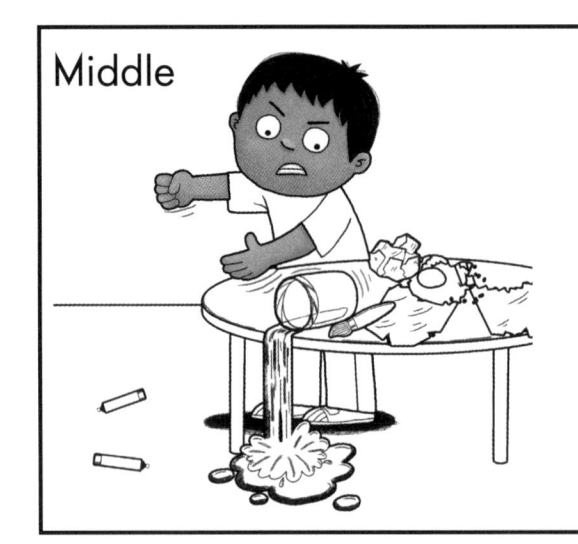

Middle

Marcos tosses markers.

End

Mm Mac and the Magnificent Masks

mask

Practice the Letter Mm

Say the letter name and the sound it stands for. Then, trace and write capital **M** and lowercase **m**.

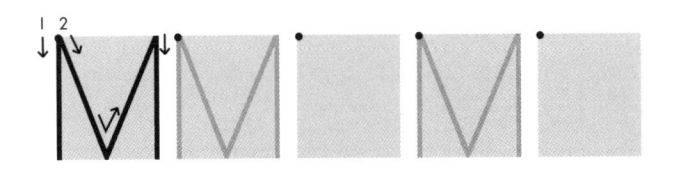

Say the name of each picture.
Write the letter that stands for the beginning sound to complete the word.

_op   _ox   _ug   _at   _ed   _ick

Look around. Find names that start with capital **M** and things that start with lowercase **m**.
Write the words.

Lola and the Lock   Ll

Understanding the Story: Events

Where does Lola look for her lock? Draw and write about three places where Lola looks.

Ll Lola and the Lock

lock

Practice the Letter Ll

Say the letter name and the sound it stands for. Then, trace and write capital **L** and lowercase **l**.

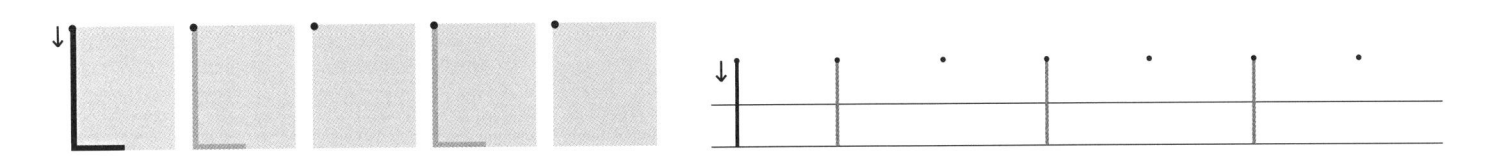

Say the name of each picture.
Write the letter that stands for the **beginning** sound to complete the word.

___eg ___un ___og ___ick ___ock ___og

Think of two things that start with the same beginning sound as **lock**. Draw them.

Kaya and the Kayak Kk

Understanding the Story: Setting

Circle the picture that shows where the story takes place.

Where is Kaya in the story? Write about the place and draw a picture.

Kk Kaya and the Kayak

kayak

Practice the Letter Kk

Say the letter name and the sound it stands for. Then, trace and write capital **K** and lowercase **k**.

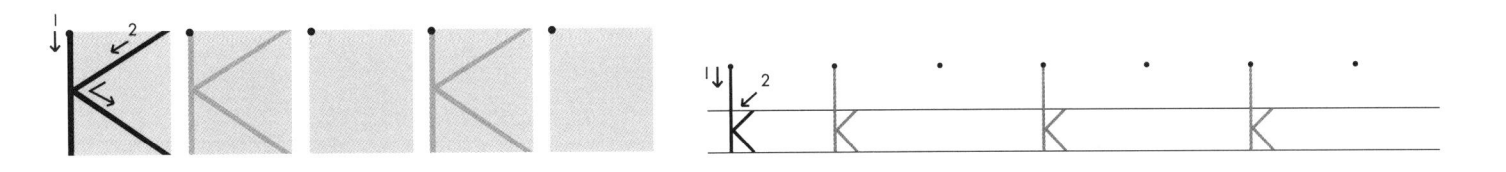

Say the name of each picture.
Write the letter that stands for the **beginning** sound to complete the word.

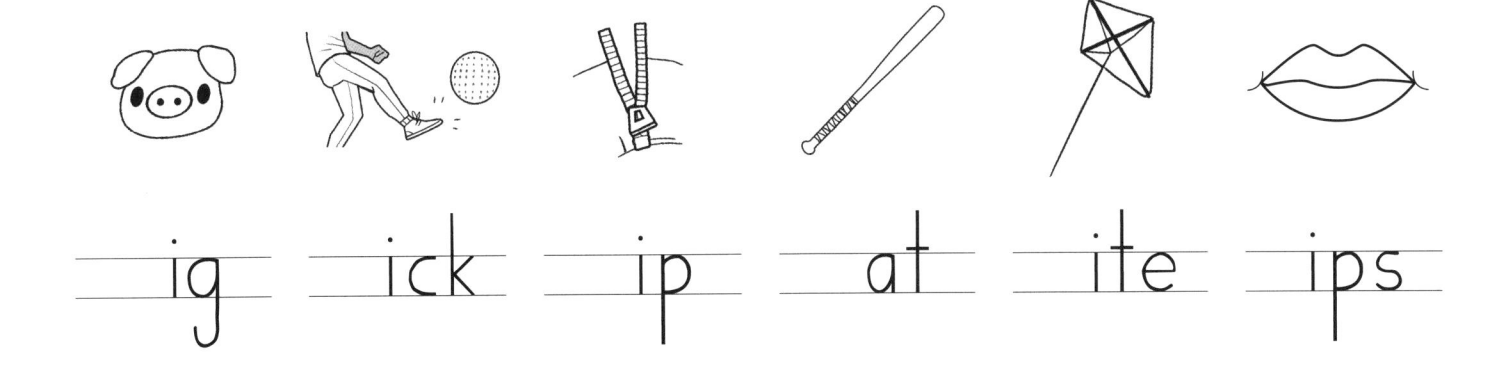

___ig   ___ick   ___ip   ___at   ___ite   ___ips

Look around. Find names that start with capital **K** and things that start with lowercase **k**.
Write the words.

Jana, Jen, and the Jellyfish — Jj

Understanding the Story: Character

Find the two main characters in the story. (Circle) two pictures.

Write about something the characters do in the story and draw a picture.

© 2022 Learning Without Tears — A–Z for Mat Man® and Me: Practice for Developing Readers - **Meaning Making**

Jj Jana, Jen, and the Jellyfish

jellyfish

Practice the Letter Jj

Say the letter name and the sound it stands for. Then, trace and write capital **J** and lowercase **j**.

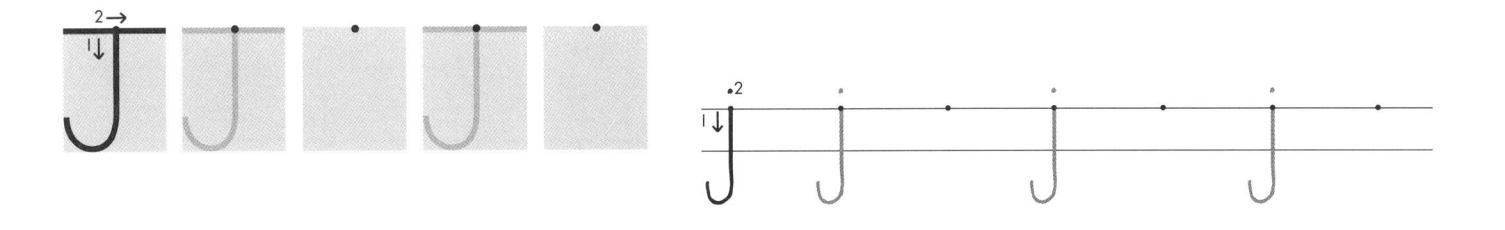

Say the name of each picture.
Write the letter that stands for the **beginning** sound to complete the word.

__un   __an   __am   __ox   __eep   __at

Think of two things that start with the same beginning sound as **jellyfish**. Draw them.

24 A–Z for Mat Man® and Me: Practice for Developing Readers - Letter Learning   © 2022 Learning Without Tears

Ikiaq and the Igloo Ii

Understanding the Story: Setting

Circle the picture that shows where the story takes place.

Write about a place from the story and draw a picture.

Ii   Ikiaq and the Igloo

igloo

Practice the Letter Ii

Say the letter name and the sound it stands for. Then, trace and write capital **I** and lowercase **i**.

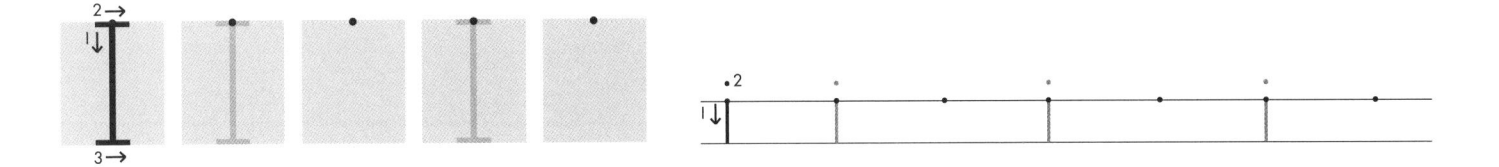

Say the name of each picture.
Write the letter that stands for the **middle** sound to complete the word.

s _ n   f _ n

z _ p   b _ x

c _ p   b _ d

p _ g   l _ ps

c _ t   d _ g

Hana has a Hammer Hh

Understanding the Story: Characters

Which animals get out in the story? Draw three that Hana has to chase. Write the names.

Hh Hana has a Hammer

hammer

Practice the Letter Hh

Say the letter name and the sound it stands for. Then, trace and write capital **H** and lowercase **h**.

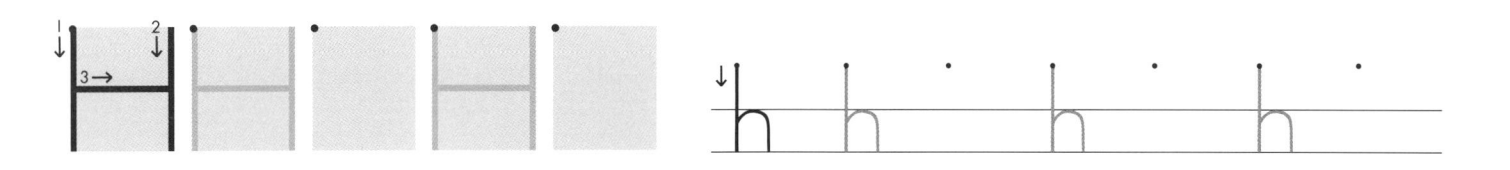

Say the name of each picture.
Write the letter that stands for the **beginning** sound to complete the word.

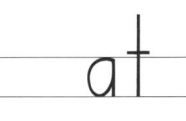

___ox   ___en   ___at   ___eg   ___og   ___ig

Look around. Find names that start with capital **H** and things that start with lowercase **h**. Write the words.

20 A–Z for Mat Man® and Me: Practice for Developing Readers - Letter Learning © 2022 Learning Without Tears

Gabby and Her Goat Gg

Understanding the Story: Events
What does Gus do in the story? Draw and write three things Gus gets.

Gg Gabby and Her Goat

goat

Practice the Letter Gg

Say the letter name and the sound it stands for. Then, trace and write capital G and lowercase g.

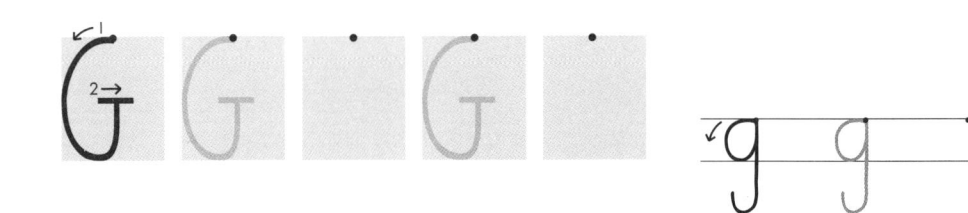

G G G G

g g g g

Say the name of each picture.
Write the letter that stands for the **ending** sound to complete the word.

ba___ mo___ do___ pi___ po___ ru___

Look around. Find names that start with capital G and things that start with lowercase g.
Write the words.

18 A–Z for Mat Man® and Me: Practice for Developing Readers - Letter Learning © 2022 Learning Without Tears

Feng, Finn, and the Fan Ff

Understanding the Story: Events

Think about what happens in the story. The middle of the story is filled in. Now, draw and write about what happens in the beginning and end.

Beginning

Middle

Feng and Finn fight.

End

Ff Feng, Finn, and the Fan

fan

Practice the Letter **Ff**

Say the letter name and the sound it stands for. Then, trace and write capital **F** and lowercase **f**.

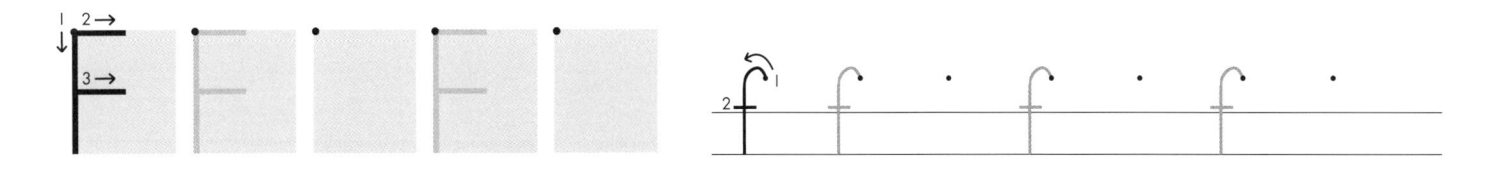

Say the name of each picture.
Write the letter that stands for the **beginning** sound to complete the word.

__at   __an   __ox   __in   __ox   __am

Think of two things that start with the same beginning sound as **fan**. Draw them.

Emma and the Elephant   Ee

Understanding the Story: Characters

Think about what Emma does and how she feels. When does Emma feel sad?
Draw and write about it.

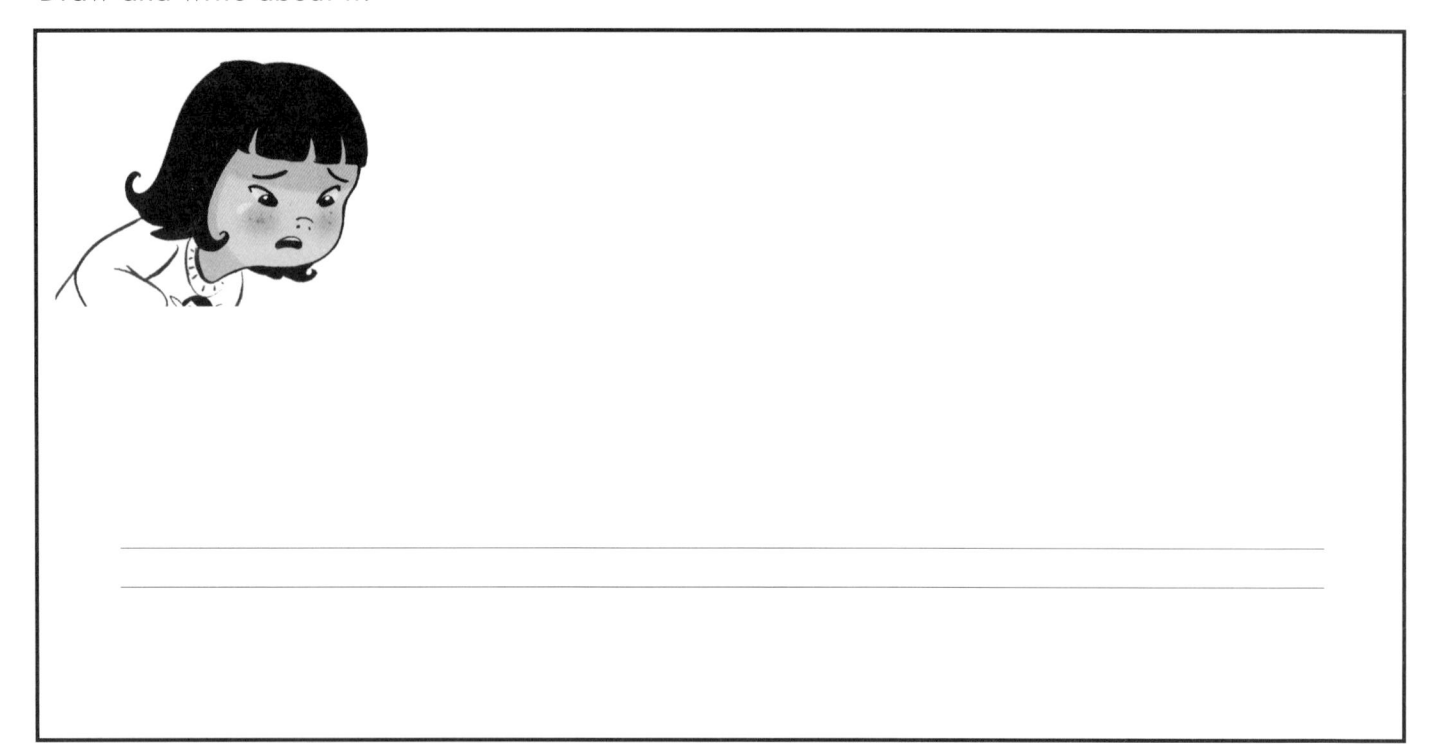

_____
_____

When does Emma feel happy in the story? Draw and write about it.

_____
_____

© 2022 Learning Without Tears   A–Z for Mat Man® and Me: Practice for Developing Readers - **Meaning Making**   15

Ee Cora and the Coconut

elephant

Practice the Letter Ee

Say the letter name and the sound it stands for. Then, trace and write capital **E** and lowercase **e**.

Say the name of each picture.
Write the letter that stands for the **middle** sound to complete the word.

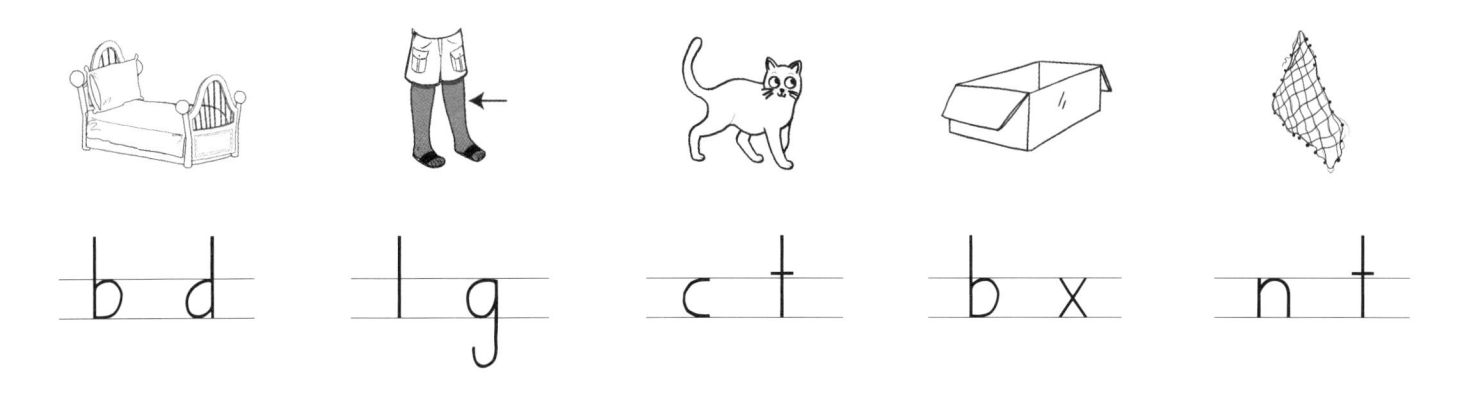

b_d   _ _g   c_t   b_x   n_t

Look around. Find names that start with capital **E** and things that start with lowercase **e**.
Write the words.

14 A–Z for Mat Man® and Me: Practice for Developing Readers - Letter Learning © 2022 Learning Without Tears

Dax and the Dolphin   Dd

Understanding the Story: Setting
Circle the picture that shows where the story takes place.

Where is Dax in the story? Write about the place and draw a picture.

Dd   Dax and the Dolphin

dolphin

Practice the Letter **Dd**

Say the letter name and the sound it stands for. Then, trace and write capital **D** and lowercase **d**.

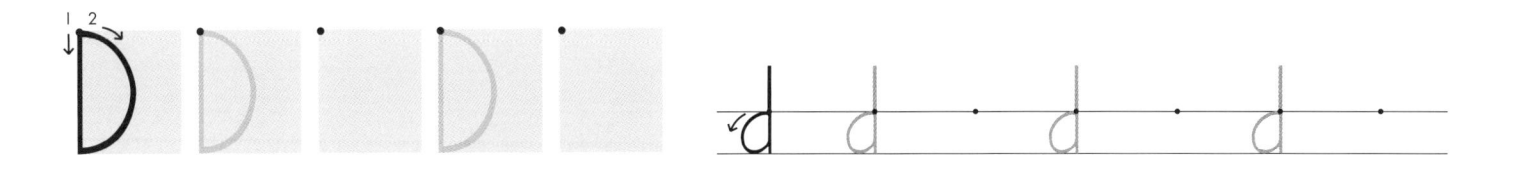

Say the name of each picture.
Write the letter that stands for the **beginning** sound to complete the word.

_ot

_uck

_op

_at

_og

_ig

_et

_an

_ox

_oll

12   *A–Z for Mat Man® and Me: Practice for Developing Readers - Letter Learning*   © 2022 Learning Without Tears

Cora and the Coconut Cc

Understanding the Story: Events

Think about what happens in the story. The middle of the story is filled in. Now, draw and write about what happens in the beginning and end.

Beginning

Middle

Cora holds up a cat.

End

© 2022 Learning Without Tears — A–Z for Mat Man® and Me: Practice for Developing Readers - Meaning Making

Cc   *Cora and the Coconut*

coconut

Practice the Letter Cc

Say the letter name and the sound it stands for. Then, trace and write capital **C** and lowercase **c**.

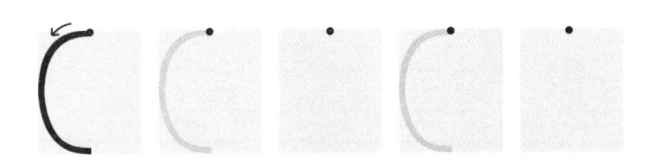

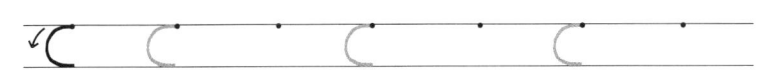

Say the name of each picture.
Write the letter that stands for the **beginning** sound to complete the word.

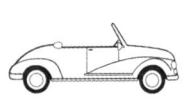

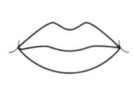

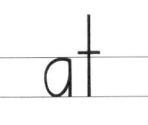

___at   ___ox   ___up   ___ar   ___ed   ___ips

Look around. Find names that start with capital **C** and things that start with lowercase **c**.
Write the words.

10   *A–Z for Mat Man® and Me: Practice for Developing Readers - Letter Learning*   © 2022 Learning Without Tears

Ben and the Big Bagels   Bb

Understanding the Story: Setting

Circle the picture that shows where the story takes place.

Where is Ben in the story? Write about the place and draw a picture.

Bb Ben and the Big Bagels

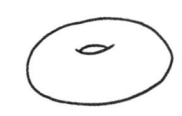

bagel

Practice the Letter **Bb**

Say the letter name and the sound it stands for. Then, trace and write capital **B** and lowercase **b**.

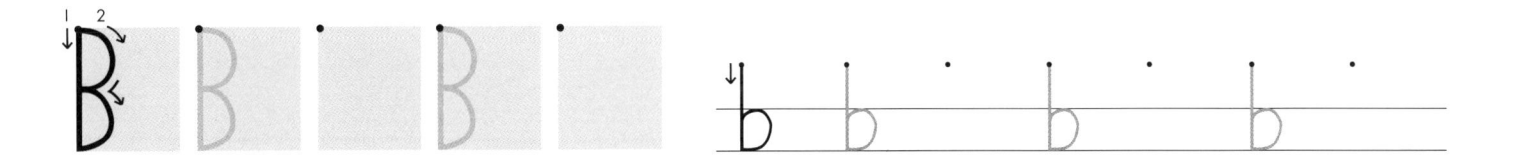

Say the name of each picture.
Write the letter that stands for the **beginning** sound to complete the word.

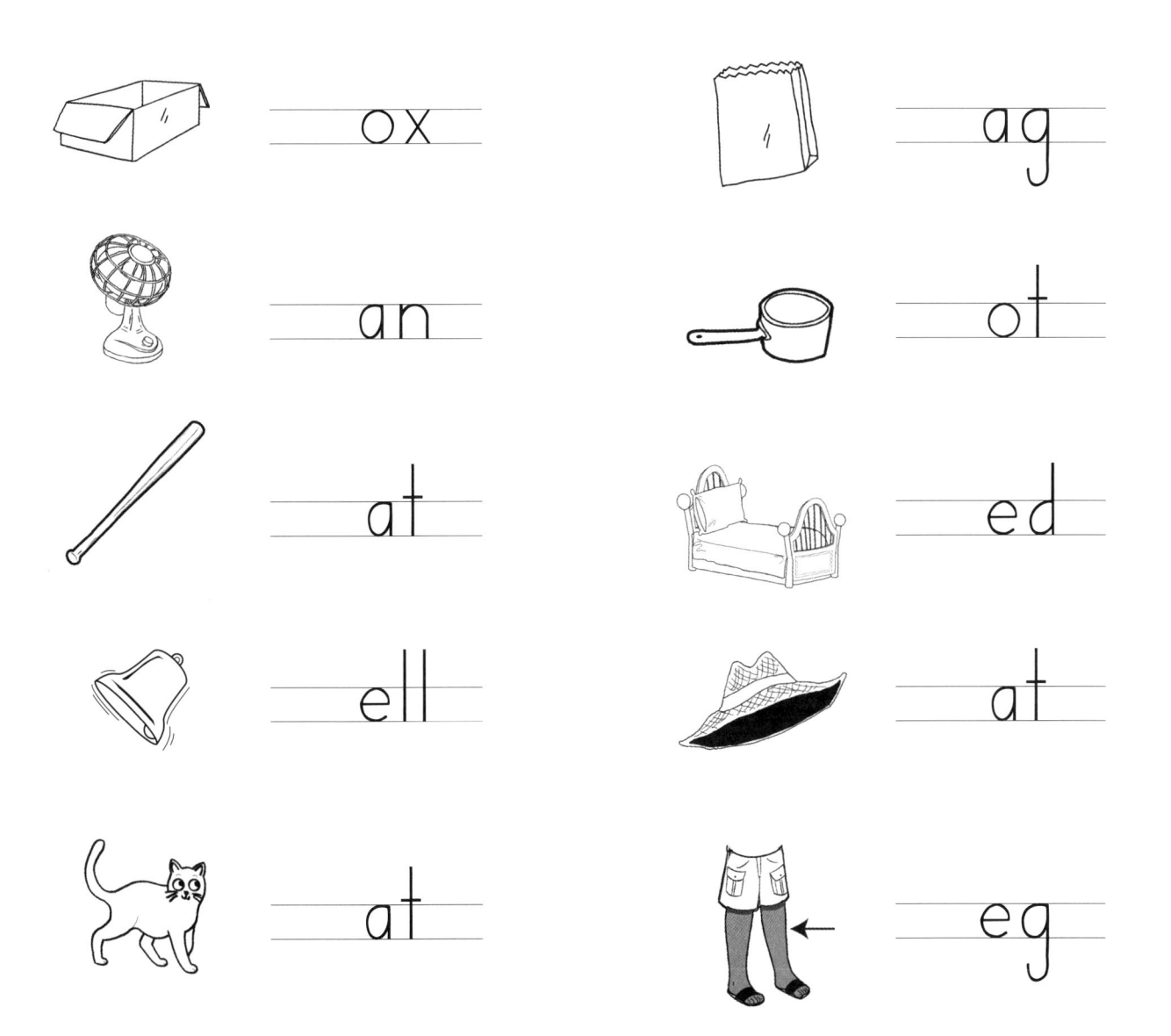

___ ox

___ ag

___ an

___ ot

___ at

___ ed

___ ell

___ at

___ at

___ eg

8   A–Z for Mat Man® and Me: Practice for Developing Readers - Letter Learning

© 2022 Learning Without Tears

Ally and the Apple   Aa

Understanding the Story: Events

Think about what happens in the story. The middle of the story is filled in. Now, draw and write about what happens in the beginning and end.

Beginning

Middle

Ally asks for help.

End

© 2022 Learning Without Tears — A–Z for Mat Man® and Me: Practice for Developing Readers - **Meaning Making**

Aa Ally and the Apple

apple

Practice the Letter Aa

Say the letter name and the sound it stands for. Then, trace and write capital **A** and lowercase **a**.

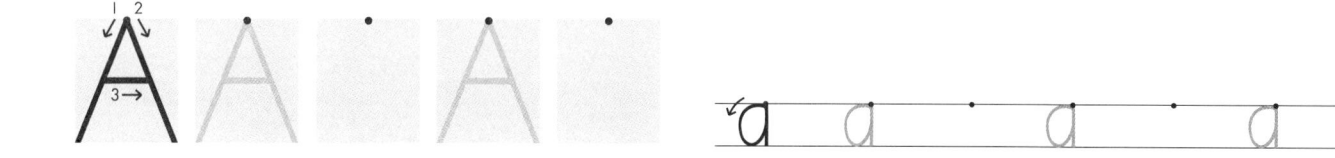

Say the name of each picture.
Write the letter that stands for the **middle** sound to complete the word.

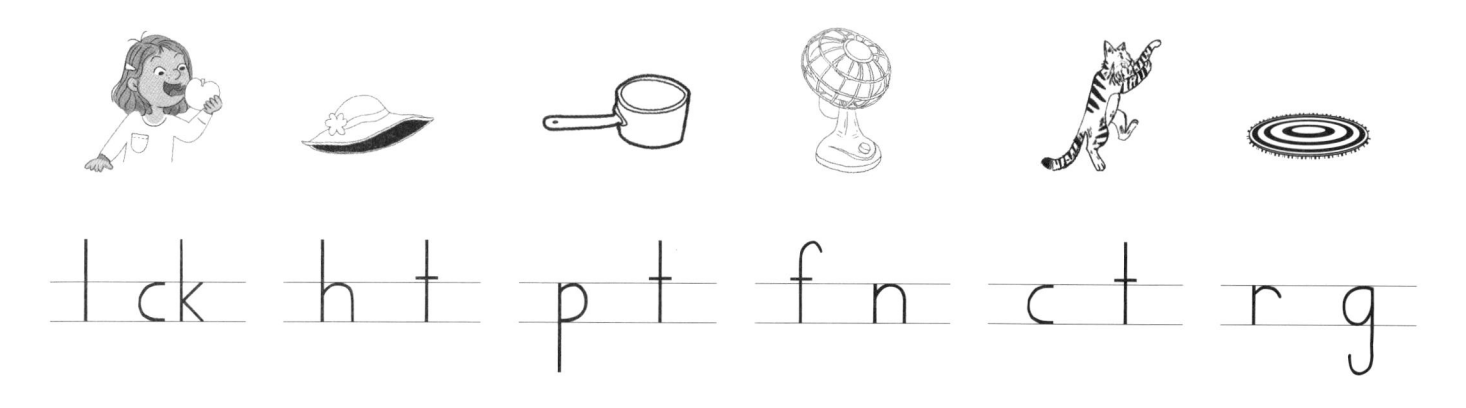

t _ ck   h _ t   p _ t   f _ n   c _ t   r _ g

Think of two things that start with the same beginning sound as **apple**. Draw them.

---

6   A–Z for Mat Man® and Me: Practice for Developing Readers - **Letter Learning**   © 2022 Learning Without Tears

Mat Man® and the Great Alphabet Parade

The First Letter in Your Name

First, ⟨circle⟩ the letter your first name starts with. Then, underline the letter your last name starts with.

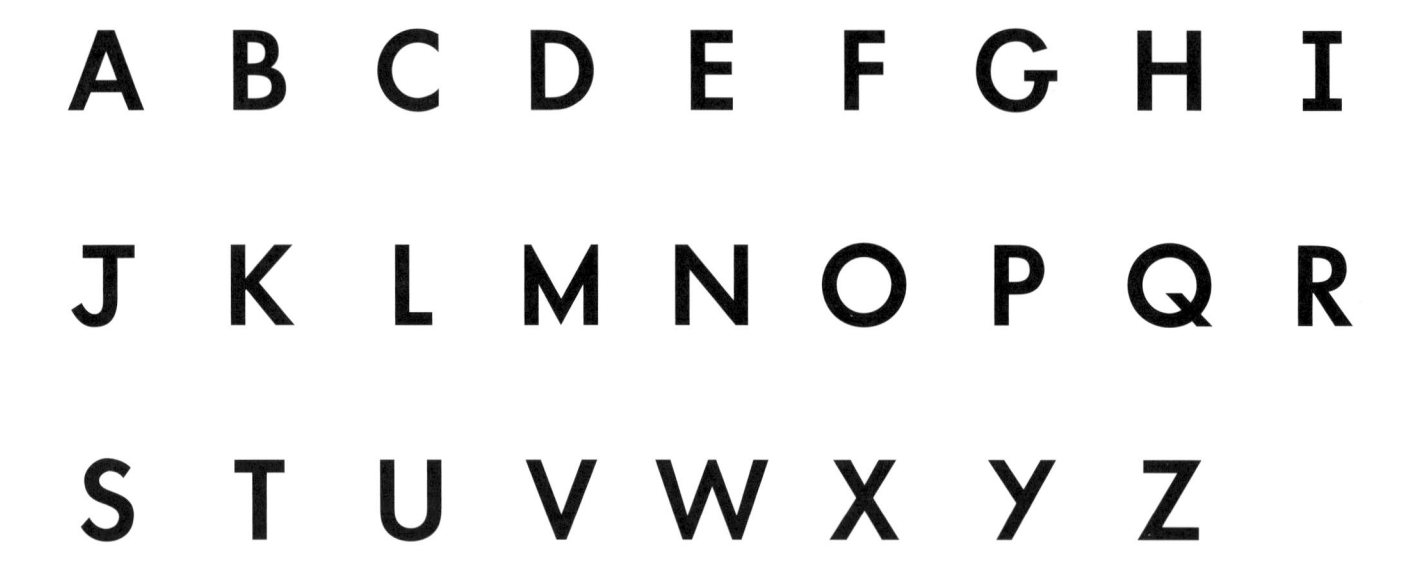

A B C D E F G H I
J K L M N O P Q R
S T U V W X Y Z

Draw a picture of something from the parade that starts with the same letter your first name starts with. Then, draw a picture of something that starts with the first letter in your last name.

© 2022 Learning Without Tears   A–Z for Mat Man® and Me: Practice for Developing Readers

Mat Man® and the Great Alphabet Parade

Sing the Alphabet Song

Help Mat Man sing the ABC song! Underline each letter as we sing it. The **a** is done for you. Then, color the pictures.

a b c d e f g

h i j k l m n o p

q r s

t u v

w x

y and z

TABLE OF CONTENTS

Sing the Alphabet Song 4
The First Letter in Your Name 5

Letter Aa: *Ally and the Apple*
Practice the Letter **Aa** 6
Understanding the Story: Events 7

Letter Bb: *Ben and the Big Bagels*
Practice the Letter **Bb** 8
Understanding the Story: Setting 9

Letter Cc: *Cora and the Coconut*
Practice the Letter **Cc** 10
Understanding the Story: Events 11

Letter Dd: *Dax and the Dolphin*
Practice the Letter **Dd** 12
Understanding the Story: Setting 13

Letter Ee: *Emma and Her Elephant*
Practice the Letter **Ee** 14
Understanding the Story: Character 15

Letter Ff: *Feng, Finn, and the Fan*
Practice the Letter **Ff** 16
Understanding the Story: Events 17

Letter Gg: *Gabby and Her Goat*
Practice the Letter **Gg** 18
Understanding the Story: Events 19

Letter Hh: *Hana Has a Hammer*
Practice the Letter **Hh** 20
Understanding the Story: Events 21

Letter Ii: *Ikiaq and the Igloo*
Practice the Letter **Ii** 22
Understanding the Story: Setting 23

Letter Jj: *Jana, Jen, and the Jellyfish*
Practice the Letter **Jj** 24
Understanding the Story: Character 25

Letter Kk: *Kaya and the Kite*
Practice the Letter **Kk** 26
Understanding the Story: Setting 27

Letter Ll: *Lola and the Lock*
Practice the Letter **Ll** 28
Understanding the Story: Events 29

Letter Mm: *Mac and the Magnificent Masks*
Practice the Letter **Mm** 30
Understanding the Story: Events 31

Letter Nn: *Nell and the Nest*
Practice the Letter **Nn** 32
Understanding the Story: Setting 33

Letter Oo: *Oz and the Octopus*
Practice the Letter **Oo** 34
Understanding the Story: Events 35

Letter Pp: *Paco and the Piano*
Practice the Letter **Pp** 36
Understanding the Story: Character 37

Letter Qq: *Quinn and the Quilt*
Practice the Letter **Qq** 38
Understanding the Story: Events 39

Letter Rr: *Rex and the Rake*
Practice the Letter **Rr** 40
Understanding the Story: Character 41

Letter Ss: *Sam in the Sun*
Practice the Letter **Ss** 42
Understanding the Story: Setting 43

Letter Tt: *Tere and the Tomato*
Practice the Letter **Tt** 44
Understanding the Story: Character 45

Letter Uu: *Umberto and the Umbrella*
Practice the Letter **Uu** 46
Understanding the Story: Events 47

Letter Vv: *Vic, Val, and the Vacuum*
Practice the Letter **Vv** 48
Understanding the Story: Character 49

Letter Ww: *Wes and the Watermelon*
Practice the Letter **Ww** 50
Understanding the Story: Setting 51

Letter Xx: *Xavier Gets an X-ray*
Practice the Letter **Xx** 52
Understanding the Story: Setting 53

Letter Yy: *Yolanda and the Yo-Yo*
Practice the Letter **Yy** 54
Understanding the Story: Events 55

Letter Zz: *Zack and His Zipper*
Practice the Letter **Zz** 56
Understanding the Story: Character 57

Letter Check 1 58
Letter Check 2 60
Letter Check 3 62
Letter Review 64

LEARNING
Without Tears®

8001 MacArthur Blvd.
Cabin John, MD 20818
LWTears.com | 888.983.8409

Art Director: Shannon Rutledge
Graphic Designer: Sammie Simon
Curriculum Designers: Adam Berkin, Nicole Iorio, Cari Meister, Casey Schultz

Copyright © 2022 Learning Without Tears
First Edition
ISBN: 978-1-954728-42-4
23456789RRD232221
Printed in Dongguan, China

The contents of this consumable workbook are protected by US copyright law. If a workbook has been purchased for a child, the author and Learning Without Tears give limited permission to copy pages for additional practice or homework for that child. No copied pages from this book can be given to another person without written permission from Learning Without Tears.

A-Z for Mat Man® and Me

Practice for Developing Readers

LEARNING Without Tears®

Letter Review

Letter Review

Say the name for each picture. Circle the letter that stands for its **beginning** sound. Write the lowercase letter on the double lines.

1.	m p s		5.	e r m	
2.	s w m		6.	t w v	
3.	c n b		7.	a p u	
4.	r p b		8.	r f l	

A–Z for Mat Man® and Me: Practice for Developing Readers

© 2022 Learning Without Tears

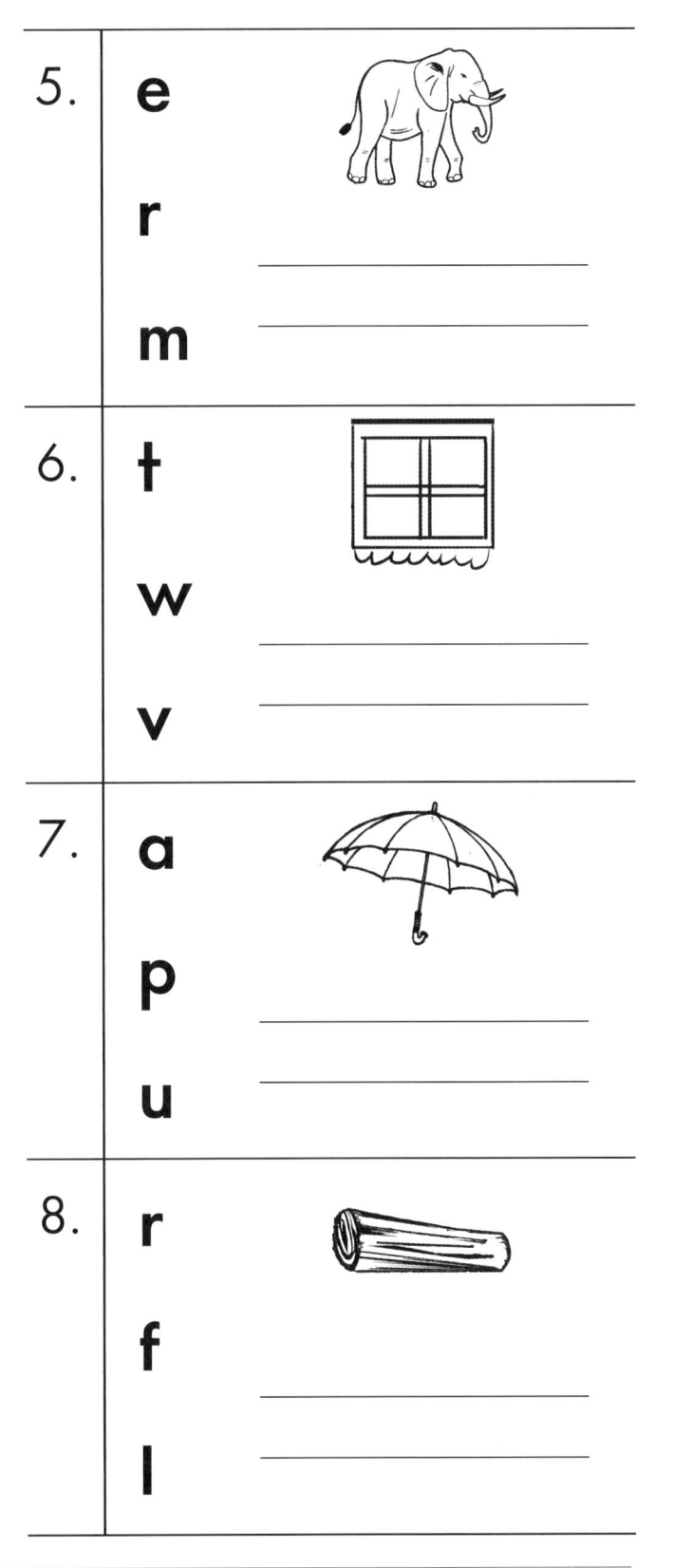

Letter Check 3

Letter Check 3, Part B

Say the name for each picture. Circle the letter that stands for its **beginning** sound. Write the lowercase letter on the double lines.

1. x
   k
   a

2. s
   j
   t

3. k
   t
   f

4. y
   j
   s

5. e
   r
   k

6. b
   n
   q

7. e
   g
   z

8. r
   w
   i

© 2022 Learning Without Tears

A–Z for Mat Man® and Me: Practice for Developing Readers   63

Letter Check 3

Letter Check 3, Part A

Say the name for each picture. Circle the letter that stands for its **beginning** sound. Write the lowercase letter on the double lines.

1. j / s / v

2. y / k / a

3. i / d / u

4. j / s / p

5. w / f / n

6. d / q / e

7. g / p / o

8. q / i / l

62 A–Z for Mat Man® and Me: Practice for Developing Readers

Letter Check 2

Letter Check 2, Part B

Say the name for each picture. Circle the letter that stands for its **beginning** sound.
Write the lowercase letter on the double lines.

1. r
   l
   g

2. c
   p
   v

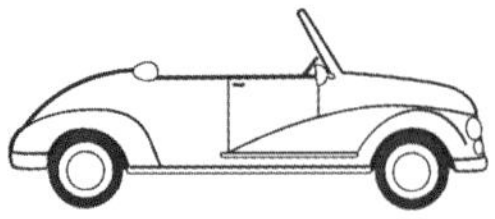

3. n
   f
   l

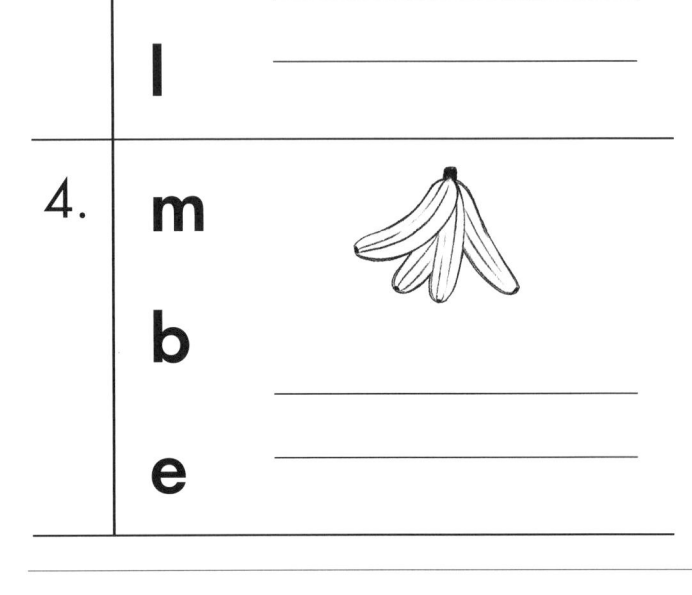

4. m
   b
   e

5. m
   d
   z

6. h
   l
   w

7. i
   d
   o

8. f
   g
   j

Letter Check 2, Part A

Say the name for each picture. Circle the letter that stands for its **beginning** sound.
Write the lowercase letter on the double lines.

1. l / d / k

2. p / h / b

3. g / w / s

4. z / t / l

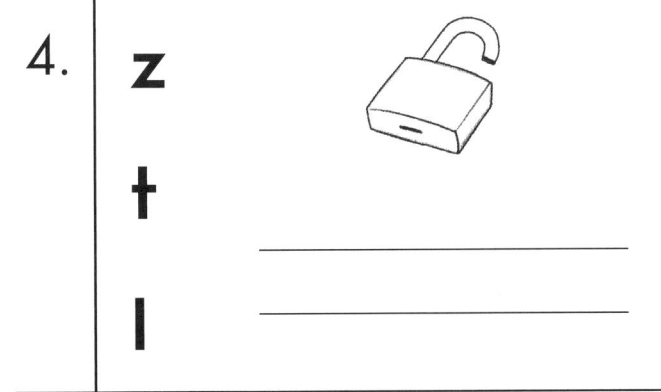

5. f / x / i

6. b / n / h

7. n / d / c

8. o / z / r

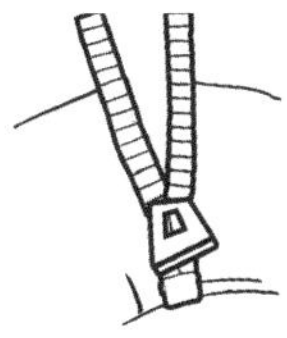

Letter Check 1

Letter Check 1, Part B

Say the name for each picture. Circle the letter that stands for its **beginning** sound.
Write the lowercase letter on the double lines.

1.	s r l		5.	a v m	
2.	i y p		6.	b v a	
3.	p n g		7.	t n r	
4.	k s r		8.	t q p	

© 2022 Learning Without Tears

A–Z for Mat Man® and Me: Practice for Developing Readers

59

Letter Check 1

Letter Check 1, Part A

Say the name for each picture. Circle the letter that stands for its **beginning** sound. Write the lowercase letter on the double lines.

1. m p a

2. s p t

3. i n b

4. r d p

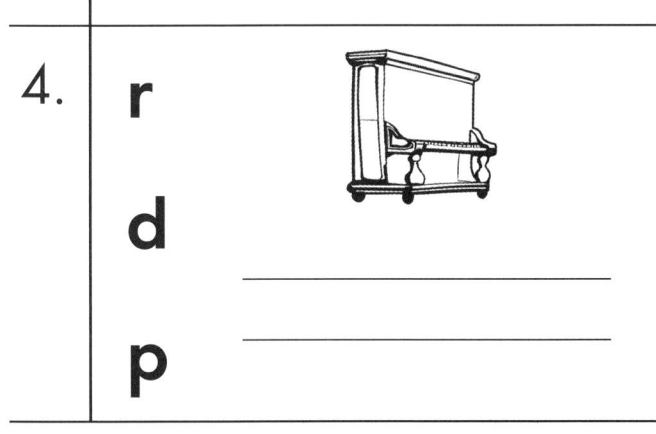

5. g r m

6. t s v

7. a b u

8. r o i

58   A–Z for Mat Man® and Me: Practice for Developing Readers

© 2022 Learning Without Tears

Zack and His Zipper Zz

Understanding the Story: Characters

Think about what Zack does and how he feels. When does Zack feel mad? Draw and write about it.

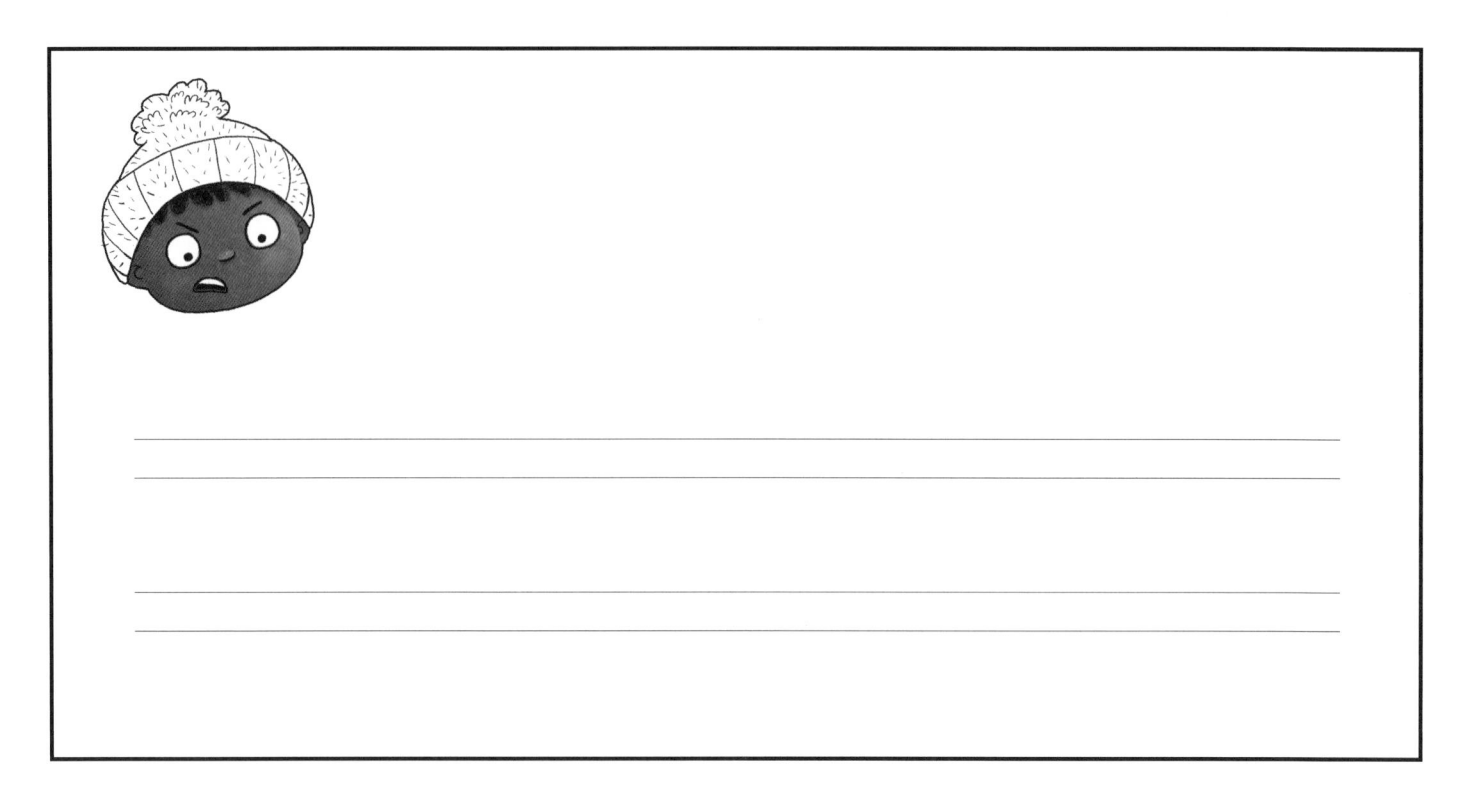

When does Zack feel happy in the story? Draw and write.

Zz Zack and His Zipper

zipper

Practice the Letter Zz

Say the letter name and the sound it stands for. Then, trace and write capital **Z** and lowercase **z**.

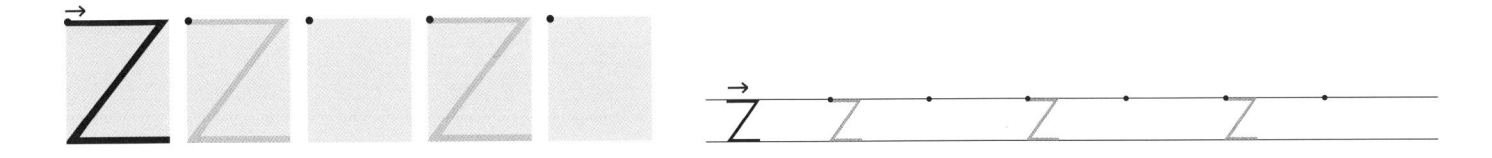

Read as much as you can. Then, circle every capital **Z** and lowercase **z** you see.

Liz zips up her coat.

It is a size too big.

It keeps out the breeze.

Liz and Zoe get to the zoo!

They look at a zebra.

Think of two things that start with the same beginning sound as **zipper**. Draw them.

Practice the Letter Yy — Yy

Understanding the Story: Events

Think about what happens in the story. The middle of the story is filled in. Now, draw and write about what happens in the beginning and end.

Beginning

Middle

Yaz does not trade back.

End

Yy Practice the Letter Yy

yo-yo

Practice the Letter **Yy**

Say the letter name and the sound it stands for. Then, trace and write capital **Y** and lowercase **y**.

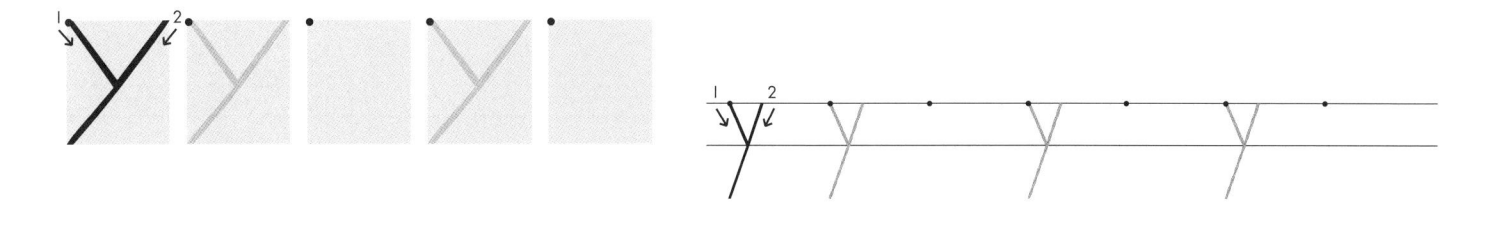

Read as much as you can. Then, circle every capital **Y** and lowercase **y** you see.

Yams are hot.
Yum! Cy says yes.
Cy gets a lot.

Jay says no.
Why yams? Yuck!
Jay gets a yogurt.

Think of two things that start with the same beginning sound as **yo-yo**. Draw them.

Xavier Gets an X-ray Xx

Understanding the Story: Setting

Where is Xavier in the story? Draw and write about three place where you see Xavier.

Xx Xavier Gets an X-ray

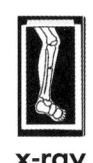

x-ray

Practice the Letter Xx

Say the letter name and the sound it stands for. Then, trace and write capital **X** and lowercase **x**.

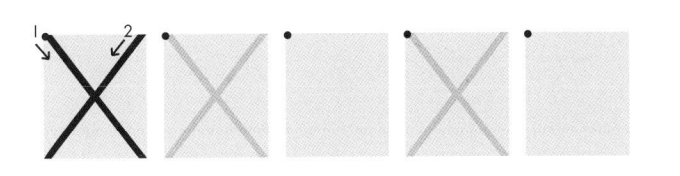

Say the name of each picture.
Write the letter that stands for the **ending** sound to complete the word.

fo___   fa___   ba___   si___   bo___   ha___

Look around. Find names and words that have an **x** in them. Write the words.

52   A–Z for Mat Man® and Me: Practice for Developing Readers - Letter Learning   © 2022 Learning Without Tears

Wes and the Watermelon Ww

Understanding the Story: Setting

Circle the picture that shows where the story takes place.

Where is Wes in the story? Write about the place and draw a picture.

Ww — Wes and the Watermelon

watermelon

Practice the Letter Ww

Say the letter name and the sound it stands for. Then, trace and write capital **W** and lowercase **w**.

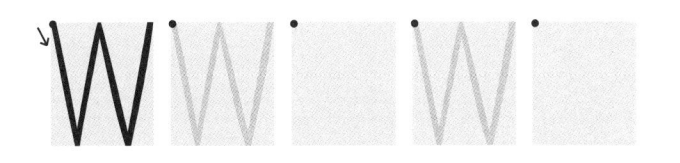

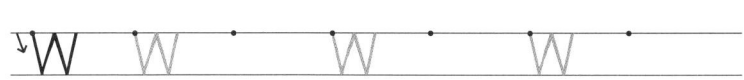

W W W   w w w w

Read as much as you can. Then, (circle) every capital **W** and lowercase **w** you see.

Will has to win.

Wu has to win, too.

Who will win the swim race?

Will swims a lap.

Wu swims a lap.

They tap the wall. Tie!

Think of two things that start with the same beginning sound as **watermelon**. Draw them.

Vic, Val, and the Vacuum   Vv

Understanding the Story: Characters

Think about what Val does and how she feels. When does Val feel mad? Draw and write about it.

When does Val feel happy and thankful in the story? Draw and write.

Vv Vic, Val, and the Vacuum

vacuum

Practice the Letter Vv

Say the letter name and the sound it stands for. Then, trace and write capital **V** and lowercase **v**.

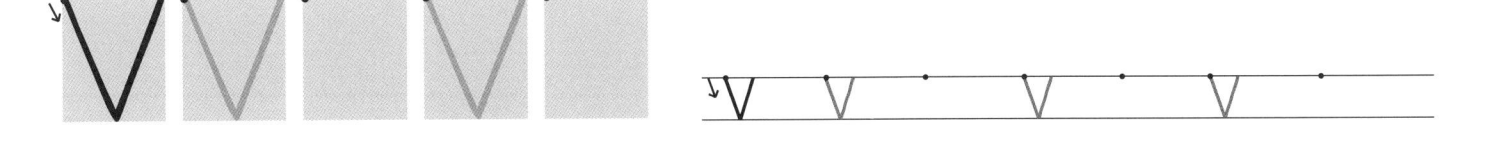

Say the name of each picture.
Write the letter that stands for the **beginning** sound to complete the word.

__ase   __at   __an   __og   __op   __ug

Think of two things that start with the same beginning sound as **vacuum**. Draw them.

48 A–Z for Mat Man® and Me: Practice for Developing Readers - Letter Learning

© 2022 Learning Without Tears

Umberto and the Umbrella Uu

Understanding the Story: Events

What does Umberto do in the story? Draw three things Umberto uses to try to stay dry.

Uu — Umberto and the Umbrella

umbrella

Practice the Letter Uu

Say the letter name and the sound it stands for. Then, trace and write capital **U** and lowercase **u**.

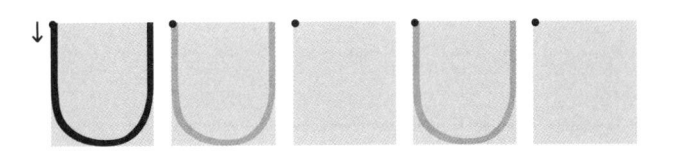

Say the name of each picture.
Write the letter that stands for the **middle** sound to complete the word.

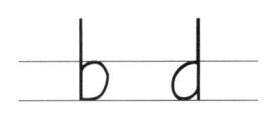

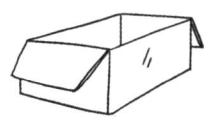

r _ cks

b _ t

s _ n

d _ ck

n _ ts

b _ d

p _ g

b _ x

c _ p

r _ g

46 A–Z for Mat Man® and Me: Practice for Developing Readers - Letter Learning © 2022 Learning Without Tears

Tere and the Tomato   Tt

Understanding the Story: Characters

Think about what Tere does and how she feels in the story. When does Tere feel worried? Draw and write about it.

When does Tere feel happy in the story? Draw and write about it.

© 2022 Learning Without Tears — A–Z for Mat Man® and Me: Practice for Developing Readers - **Meaning Making**

Tt Tere and the Tomato

tomato

Practice the Letter Tt

Say the letter name and the sound it stands for. Then, trace and write capital **T** and lowercase **t**.

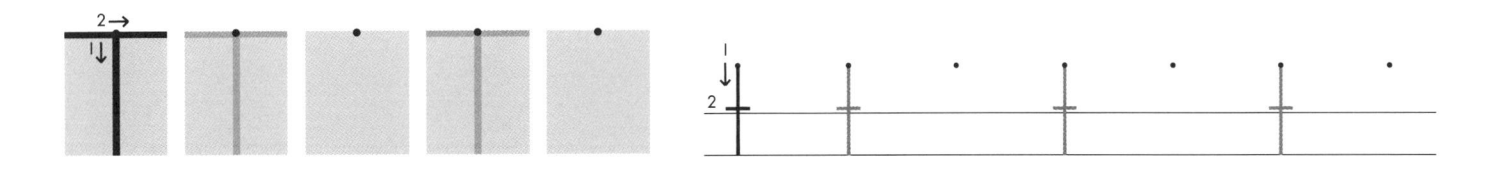

Say the name of each picture.
Write the letter that stands for the **beginning** sound to complete the word.

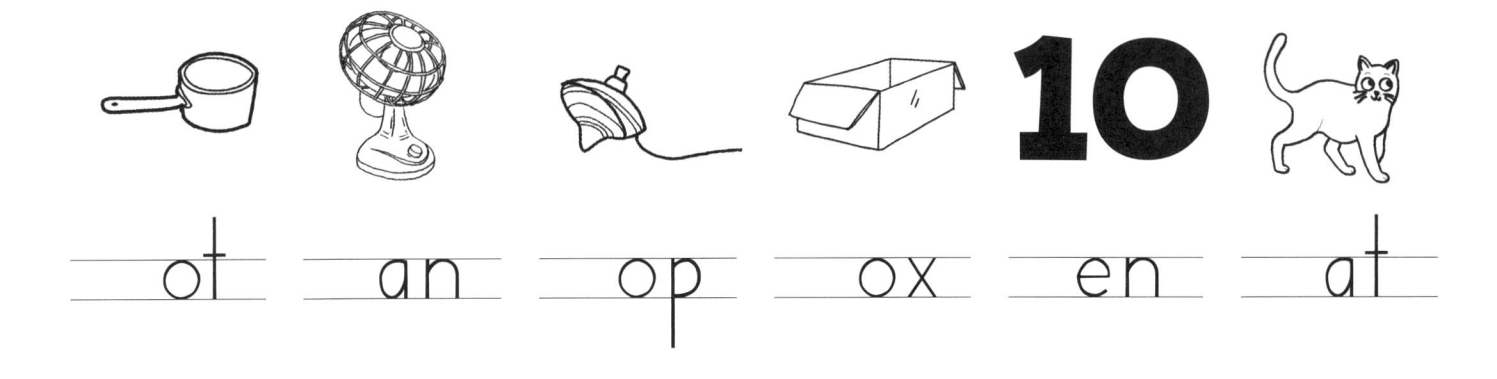

_ot   _an   _op   _ox   _en   _at

Look around. Find names that start with capital **T** and things that start with lowercase **t**.
Write the words.

Sam in the Sun Ss

Understanding the Story: Setting

Circle the picture that shows where the story takes place.

Where is Sam in the story? Write about the place and draw a picture.

Ss Sam in the Sun

sun

Practice the Letter Ss

Say the letter name and the sound it stands for. Then, trace and write capital **S** and lowercase **s**.

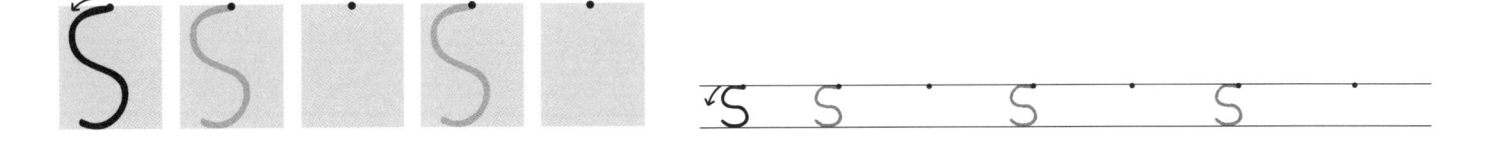

Say the name of each picture.
Write the letter that stands for the **beginning** sound to complete the word.

__at   __un   __ink   __og   __ix   __an

Think of two things that start with the same beginning sound as **sun**. Draw them.

Rex and the Rake — Rr

Understanding the Story: Characters

Think about what Rex does and how he feels.
When does Rex feel confused about something in the story? Write and draw about it.

When does Rex feel upset and frustrated in the story? Write and draw about it.

© 2022 Learning Without Tears — *A–Z for Mat Man® and Me: Practice for Developing Readers* - **Meaning Making**

Rr Rex and the Rake

rake

Practice the Letter **Rr**

Say the letter name and the sound it stands for. Then, trace and write capital **R** and lowercase **r**.

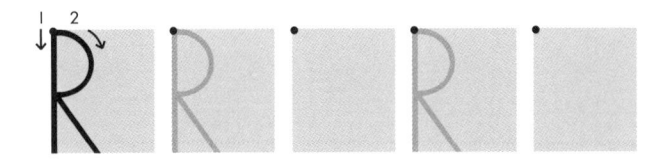

Say the name of each picture.
Write the letter that stands for the **beginning** sound to complete the word.

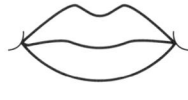

_oof _an _ocks _un _ug _ips

Look around. Find names that start with capital **R** and things that start with lowercase **r**.
Write the words.

Quinn and the Quilt   Qq

Understanding the Story: Events

Think about what happens in the story. The middle of the story is filled in. Now, draw and write about what happens in the beginning and end.

Beginning

Middle

"Dad!"

The quilt gets wet.

End

© 2022 Learning Without Tears — A–Z for Mat Man® and Me: Practice for Developing Readers - **Meaning Making**

Qq Quinn and the Quilt

quilt

Practice the Letter Qq

Say the letter name and the sound it stands for. Then, trace and write capital **Q** and lowercase **q**.

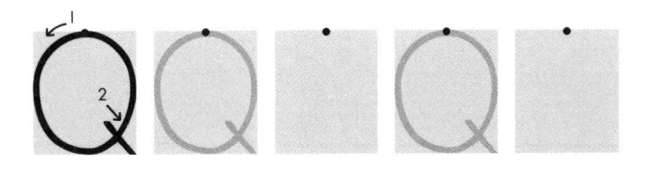

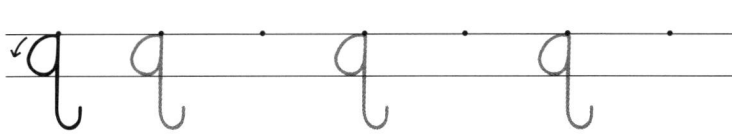

Read as much as you can. Then, circle every capital **Q** and lowercase **q** you see.

Monique has a duck.

Quack! Quack! Quack!

It is not quiet.

Raquan will get it.

Raquan can not.

The duck is quick!

Think of two things that start with the same beginning sound as **quilt**. Draw them.

Paco and the Piano Pp

Understanding the Story: Setting

Circle the picture that shows where the story takes place.

Write and draw about where Paco goes in the story.

Pp Paco and the Piano

piano

Practice the Letter **Pp**

Say the letter name and the sound it stands for. Then, trace and write capital **P** and lowercase **p**.

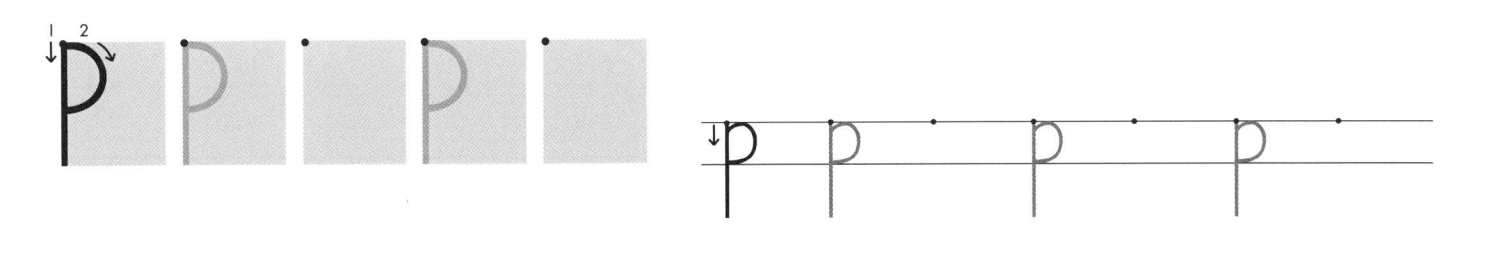

Say the name of each picture.
Write the letter that stands for the **beginning** sound to complete the word.

___ ot   ___ at   ___ up   ___ ig   ___ ug   ___ an

Look around. Find names that start with capital **P** and things that start with lowercase **p**. Write the words.

Oz and the Octopus   Oo

Understanding the Story: Events

Think about what happens in the story. The middle of the story is filled in. Now, draw and write about what happens in the beginning and end.

Beginning

Middle

The octopus is on the tank.

End

© 2022 Learning Without Tears — A–Z for Mat Man® and Me: Practice for Developing Readers - **Meaning Making**   35

Oo Oz and the Octopus

octopus

Practice the Letter Oo

Say the letter name and the sound it stands for. Then, trace and write capital **O** and lowercase **o**.

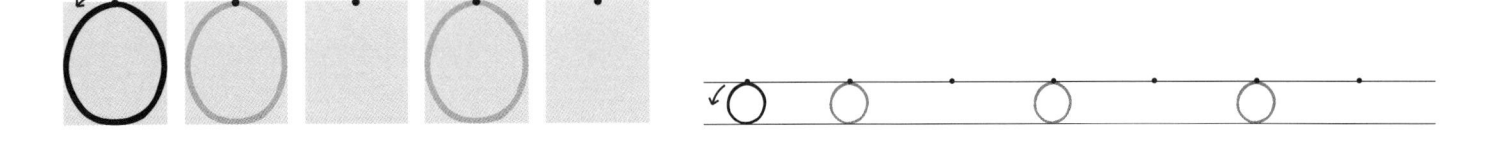

Say the name of each picture.
Write the letter that stands for the **middle** sound to complete the word.

f_sh   m_p

p_t   l_g

f_n   d_g

b_d   c_t

f_x   b_x

34 A–Z for Mat Man® and Me: Practice for Developing Readers - Letter Learning   © 2022 Learning Without Tears

Nell and the Nest — Nn

Understanding the Story: Setting

Circle the picture that shows where the story takes place.

Write and draw about the place where Nell is and why it is important to what happens in the story.

Nn Nell and the Nest

Practice the Letter **Nn**

Say the letter name and the sound it stands for. Then, trace and write capital **N** and lowercase **n**.

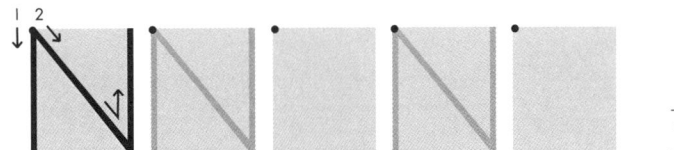

nest

Say the name of each picture.
Write the letter that stands for the **beginning** sound to complete the word.

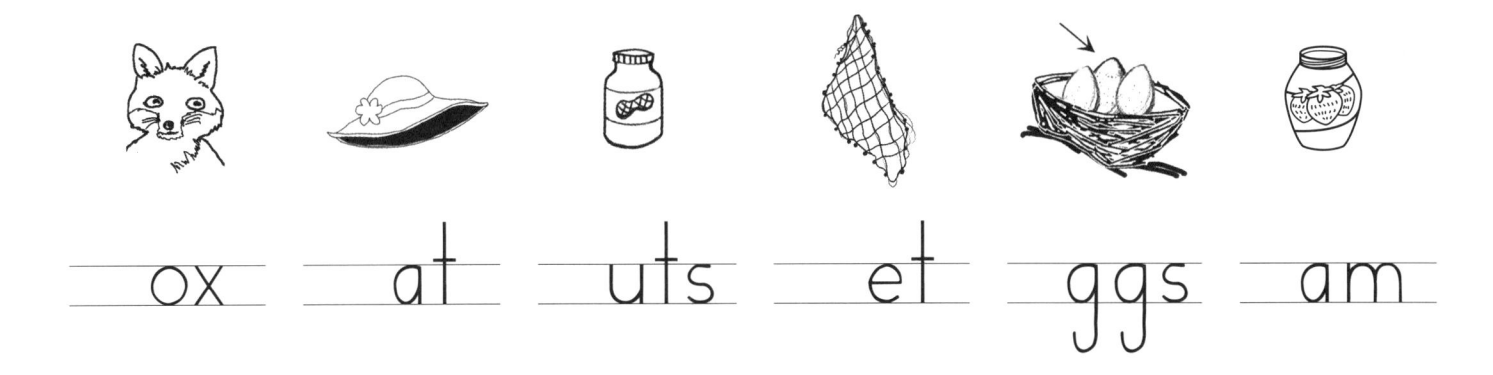

___ox   ___at   ___uts   ___et   ___ggs   ___am

Think of two things that start with the same beginning sound as **nest**. Draw them.

32 A–Z for Mat Man® and Me: Practice for Developing Readers - Letter Learning   © 2022 Learning Without Tears

Mac and the Magnificent Masks   Mm

Understanding the Story: Events

Think about what happens in the story. The middle of the story is filled in. Now, draw and write about what happens in the beginning and end.

Beginning

Middle

Marcos tosses markers.

End

© 2022 Learning Without Tears — A–Z for Mat Man® and Me: Practice for Developing Readers - **Meaning Making**

Mm Mac and the Magnificent Masks

mask

Practice the Letter Mm

Say the letter name and the sound it stands for. Then, trace and write capital **M** and lowercase **m**.

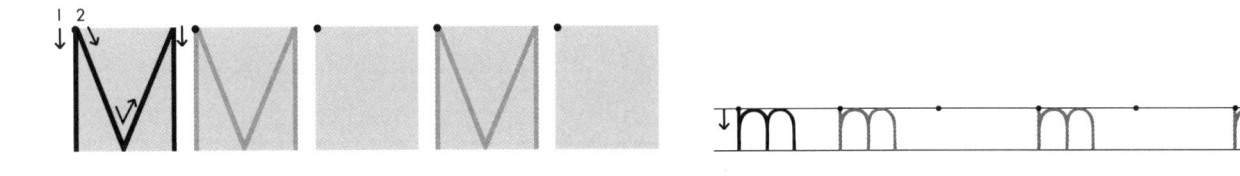

M M M   m m m m

Say the name of each picture.
Write the letter that stands for the beginning sound to complete the word.

__op   __ox   __ug   __at   __ed   __ick

Look around. Find names that start with capital **M** and things that start with lowercase **m**.
Write the words.

Understanding the Story: Events

Where does Lola look for her lock? Draw and write about three places where Lola looks.

Ll Lola and the Lock

lock

Practice the Letter Ll

Say the letter name and the sound it stands for. Then, trace and write capital **L** and lowercase **l**.

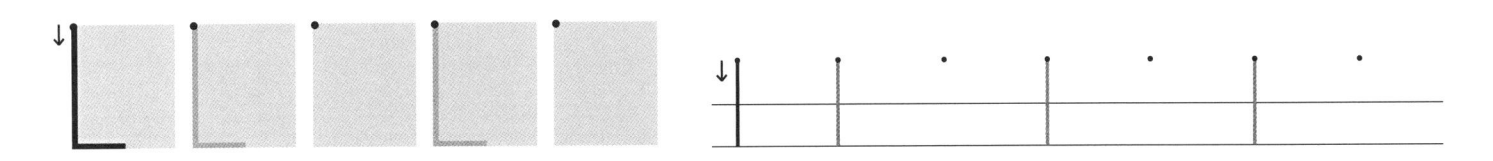

Say the name of each picture.
Write the letter that stands for the **beginning** sound to complete the word.

___eg   ___un   ___og   ___ick   ___ock   ___og

Think of two things that start with the same beginning sound as **lock**. Draw them.

28 A–Z for Mat Man® and Me: Practice for Developing Readers - Letter Learning © 2022 Learning Without Tears

Kaya and the Kayak Kk

Understanding the Story: Setting

Circle the picture that shows where the story takes place.

Where is Kaya in the story? Write about the place and draw a picture.

Kk Kaya and the Kayak

kayak

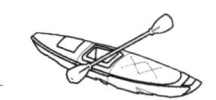

Practice the Letter **Kk**

Say the letter name and the sound it stands for. Then, trace and write capital **K** and lowercase **k**.

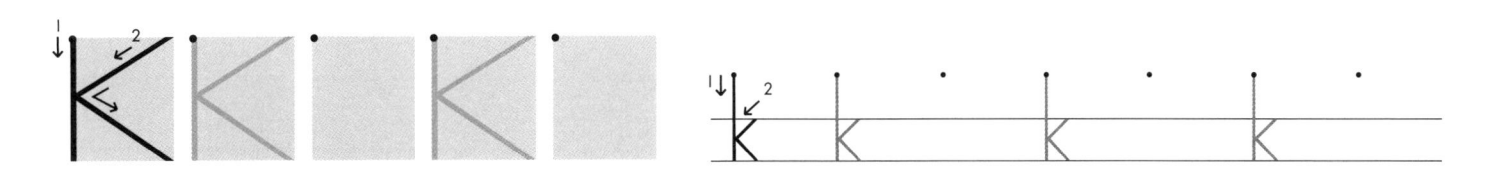

Say the name of each picture.
Write the letter that stands for the **beginning** sound to complete the word.

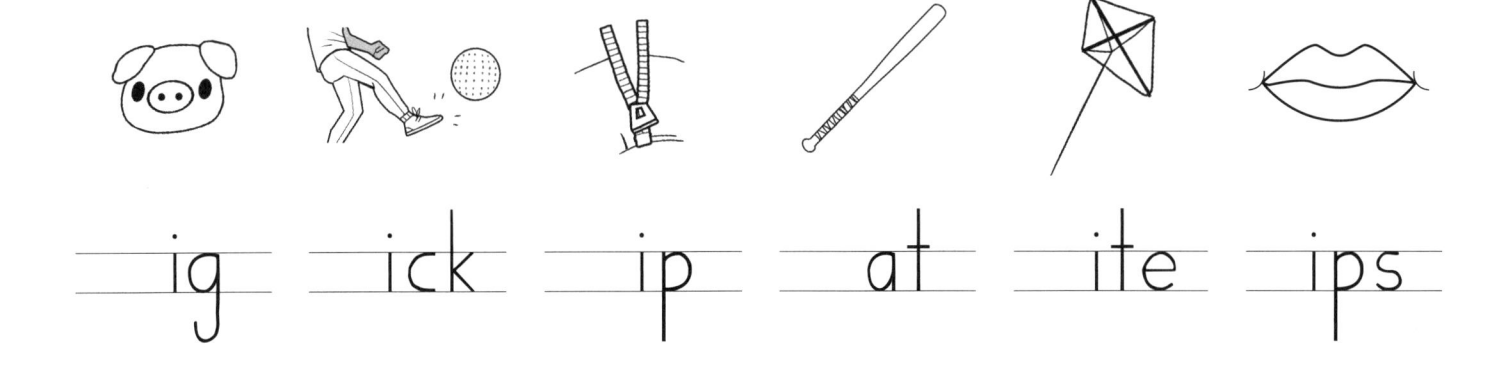

___ig   ___ick   ___ip   ___at   ___ite   ___ips

Look around. Find names that start with capital **K** and things that start with lowercase **k**.
Write the words.

Jana, Jen, and the Jellyfish   Jj

Understanding the Story: Character

Find the two main characters in the story. (Circle) two pictures.

Write about something the characters do in the story and draw a picture.

Jj Jana, Jen, and the Jellyfish

jellyfish

Practice the Letter Jj

Say the letter name and the sound it stands for. Then, trace and write capital **J** and lowercase **j**.

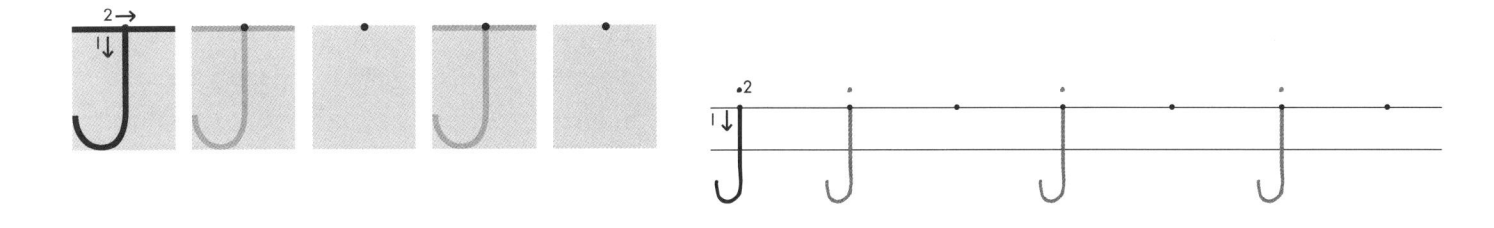

Say the name of each picture.
Write the letter that stands for the **beginning** sound to complete the word.

_un   _an   _am   _ox   _eep   _at

Think of two things that start with the same beginning sound as **jellyfish**. Draw them.

24 A–Z for Mat Man® and Me: Practice for Developing Readers - Letter Learning   © 2022 Learning Without Tears

Ikiaq and the Igloo   Ii

Understanding the Story: Setting

Circle the picture that shows where the story takes place.

Write about a place from the story and draw a picture.

Ii Ikiaq and the Igloo

igloo

Practice the Letter Ii

Say the letter name and the sound it stands for. Then, trace and write capital **I** and lowercase **i**.

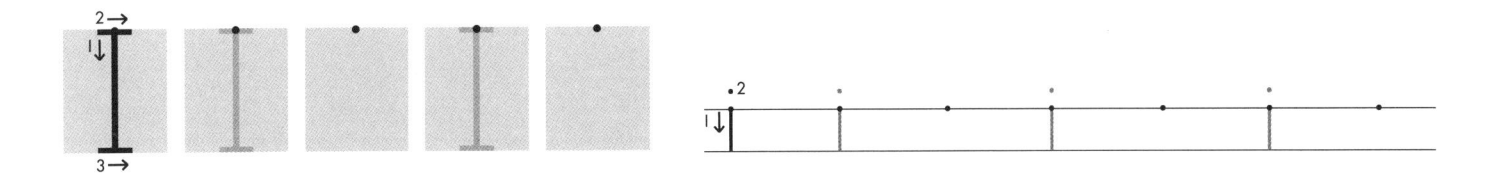

Say the name of each picture.
Write the letter that stands for the **middle** sound to complete the word.

s _ n   f _ n

z _ p   b _ x

c _ p   b _ d

p _ g   l _ ps

c _ t   d _ g

Hana has a Hammer   Hh

Understanding the Story: Characters

Which animals get out in the story? Draw three that Hana has to chase. Write the names.

21

Hh Hana has a Hammer

hammer

Practice the Letter Hh

Say the letter name and the sound it stands for. Then, trace and write capital **H** and lowercase **h**.

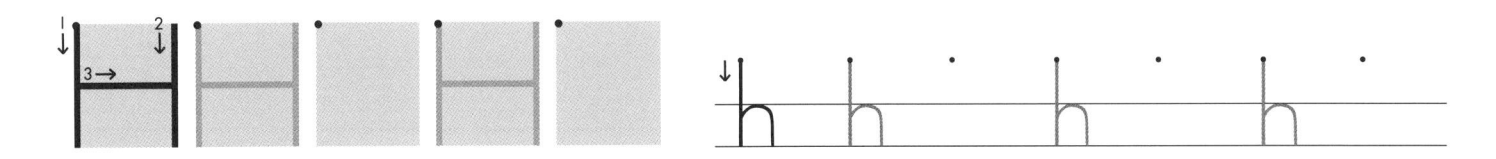

Say the name of each picture.
Write the letter that stands for the **beginning** sound to complete the word.

___ox   ___en   ___at   ___eg   ___og   ___ig

Look around. Find names that start with capital **H** and things that start with lowercase **h**.
Write the words.

Understanding the Story: Events

What does Gus do in the story? Draw and write three things Gus gets.

Gg Gabby and Her Goat

goat

Practice the Letter Gg

Say the letter name and the sound it stands for. Then, trace and write capital **G** and lowercase **g**.

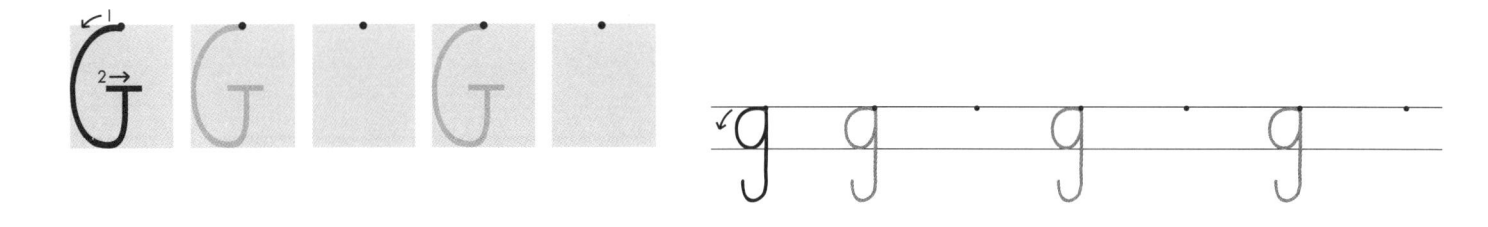

Say the name of each picture.
Write the letter that stands for the **ending** sound to complete the word.

ba___   mo___   do___   pi___   po___   ru___

Look around. Find names that start with capital **G** and things that start with lowercase **g**.
Write the words.

Feng, Finn, and the Fan Ff

Understanding the Story: Events

Think about what happens in the story. The middle of the story is filled in. Now, draw and write about what happens in the beginning and end.

Beginning

Middle

Feng and Finn fight.

End

A–Z for Mat Man® and Me: Practice for Developing Readers - Meaning Making

Ff Feng, Finn, and the Fan

fan

Practice the Letter Ff

Say the letter name and the sound it stands for. Then, trace and write capital **F** and lowercase **f**.

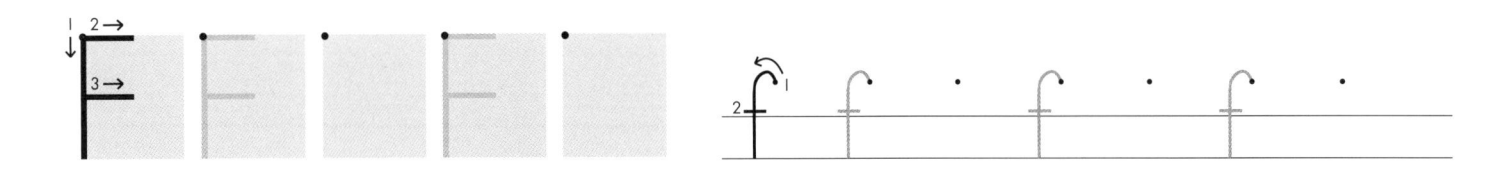

Say the name of each picture.
Write the letter that stands for the **beginning** sound to complete the word.

_at   _an   _ox   _in   _ox   _am

Think of two things that start with the same beginning sound as **fan**. Draw them.

Emma and the Elephant   Ee

Understanding the Story: Characters

Think about what Emma does and how she feels. When does Emma feel sad?
Draw and write about it.

When does Emma feel happy in the story? Draw and write about it.

© 2022 Learning Without Tears — A–Z for Mat Man® and Me: Practice for Developing Readers - **Meaning Making**   15

Ee Cora and the Coconut

Practice the Letter Ee

Say the letter name and the sound it stands for. Then, trace and write capital **E** and lowercase **e**.

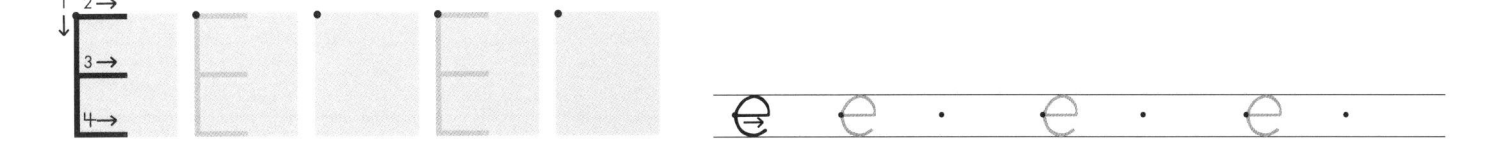

elephant

Say the name of each picture.
Write the letter that stands for the **middle** sound to complete the word.

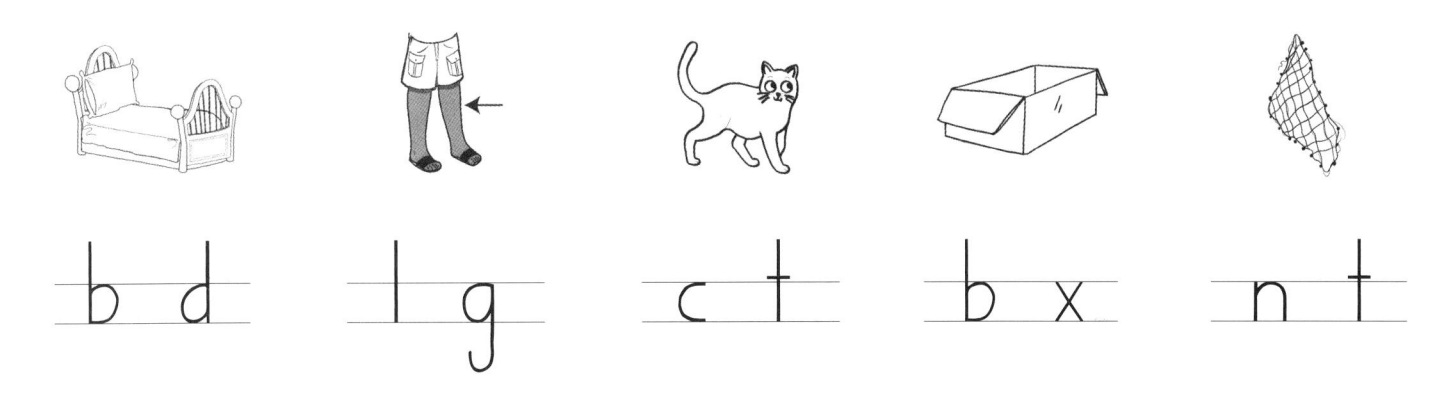

b __ d   l __ g   c __ t   b __ x   n __ t

Look around. Find names that start with capital **E** and things that start with lowercase **e**.
Write the words.

14   *A–Z for Mat Man® and Me: Practice for Developing Readers - Letter Learning*   © 2022 Learning Without Tears

Dax and the Dolphin   Dd

Understanding the Story: Setting

Circle the picture that shows where the story takes place.

Where is Dax in the story? Write about the place and draw a picture.

Dd Dax and the Dolphin

dolphin

Practice the Letter **Dd**
Say the letter name and the sound it stands for. Then, trace and write capital **D** and lowercase **d**.

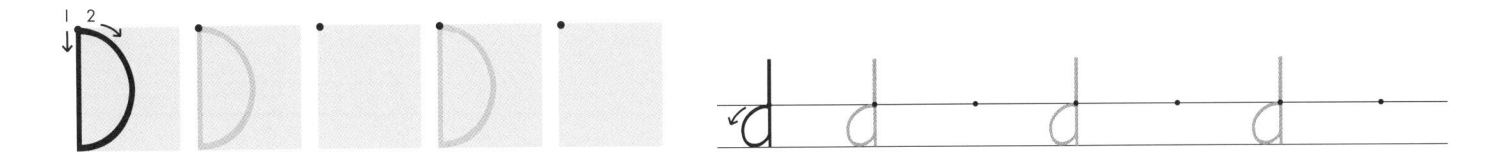

Say the name of each picture.
Write the letter that stands for the **beginning** sound to complete the word.

_ot

_uck

_op

_at

_og

_ig

_et

_an

_ox

_oll

12 *A–Z for Mat Man® and Me: Practice for Developing Readers - Letter Learning*   © 2022 Learning Without Tears

Cora and the Coconut Cc

Understanding the Story: Events

Think about what happens in the story. The middle of the story is filled in. Now, draw and write about what happens in the beginning and end.

Beginning

Middle

Cora holds up a cat.

End

© 2022 Learning Without Tears — *A–Z for Mat Man® and Me: Practice for Developing Readers* - **Meaning Making**

Cc Cora and the Coconut

coconut

Practice the Letter Cc

Say the letter name and the sound it stands for. Then, trace and write capital **C** and lowercase **c**.

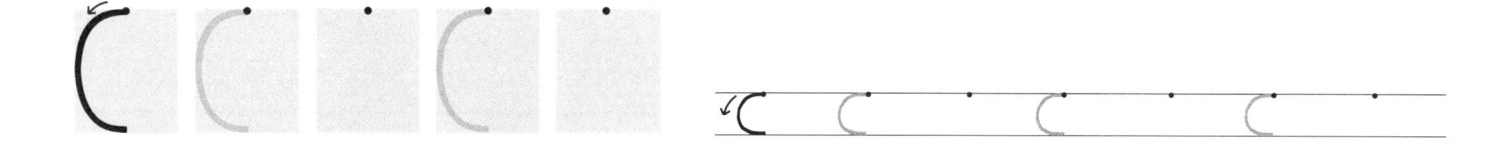

Say the name of each picture.
Write the letter that stands for the **beginning** sound to complete the word.

_c_at   _f_ox   _c_up   _c_ar   _b_ed   _l_ips

Look around. Find names that start with capital **C** and things that start with lowercase **c**.
Write the words.

Ben and the Big Bagels Bb

Understanding the Story: Setting

Circle the picture that shows where the story takes place.

Where is Ben in the story? Write about the place and draw a picture.

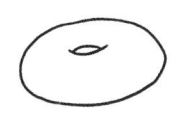

Bb Ben and the Big Bagels

bagel

Practice the Letter Bb

Say the letter name and the sound it stands for. Then, trace and write capital **B** and lowercase **b**.

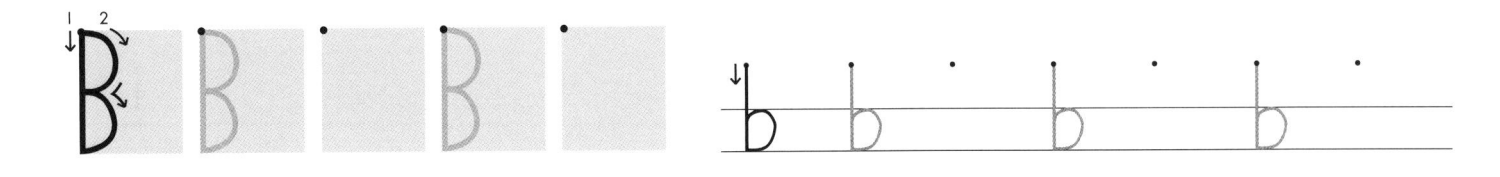

B B B b b b b

Say the name of each picture.
Write the letter that stands for the **beginning** sound to complete the word.

_ox   _ag

_an   _ot

_at   _ed

_ell   _at

_at   _eg

8 A–Z for Mat Man® and Me: Practice for Developing Readers - Letter Learning   © 2022 Learning Without Tears

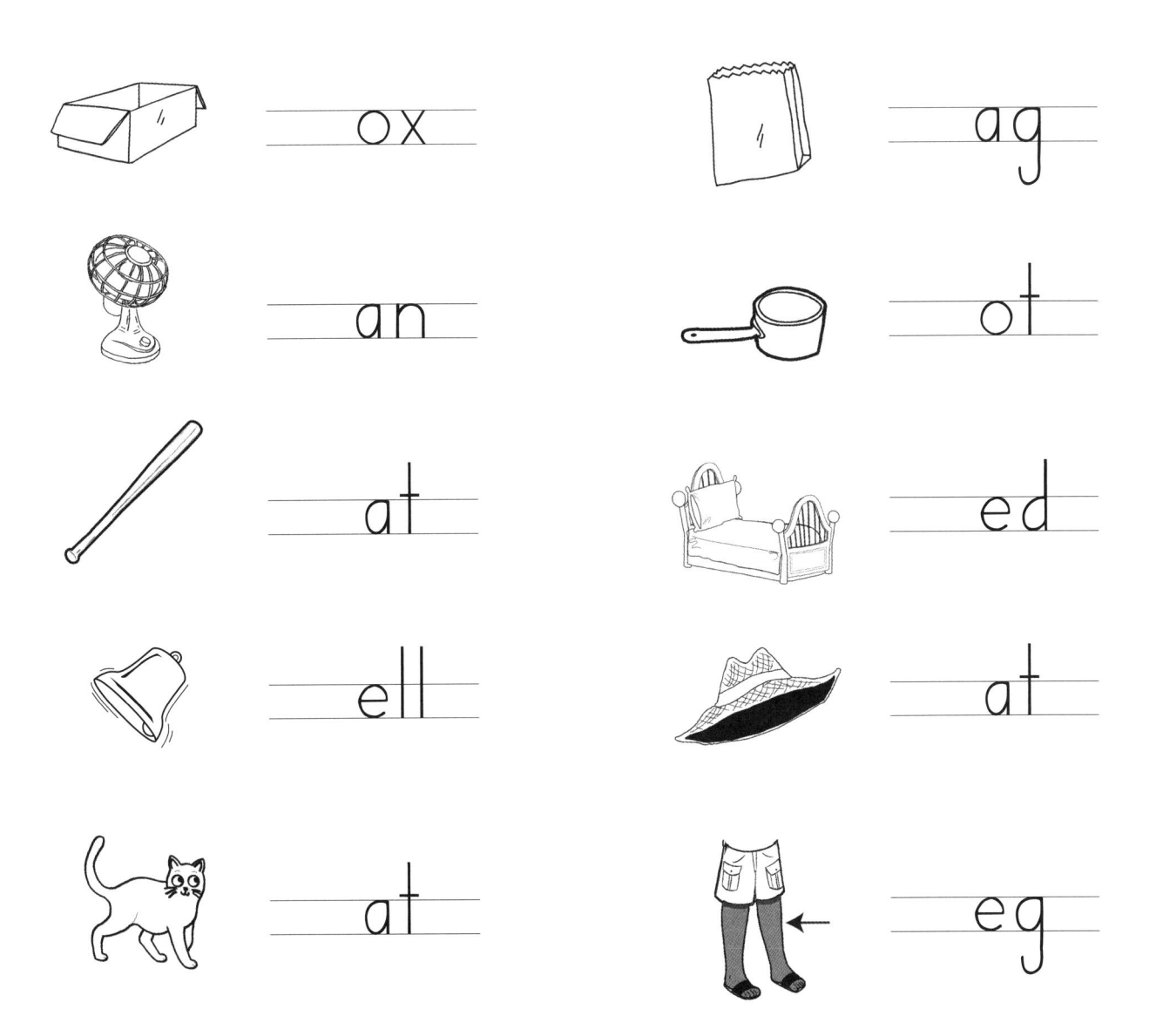

Ally and the Apple   Aa

Understanding the Story: Events

Think about what happens in the story. The middle of the story is filled in. Now, draw and write about what happens in the beginning and end.

Beginning

Middle

Ally asks for help.

End

Aa   Ally and the Apple

apple

Practice the Letter Aa

Say the letter name and the sound it stands for. Then, trace and write capital **A** and lowercase **a**.

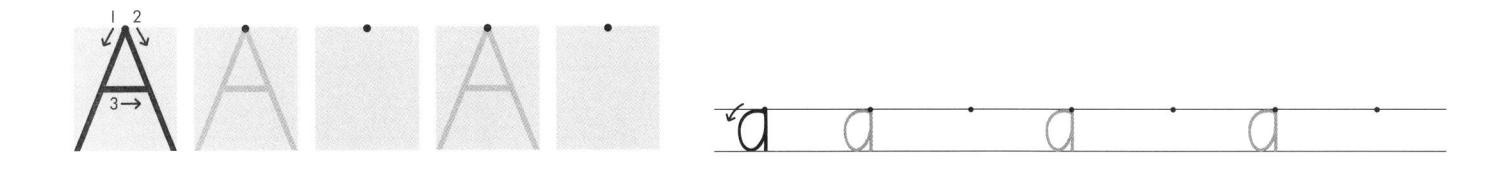

Say the name of each picture.
Write the letter that stands for the **middle** sound to complete the word.

_ck   h_t   p_t   f_n   c_t   r_g

Think of two things that start with the same beginning sound as **apple**. Draw them.

Mat Man® and the Great Alphabet Parade

The First Letter in Your Name

First, (circle) the letter your first name starts with. Then, underline the letter your last name starts with.

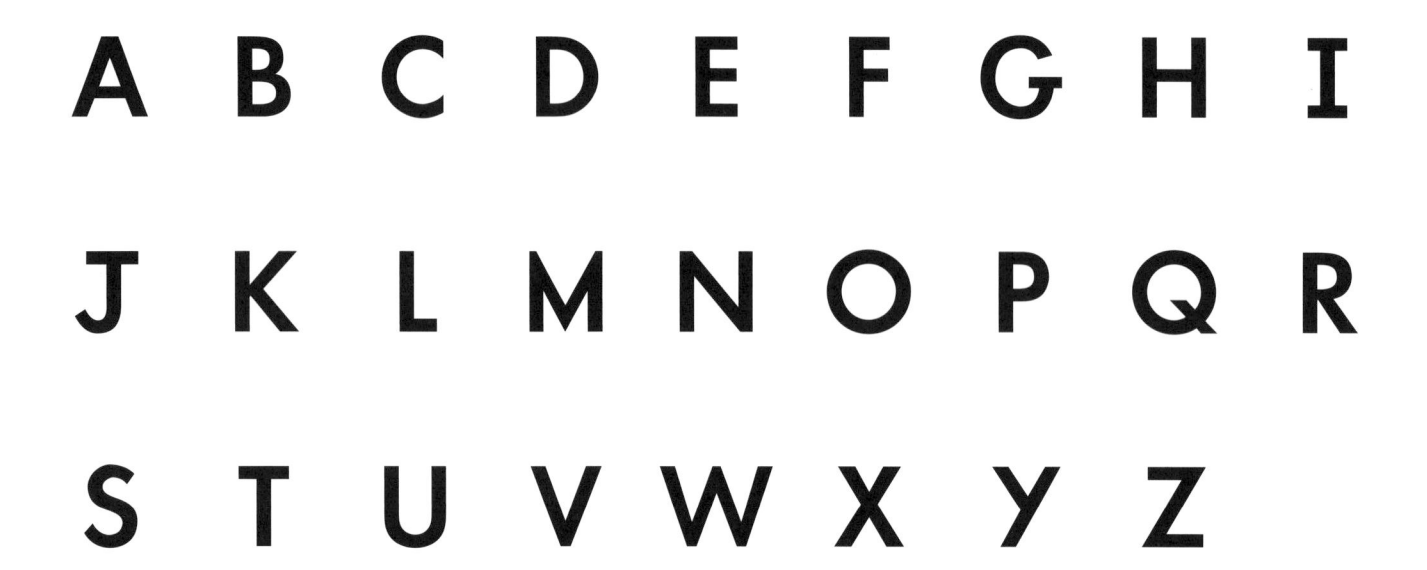

A B C D E F G H I
J K L M N O P Q R
S T U V W X Y Z

Draw a picture of something from the parade that starts with the same letter your first name starts with. Then, draw a picture of something that starts with the first letter in your last name.

Mat Man® and the Great Alphabet Parade

Sing the Alphabet Song

Help Mat Man sing the ABC song! Underline each letter as we sing it. The **a** is done for you. Then, color the pictures.

a b c d e f g

h i j k l m n o p

q r s

t u v

w x

y and z

TABLE OF CONTENTS

Sing the Alphabet Song 4

The First Letter in Your Name 5

Letter Aa: *Ally and the Apple*
   Practice the Letter **Aa** 6
   Understanding the Story: Events 7

Letter Bb: *Ben and the Big Bagels*
   Practice the Letter **Bb** 8
   Understanding the Story: Setting 9

Letter Cc: *Cora and the Coconut*
   Practice the Letter **Cc** 10
   Understanding the Story: Events 11

Letter Dd: *Dax and the Dolphin*
   Practice the Letter **Dd** 12
   Understanding the Story: Setting 13

Letter Ee: *Emma and Her Elephant*
   Practice the Letter **Ee** 14
   Understanding the Story: Character 15

Letter Ff: *Feng, Finn, and the Fan*
   Practice the Letter **Ff** 16
   Understanding the Story: Events 17

Letter Gg: *Gabby and Her Goat*
   Practice the Letter **Gg** 18
   Understanding the Story: Events 19

Letter Hh: *Hana Has a Hammer*
   Practice the Letter **Hh** 20
   Understanding the Story: Events 21

Letter Ii: *Ikiaq and the Igloo*
   Practice the Letter **Ii** 22
   Understanding the Story: Setting 23

Letter Jj: *Jana, Jen, and the Jellyfish*
   Practice the Letter **Jj** 24
   Understanding the Story: Character 25

Letter Kk: *Kaya and the Kite*
   Practice the Letter **Kk** 26
   Understanding the Story: Setting 27

Letter Ll: *Lola and the Lock*
   Practice the Letter **Ll** 28
   Understanding the Story: Events 29

Letter Mm: *Mac and the Magnificent Masks*
   Practice the Letter **Mm** 30
   Understanding the Story: Events 31

Letter Nn: *Nell and the Nest*
   Practice the Letter **Nn** 32
   Understanding the Story: Setting 33

Letter Oo: *Oz and the Octopus*
   Practice the Letter **Oo** 34
   Understanding the Story: Events 35

Letter Pp: *Paco and the Piano*
   Practice the Letter **Pp** 36
   Understanding the Story: Character 37

Letter Qq: *Quinn and the Quilt*
   Practice the Letter **Qq** 38
   Understanding the Story: Events 39

Letter Rr: *Rex and the Rake*
   Practice the Letter **Rr** 40
   Understanding the Story: Character 41

Letter Ss: *Sam in the Sun*
   Practice the Letter **Ss** 42
   Understanding the Story: Setting 43

Letter Tt: *Tere and the Tomato*
   Practice the Letter **Tt** 44
   Understanding the Story: Character 45

Letter Uu: *Umberto and the Umbrella*
   Practice the Letter **Uu** 46
   Understanding the Story: Events 47

Letter Vv: *Vic, Val, and the Vacuum*
   Practice the Letter **Vv** 48
   Understanding the Story: Character 49

Letter Ww: *Wes and the Watermelon*
   Practice the Letter **Ww** 50
   Understanding the Story: Setting 51

Letter Xx: *Xavier Gets an X-ray*
   Practice the Letter **Xx** 52
   Understanding the Story: Setting 53

Letter Yy: *Yolanda and the Yo-Yo*
   Practice the Letter **Yy** 54
   Understanding the Story: Events 55

Letter Zz: *Zack and His Zipper*
   Practice the Letter **Zz** 56
   Understanding the Story: Character 57

Letter Check 1 58

Letter Check 2 60

Letter Check 3 62

Letter Review 64

© 2022 Learning Without Tears

LEARNING
Without Tears®

8001 MacArthur Blvd.
Cabin John, MD 20818
LWTears.com | 888.983.8409

Art Director: Shannon Rutledge
Graphic Designer: Sammie Simon
Curriculum Designers: Adam Berkin, Nicole Iorio, Cari Meister, Casey Schultz

Copyright © 2022 Learning Without Tears
First Edition
ISBN: 978-1-954728-42-4
23456789RRD232221
Printed in Dongguan, China

The contents of this consumable workbook are protected by US copyright law. If a workbook has been purchased for a child, the author and Learning Without Tears give limited permission to copy pages for additional practice or homework for that child. No copied pages from this book can be given to another person without written permission from Learning Without Tears.

A-Z for Mat Man® and Me

Practice for Developing Readers

LEARNING
Without Tears®

Letter Review

Say the name for each picture. Circle the letter that stands for its **beginning** sound. Write the lowercase letter on the double lines.

1. m / p / s

2. s / w / m

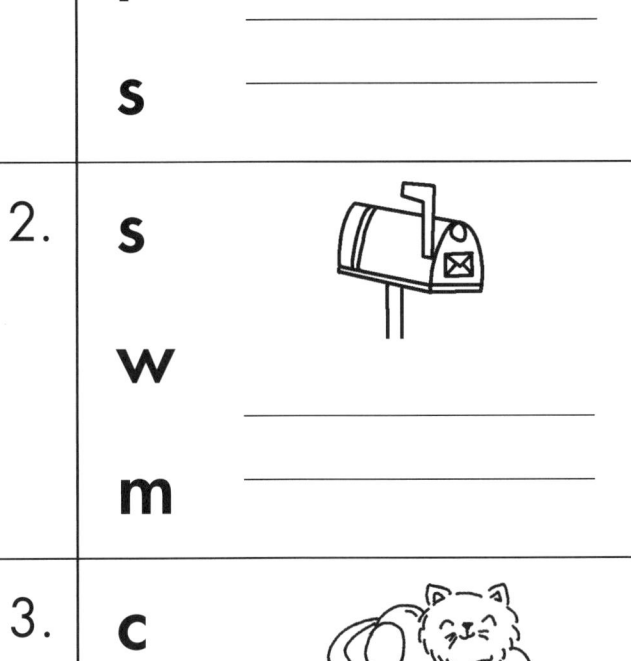

3. c / n / b

4. r / p / b

5. e / r / m

6. t / w / v

7. a / p / u

8. r / f / l

Letter Check 3

Letter Check 3, Part B

Say the name for each picture. Circle the letter that stands for its **beginning** sound.
Write the lowercase letter on the double lines.

1. x / k / a

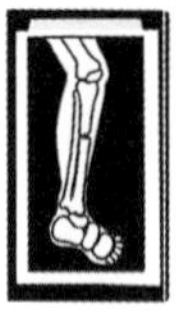

2. s / j / t

3. k / t / f

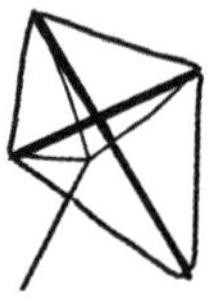

4. y / j / s

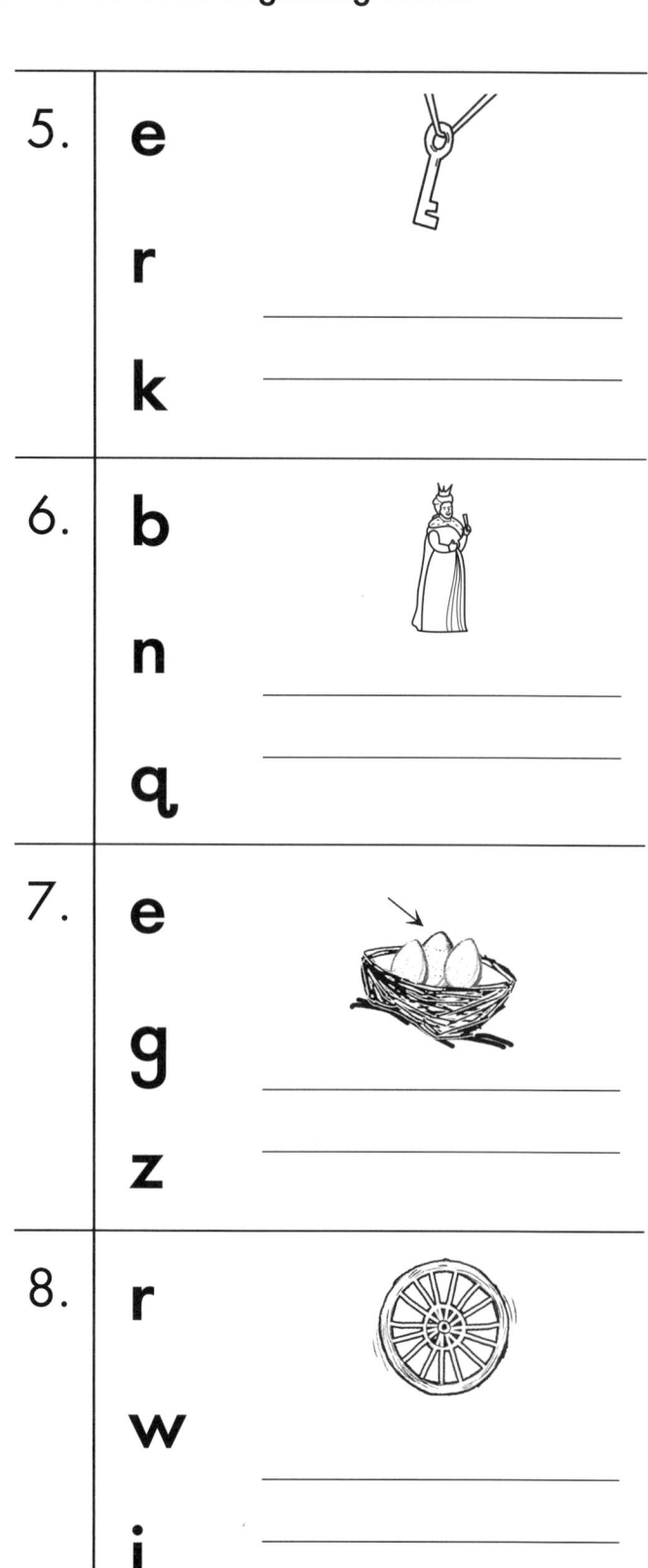

5. e / r / k

6. b / n / q

7. e / g / z

8. r / w / i

Letter Check 3

Letter Check 3, Part A

Say the name for each picture. Circle the letter that stands for its **beginning** sound. Write the lowercase letter on the double lines.

1. j / s / v

2. y / k / a

3. i / d / u

4. j / s / p

5. w / f / n

6. d / q / e

7. g / p / o

8. q / i / l

62 A–Z for Mat Man® and Me: Practice for Developing Readers

Letter Check 2

Letter Check 2, Part B

Say the name for each picture. Circle the letter that stands for its **beginning** sound. Write the lowercase letter on the double lines.

1.	r l g		5.	m d z
2.	c p v		6.	h l w
3.	n f l		7.	i d o
4.	m b e		8.	f g j

© 2022 Learning Without Tears

A–Z for Mat Man® and Me: Practice for Developing Readers

Letter Check 2

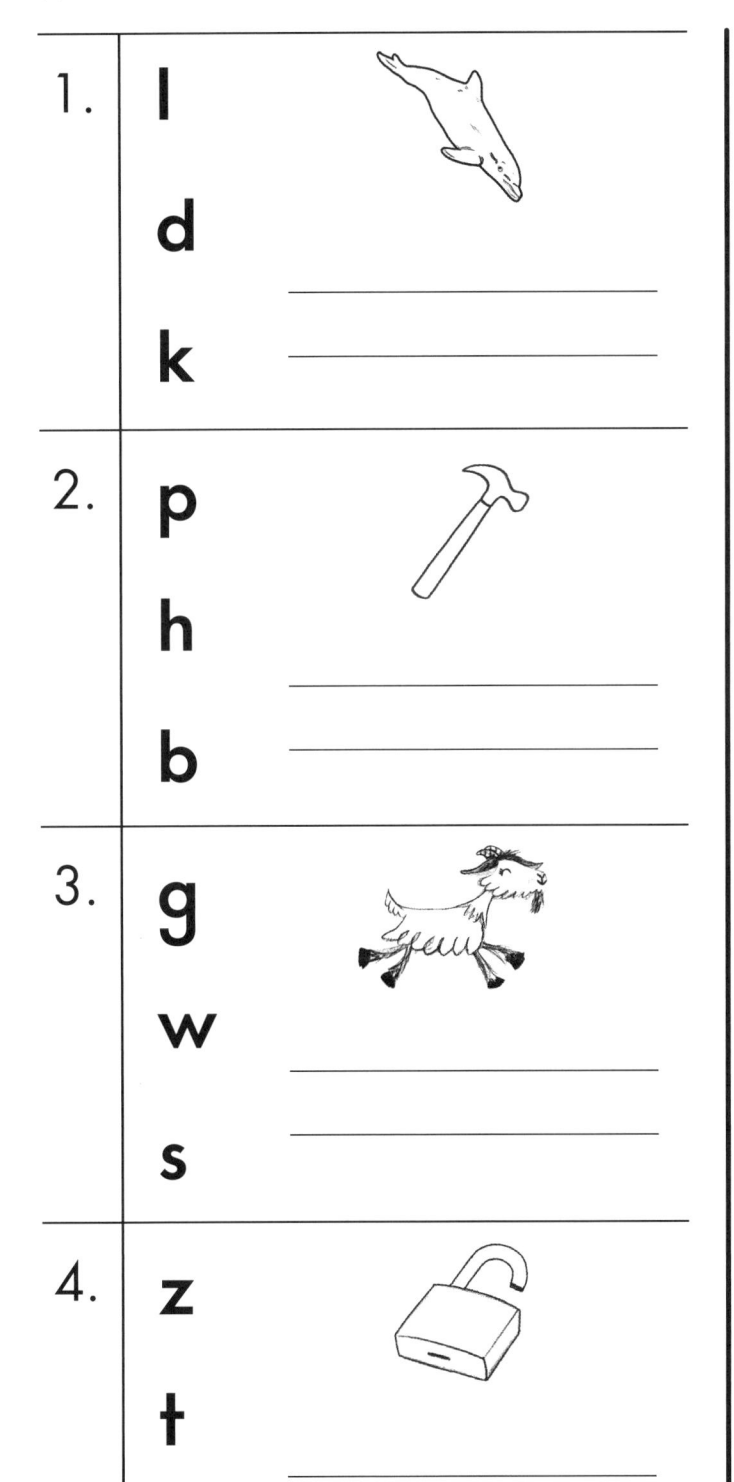

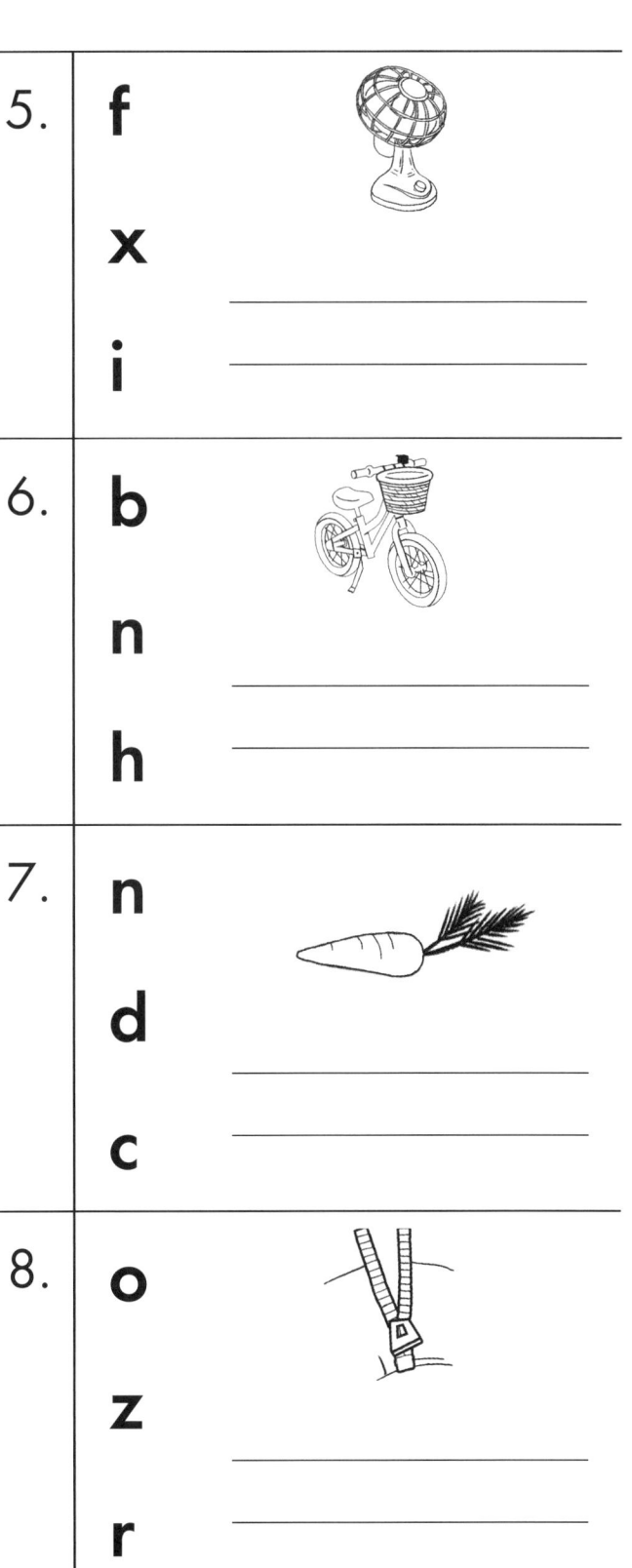

Letter Check 2, Part A

Say the name for each picture. Circle the letter that stands for its **beginning** sound. Write the lowercase letter on the double lines.

1. l / d / k

2. p / h / b

3. g / w / s

4. z / t / l

5. f / x / i

6. b / n / h

7. n / d / c

8. o / z / r

Letter Check 1

Letter Check 1, Part B

Say the name for each picture. (Circle) the letter that stands for its **beginning** sound.
Write the lowercase letter on the double lines.

1. s
   r
   l

2. i
   y
   p

3. p
   n
   g

4. k
   s
   r

5. a
   v
   m

6. b
   v
   a

7. t
   n
   r

8. t
   q
   p

Letter Check 1

Letter Check 1, Part A

Say the name for each picture. Circle the letter that stands for its **beginning** sound. Write the lowercase letter on the double lines.

1.	m p a		5.	g r m	
2.	s p t		6.	t s v	
3.	i n b		7.	a b u	
4.	r d p		8.	r o i	

58   A–Z for Mat Man® and Me: Practice for Developing Readers

Zack and His Zipper Zz

Understanding the Story: Characters

Think about what Zack does and how he feels. When does Zack feel mad? Draw and write about it.

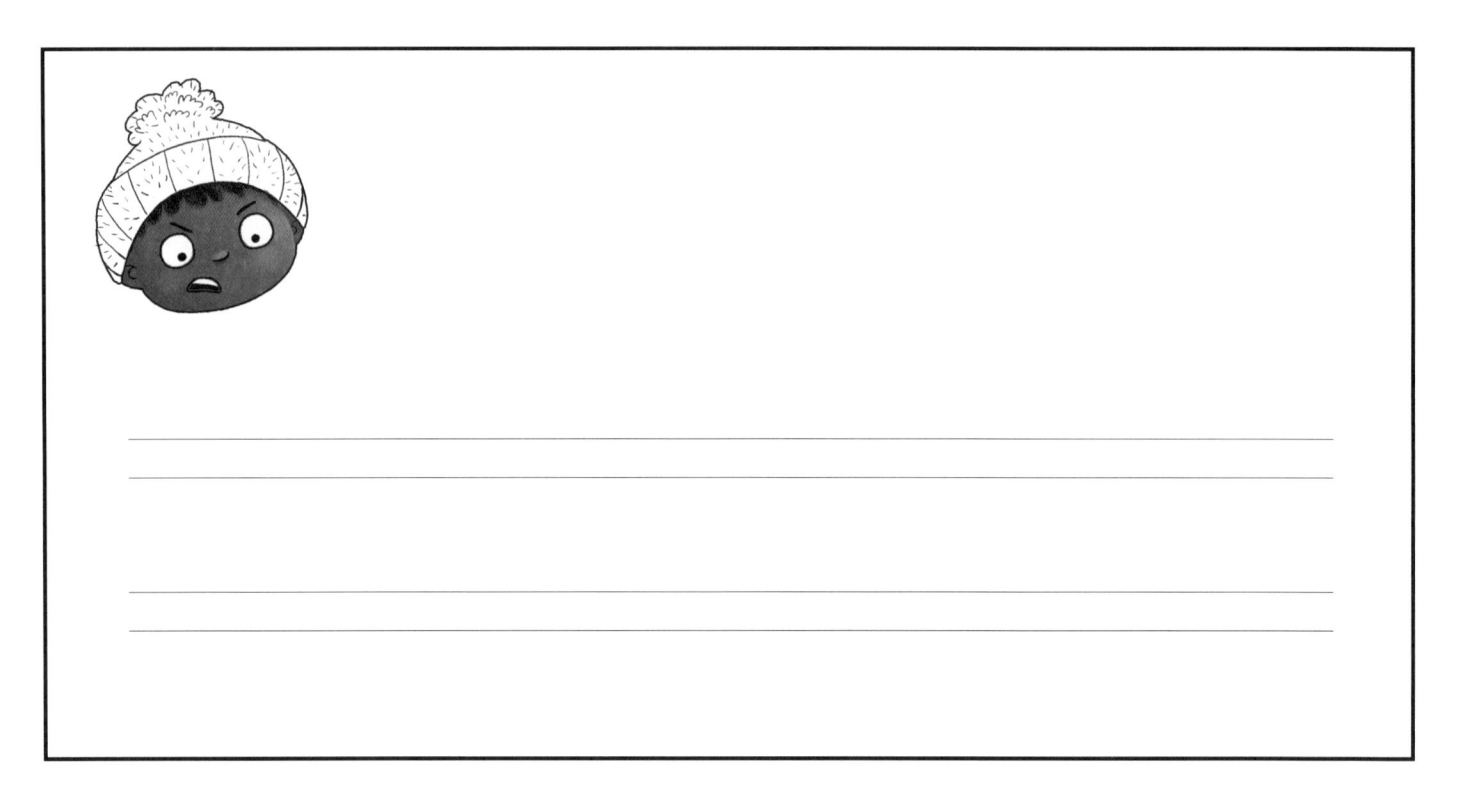

When does Zack feel happy in the story? Draw and write.

Zz Zack and His Zipper

zipper

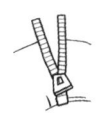

Practice the Letter Zz

Say the letter name and the sound it stands for. Then, trace and write capital Z and lowercase z.

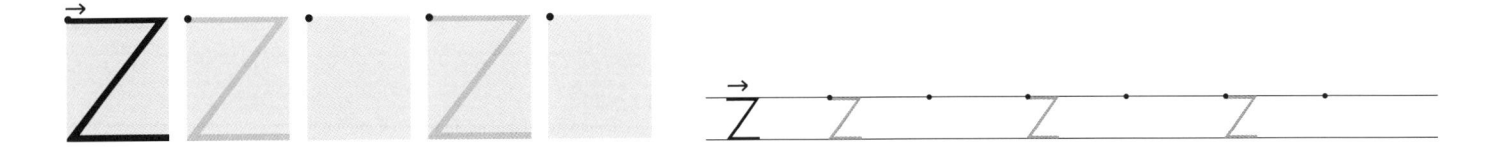

Read as much as you can. Then, circle every capital Z and lowercase z you see.

Liz zips up her coat.

It is a size too big.

It keeps out the breeze.

Liz and Zoe get to the zoo!

They look at a zebra.

Think of two things that start with the same beginning sound as **zipper**. Draw them.

Practice the Letter Yy

Understanding the Story: Events

Think about what happens in the story. The middle of the story is filled in. Now, draw and write about what happens in the beginning and end.

Beginning

Middle

Yaz does not trade back.

End

© 2022 Learning Without Tears — A–Z for Mat Man® and Me: Practice for Developing Readers - **Meaning Making**

Yy Practice the Letter Yy

yo-yo

Practice the Letter **Yy**

Say the letter name and the sound it stands for. Then, trace and write capital **Y** and lowercase **y**.

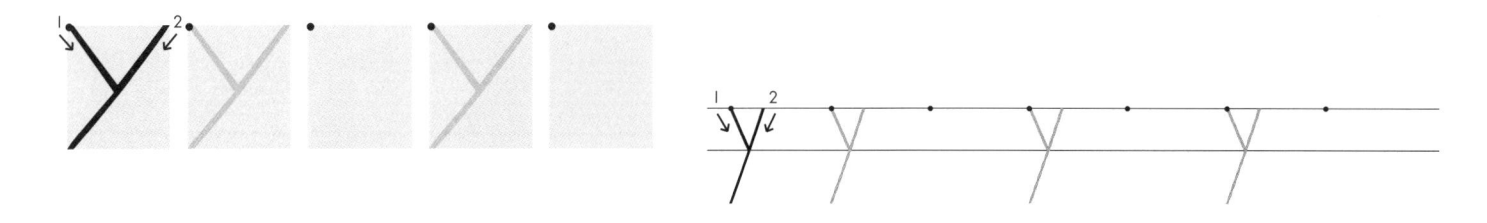

Read as much as you can. Then, circle every capital **Y** and lowercase **y** you see.

Yams are hot.

Yum! Cy says yes.

Cy gets a lot.

Jay says no.

Why yams? Yuck!

Jay gets a yogurt.

Think of two things that start with the same beginning sound as **yo-yo**. Draw them.

Xavier Gets an X-ray **Xx**

Understanding the Story: Setting

Where is Xavier in the story? Draw and write about three place where you see Xavier.

Xx Xavier Gets an X-ray

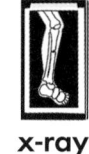

x-ray

Practice the Letter Xx

Say the letter name and the sound it stands for. Then, trace and write capital **X** and lowercase **x**.

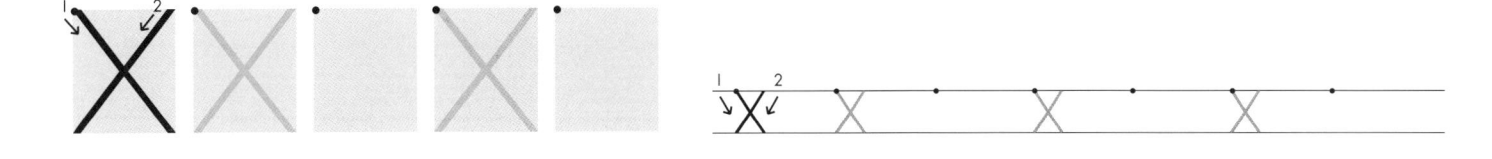

Say the name of each picture.
Write the letter that stands for the **ending** sound to complete the word.

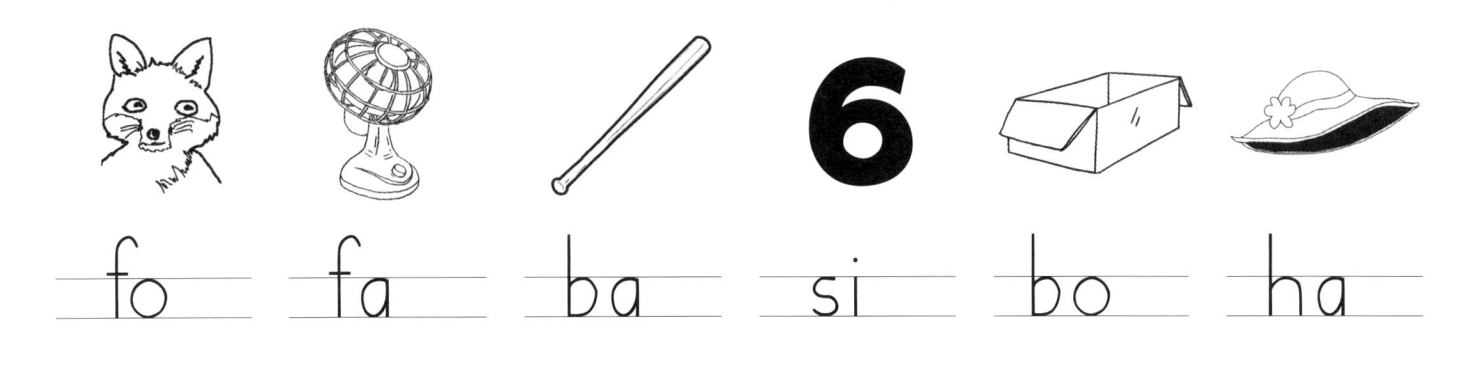

fo___   fa___   ba___   si___   bo___   ha___

Look around. Find names and words that have an **x** in them. Write the words.

Vic, Val, and the Vacuum   Vv

Understanding the Story: Characters

Think about what Val does and how she feels. When does Val feel mad? Draw and write about it.

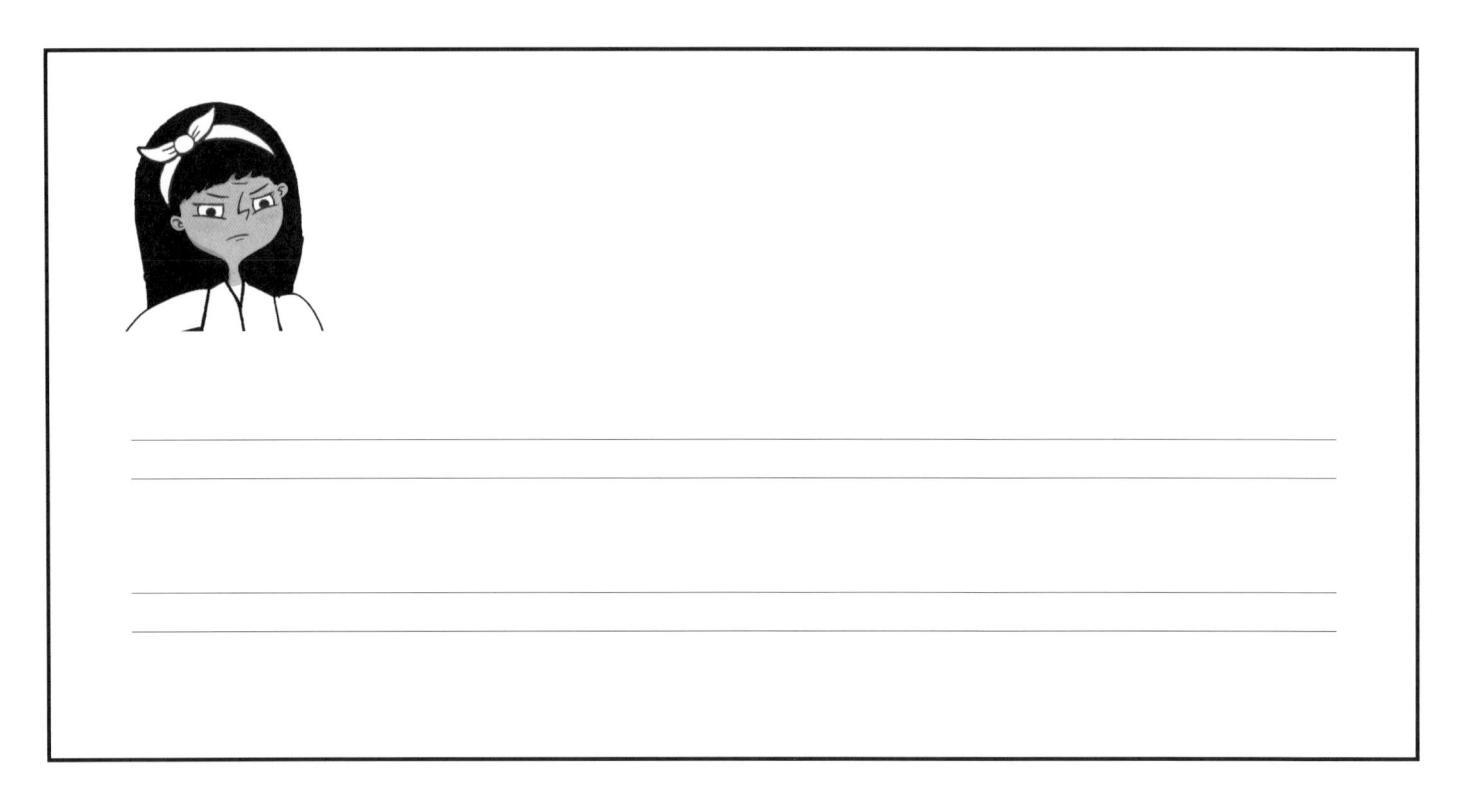

When does Val feel happy and thankful in the story? Draw and write.

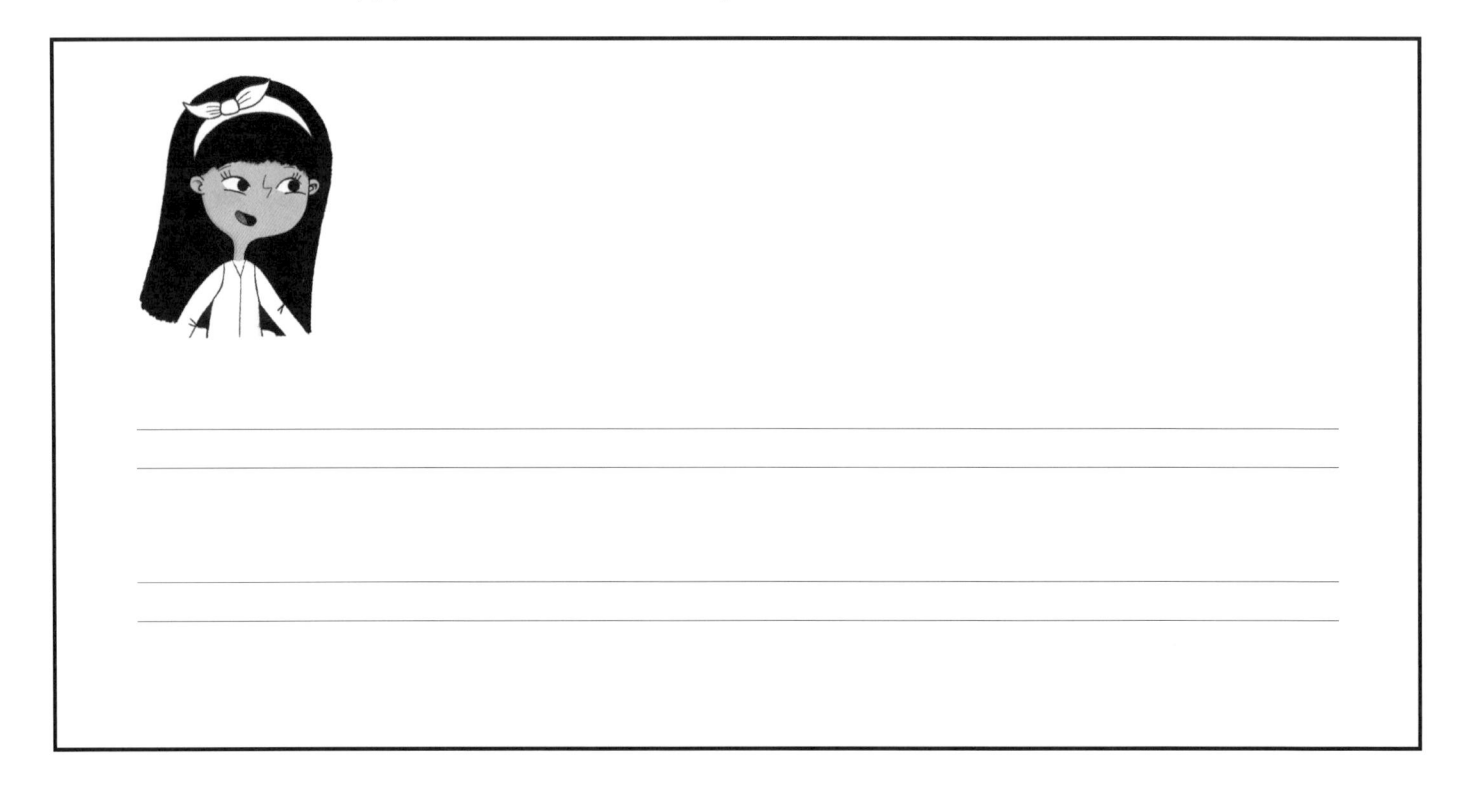

Wes and the Watermelon

Understanding the Story: Setting

Circle the picture that shows where the story takes place.

Where is Wes in the story? Write about the place and draw a picture.

Ww Wes and the Watermelon

watermelon

Practice the Letter Ww

Say the letter name and the sound it stands for. Then, trace and write capital **W** and lowercase **w**.

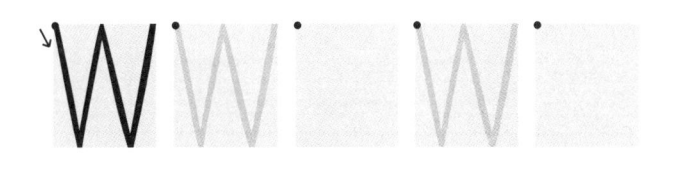

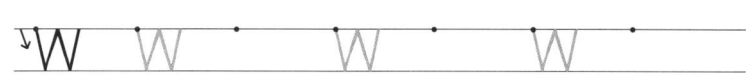

Read as much as you can. Then, circle every capital **W** and lowercase **w** you see.

Will has to win.

Wu has to win, too.

Who will win the swim race?

Will swims a lap.

Wu swims a lap.

They tap the wall. Tie!

Think of two things that start with the same beginning sound as **watermelon**. Draw them.

Vv Vic, Val, and the Vacuum

vacuum

Practice the Letter Vv

Say the letter name and the sound it stands for. Then, trace and write capital **V** and lowercase **v**.

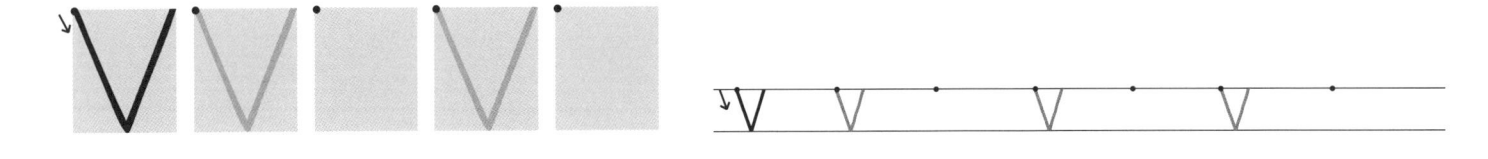

Say the name of each picture.
Write the letter that stands for the **beginning** sound to complete the word.

___ase   ___at   ___an   ___og   ___op   ___ug

Think of two things that start with the same beginning sound as **vacuum**. Draw them.

48 A–Z for Mat Man® and Me: Practice for Developing Readers - Letter Learning © 2022 Learning Without Tears

Umberto and the Umbrella   Uu

Understanding the Story: Events
What does Umberto do in the story? Draw three things Umberto uses to try to stay dry.

Uu — Umberto and the Umbrella

umbrella

Practice the Letter Uu

Say the letter name and the sound it stands for. Then, trace and write capital **U** and lowercase **u**.

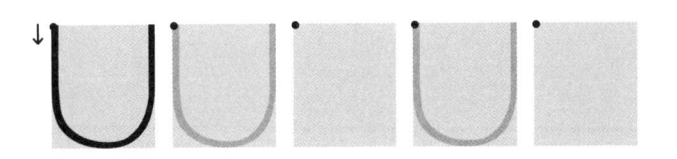

Say the name of each picture.
Write the letter that stands for the **middle** sound to complete the word.

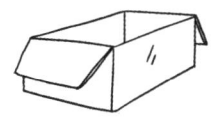

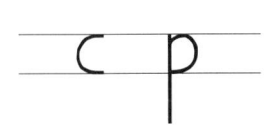

r _ cks

b _ t

s _ n

d _ ck

n _ ts

b _ d

p _ g

b _ x

c _ p

r _ g

46 A–Z for Mat Man® and Me: Practice for Developing Readers - Letter Learning © 2022 Learning Without Tears

Tere and the Tomato — Tt

Understanding the Story: Characters

Think about what Tere does and how she feels in the story. When does Tere feel worried? Draw and write about it.

When does Tere feel happy in the story? Draw and write about it.

Tt   Tere and the Tomato

tomato

Practice the Letter **Tt**

Say the letter name and the sound it stands for. Then, trace and write capital **T** and lowercase **t**.

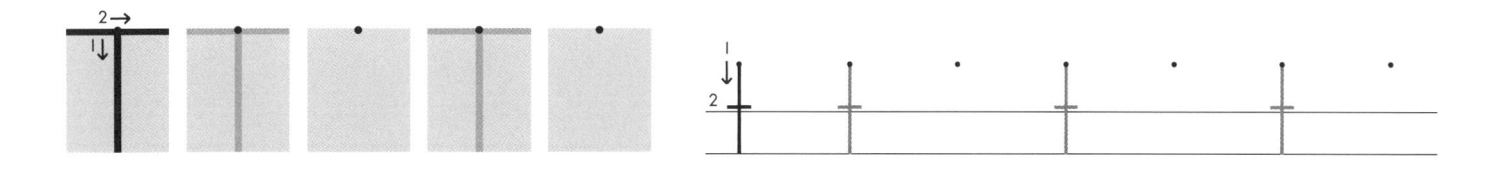

Say the name of each picture.
Write the letter that stands for the **beginning** sound to complete the word.

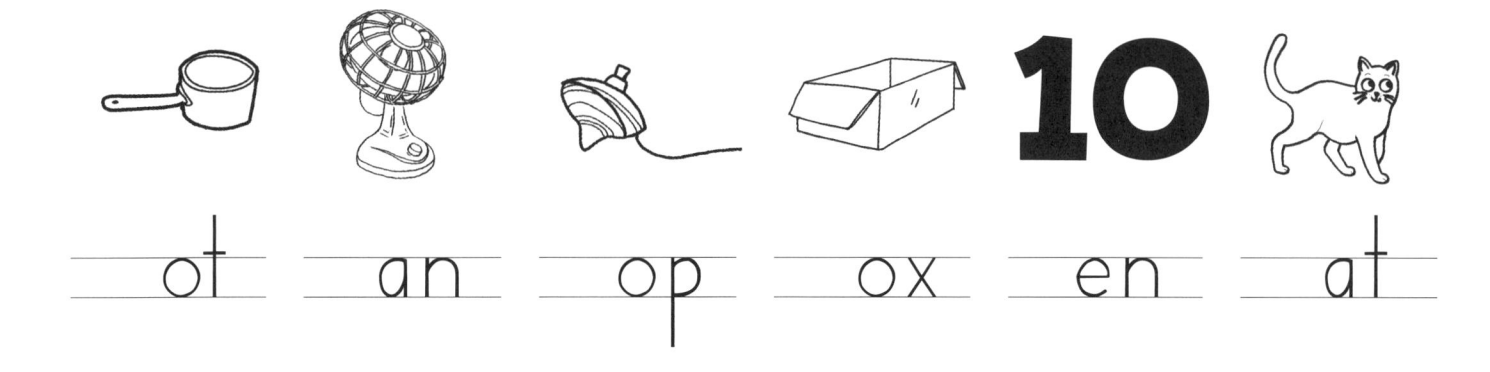

___ ot   ___ an   ___ op   ___ ox   ___ en   ___ at

Look around. Find names that start with capital **T** and things that start with lowercase **t**.
Write the words.

44   A–Z for Mat Man® and Me: Practice for Developing Readers - Letter Learning   © 2022 Learning Without Tears

Sam in the Sun Ss

Understanding the Story: Setting

Circle the picture that shows where the story takes place.

Where is Sam in the story? Write about the place and draw a picture.

Ss Sam in the Sun

sun

Practice the Letter Ss

Say the letter name and the sound it stands for. Then, trace and write capital **S** and lowercase **s**.

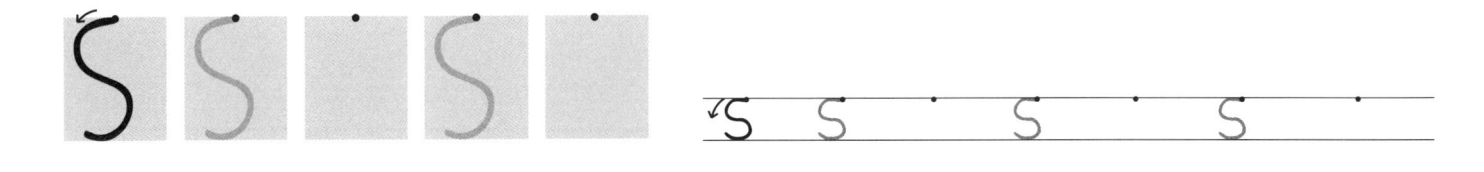

S S S S S   s s s s

Say the name of each picture.
Write the letter that stands for the **beginning** sound to complete the word.

__at   __un   __ink   __og   __ix   __an

Think of two things that start with the same beginning sound as **sun**. Draw them.

42 A–Z for Mat Man® and Me: Practice for Developing Readers - Letter Learning   © 2022 Learning Without Tears

Understanding the Story: Characters

Think about what Rex does and how he feels.
When does Rex feel confused about something in the story? Write and draw about it.

When does Rex feel upset and frustrated in the story? Write and draw about it.

Rr Rex and the Rake

rake

Practice the Letter Rr

Say the letter name and the sound it stands for. Then, trace and write capital **R** and lowercase **r**.

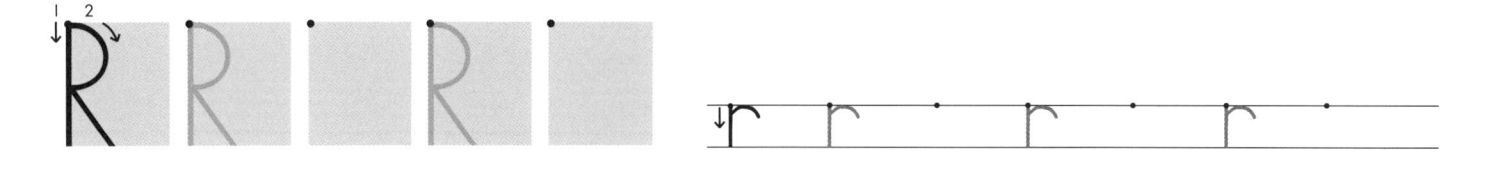

R R R   r r r r

Say the name of each picture.
Write the letter that stands for the **beginning** sound to complete the word.

_oof   _an   _ocks   _un   _ug   _ips

Look around. Find names that start with capital **R** and things that start with lowercase **r**. Write the words.

Quinn and the Quilt   Qq

Understanding the Story: Events

Think about what happens in the story. The middle of the story is filled in. Now, draw and write about what happens in the beginning and end.

Beginning

Middle

The quilt gets wet.

End

© 2022 Learning Without Tears — A–Z for Mat Man® and Me: Practice for Developing Readers - Meaning Making

Qq Quinn and the Quilt

quilt

Practice the Letter Qq

Say the letter name and the sound it stands for. Then, trace and write capital **Q** and lowercase **q**.

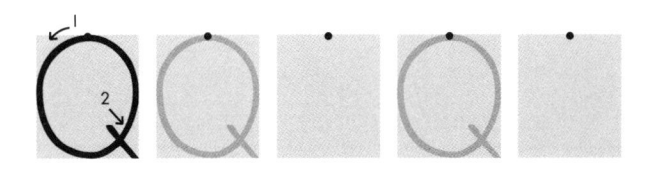

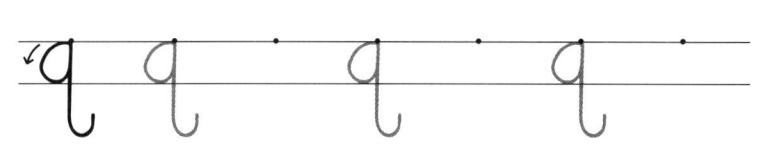

Read as much as you can. Then, circle every capital **Q** and lowercase **q** you see.

Monique has a duck.

Quack! Quack! Quack!

It is not quiet.

Raquan will get it.

Raquan can not.

The duck is quick!

Think of two things that start with the same beginning sound as **quilt**. Draw them.

Paco and the Piano — Pp

Understanding the Story: Setting

Circle the picture that shows where the story takes place.

Write and draw about where Paco goes in the story.

Pp Paco and the Piano

piano

Practice the Letter Pp

Say the letter name and the sound it stands for. Then, trace and write capital **P** and lowercase **p**.

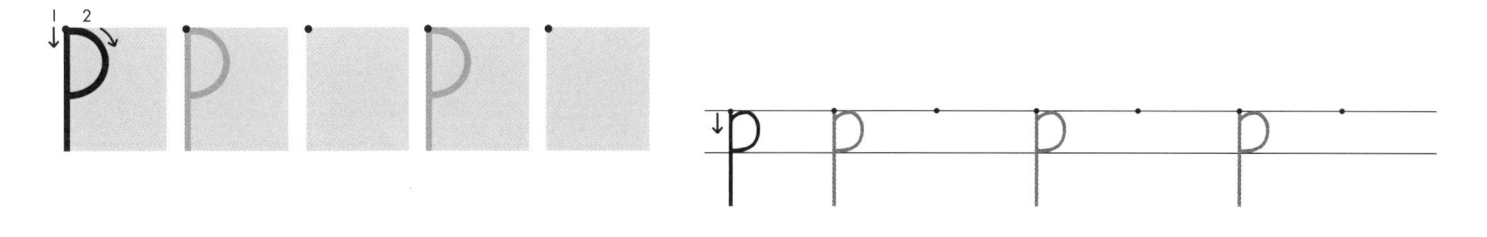

Say the name of each picture.
Write the letter that stands for the **beginning** sound to complete the word.

__ot   __at   __up   __ig   __ug   __an

Look around. Find names that start with capital **P** and things that start with lowercase **p**.
Write the words.

36 A–Z for Mat Man® and Me: Practice for Developing Readers - Letter Learning   © 2022 Learning Without Tears

Oz and the Octopus Oo

Understanding the Story: Events

Think about what happens in the story. The middle of the story is filled in. Now, draw and write about what happens in the beginning and end.

Beginning

Middle

The octopus is on the tank.

End

Oo Oz and the Octopus

octopus

Practice the Letter Oo

Say the letter name and the sound it stands for. Then, trace and write capital **O** and lowercase **o**.

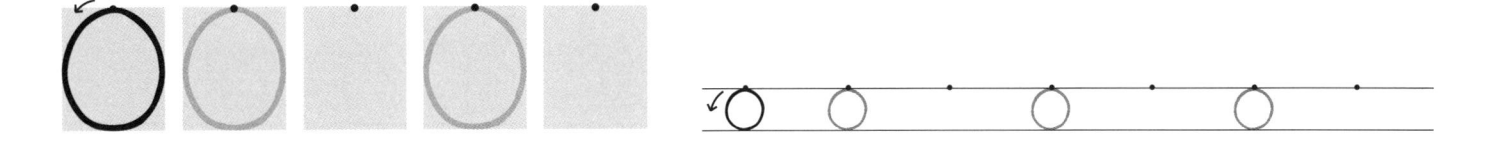

Say the name of each picture.
Write the letter that stands for the **middle** sound to complete the word.

f_sh   m_p

p_t   _l_g

f_n   d_g

b_d   c_t

f_x   b_x

34 A–Z for Mat Man® and Me: Practice for Developing Readers - Letter Learning

© 2022 Learning Without Tears

Nell and the Nest Nn

Understanding the Story: Setting

Circle the picture that shows where the story takes place.

Write and draw about the place where Nell is and why it is important to what happens in the story.

Nn Nell and the Nest

nest

Practice the Letter **Nn**

Say the letter name and the sound it stands for. Then, trace and write capital **N** and lowercase **n**.

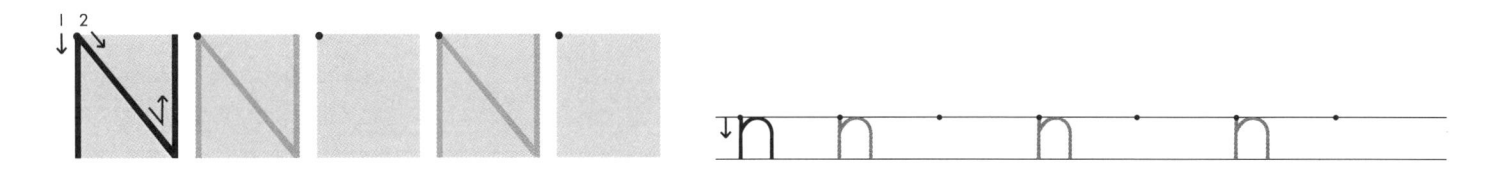

N N N   n n n n

Say the name of each picture.
Write the letter that stands for the **beginning** sound to complete the word.

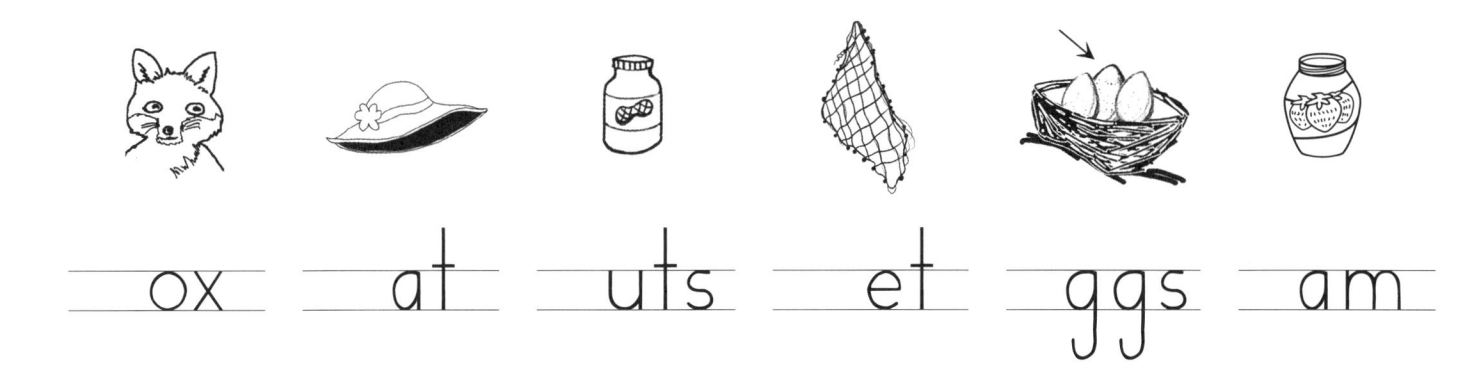

_ox   _at   _uts   _et   _ggs   _am

Think of two things that start with the same beginning sound as **nest**. Draw them.

Mac and the Magnificent Masks   Mm

Understanding the Story: Events

Think about what happens in the story. The middle of the story is filled in. Now, draw and write about what happens in the beginning and end.

Beginning

Middle

Marcos tosses markers.

End

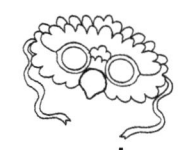

Mm Mac and the Magnificent Masks

mask

Practice the Letter Mm

Say the letter name and the sound it stands for. Then, trace and write capital **M** and lowercase **m**.

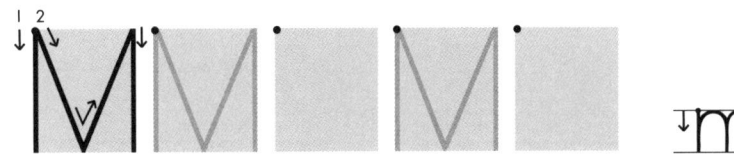

Say the name of each picture.
Write the letter that stands for the beginning sound to complete the word.

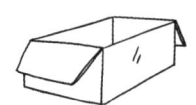

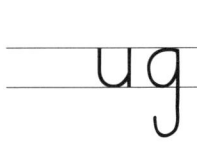

__op   __ox   __ug   __at   __ed   __ick

Look around. Find names that start with capital **M** and things that start with lowercase **m**.
Write the words.

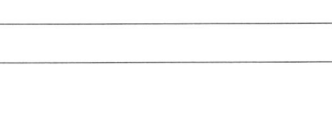

30   A–Z for Mat Man® and Me: Practice for Developing Readers - **Letter Learning**   © 2022 Learning Without Tears

Lola and the Lock — Ll

Understanding the Story: Events

Where does Lola look for her lock? Draw and write about three places where Lola looks.

Ll Lola and the Lock

lock

Practice the Letter Ll

Say the letter name and the sound it stands for. Then, trace and write capital **L** and lowercase **l**.

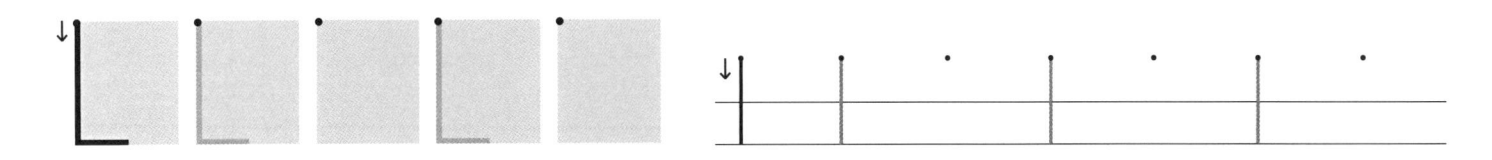

Say the name of each picture.
Write the letter that stands for the **beginning** sound to complete the word.

___eg   ___un   ___og   ___ick   ___ock   ___og

Think of two things that start with the same beginning sound as **lock**. Draw them.

Kaya and the Kayak Kk

Understanding the Story: Setting

Circle the picture that shows where the story takes place.

Where is Kaya in the story? Write about the place and draw a picture.

Kk Kaya and the Kayak

kayak

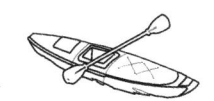

Practice the Letter **Kk**

Say the letter name and the sound it stands for. Then, trace and write capital **K** and lowercase **k**.

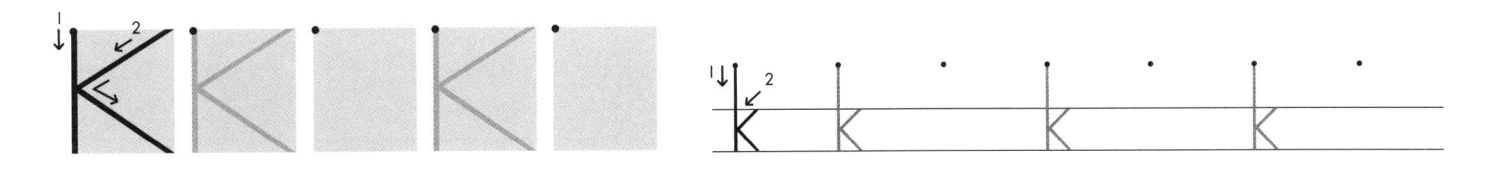

Say the name of each picture.
Write the letter that stands for the **beginning** sound to complete the word.

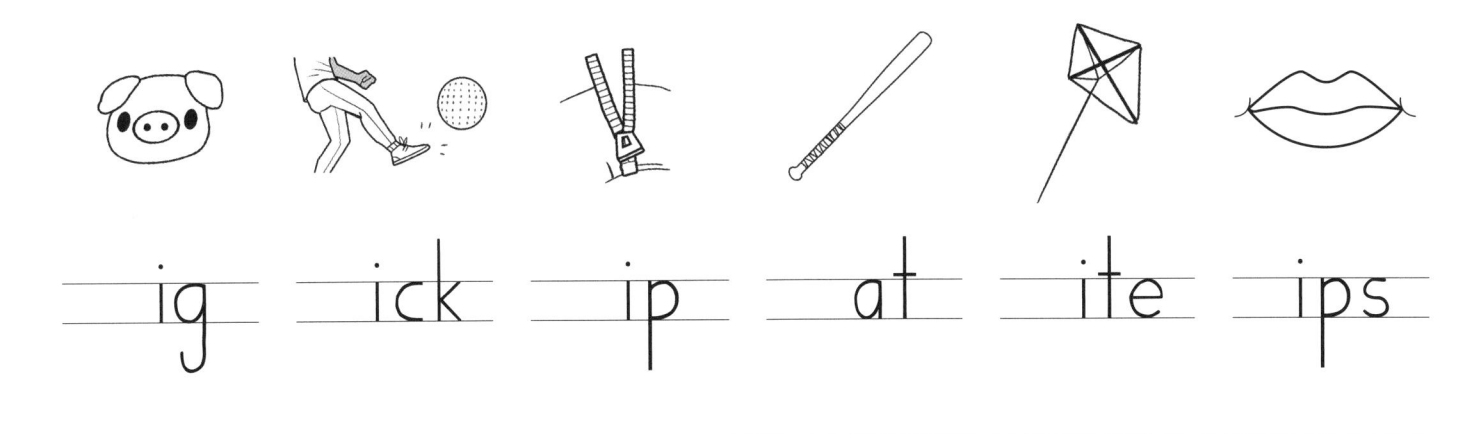

_ig   _ick   _ip   _at   _ite   _ips

Look around. Find names that start with capital **K** and things that start with lowercase **k**.
Write the words.

Jana, Jen, and the Jellyfish Jj

Understanding the Story: Character

Find the two main characters in the story. Circle two pictures.

Write about something the characters do in the story and draw a picture.

Jj Jana, Jen, and the Jellyfish

jellyfish

Practice the Letter Jj

Say the letter name and the sound it stands for. Then, trace and write capital **J** and lowercase **j**.

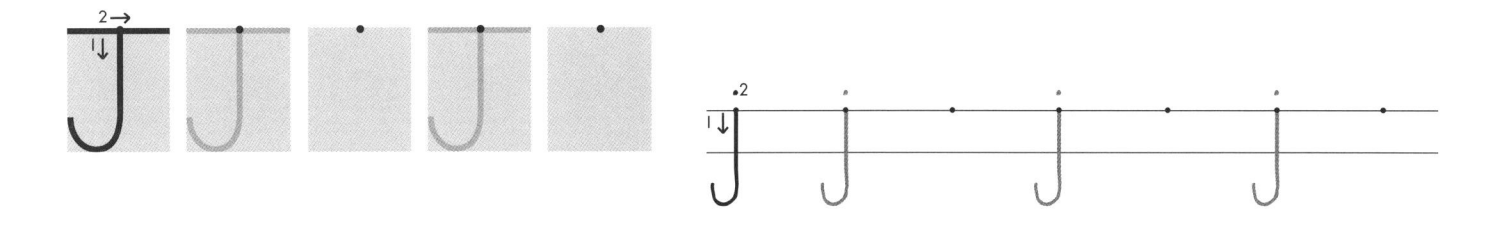

Say the name of each picture.
Write the letter that stands for the **beginning** sound to complete the word.

___un   ___an   ___am   ___ox   ___eep   ___at

Think of two things that start with the same beginning sound as **jellyfish**. Draw them.

Ikiaq and the Igloo Ii

Understanding the Story: Setting

Circle the picture that shows where the story takes place.

Write about a place from the story and draw a picture.

Ii Ikiaq and the Igloo

igloo

Practice the Letter **I**i

Say the letter name and the sound it stands for. Then, trace and write capital **I** and lowercase **i**.

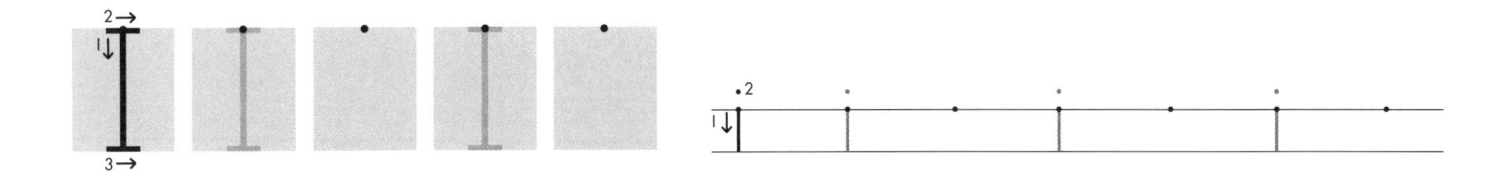

Say the name of each picture.
Write the letter that stands for the **middle** sound to complete the word.

s _ n   f _ n

z _ p   b _ x

c _ p   b _ d

p _ g   l _ ps

c _ t   d _ g

22   A–Z for Mat Man® and Me: Practice for Developing Readers - Letter Learning   © 2022 Learning Without Tears

Hana has a Hammer   Hh

Understanding the Story: Characters

Which animals get out in the story? Draw three that Hana has to chase. Write the names.

© 2022 Learning Without Tears — A–Z for Mat Man® and Me: Practice for Developing Readers - **Meaning Making**   21

Hh Hana has a Hammer

hammer

Practice the Letter Hh

Say the letter name and the sound it stands for. Then, trace and write capital **H** and lowercase **h**.

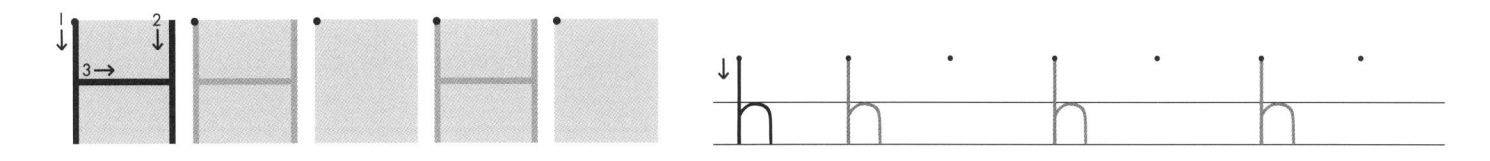

Say the name of each picture.
Write the letter that stands for the **beginning** sound to complete the word.

___ox   ___en   ___at   ___eg   ___og   ___ig

Look around. Find names that start with capital **H** and things that start with lowercase **h**. Write the words.

Gabby and Her Goat Gg

Understanding the Story: Events

What does Gus do in the story? Draw and write three things Gus gets.

Gg Gabby and Her Goat

goat

Practice the Letter Gg

Say the letter name and the sound it stands for. Then, trace and write capital **G** and lowercase **g**.

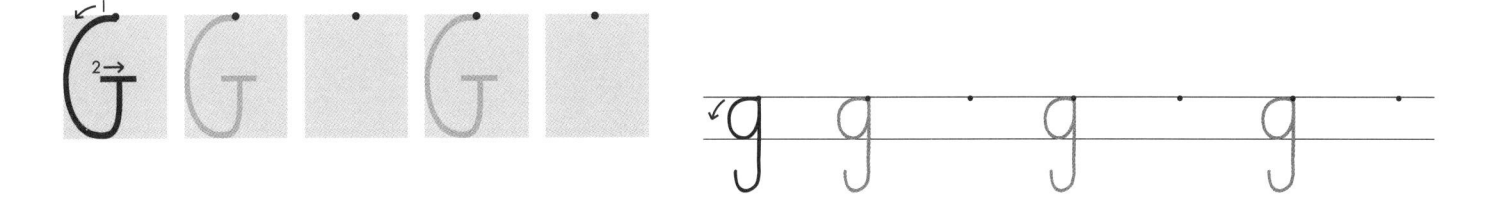

Say the name of each picture.
Write the letter that stands for the **ending** sound to complete the word.

ba____   mo____   do____   pi____   po____   ru____

Look around. Find names that start with capital **G** and things that start with lowercase **g**.
Write the words.

18   A–Z for Mat Man® and Me: Practice for Developing Readers - Letter Learning   © 2022 Learning Without Tears

Feng, Finn, and the Fan   Ff

Understanding the Story: Events

Think about what happens in the story. The middle of the story is filled in. Now, draw and write about what happens in the beginning and end.

Beginning

Middle

Feng and Finn fight.

End

A–Z for Mat Man® and Me: Practice for Developing Readers - **Meaning Making**

Ff Feng, Finn, and the Fan

fan

Practice the Letter Ff

Say the letter name and the sound it stands for. Then, trace and write capital **F** and lowercase **f**.

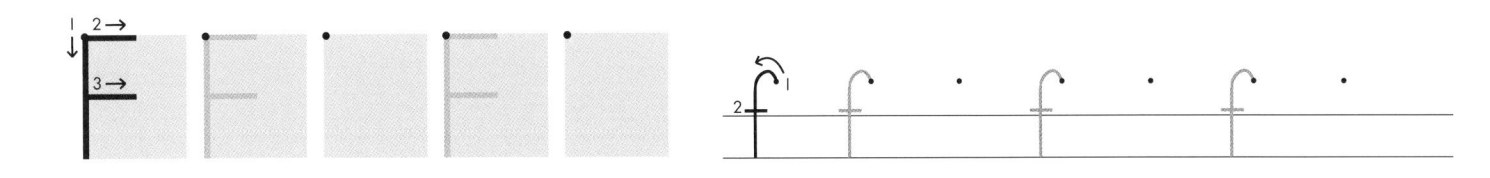

Say the name of each picture.
Write the letter that stands for the **beginning** sound to complete the word.

___at   ___an   ___ox   ___in   ___ox   ___am

Think of two things that start with the same beginning sound as **fan**. Draw them.

Emma and the Elephant   Ee

Understanding the Story: Characters

Think about what Emma does and how she feels. When does Emma feel sad?
Draw and write about it.

_____
_____

When does Emma feel happy in the story? Draw and write about it.

_____
_____

Ee   Cora and the Coconut

elephant

Practice the Letter Ee

Say the letter name and the sound it stands for. Then, trace and write capital **E** and lowercase **e**.

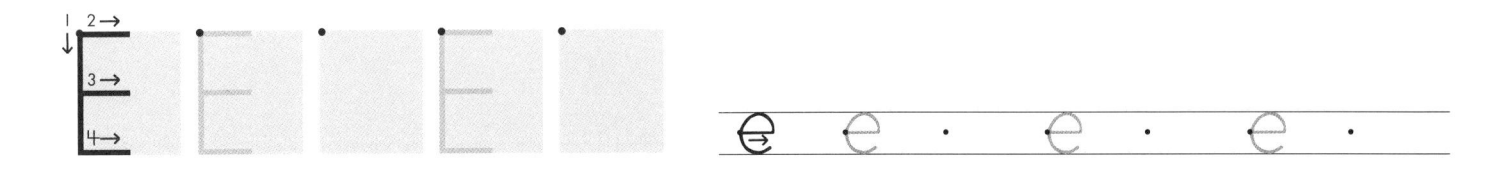

Say the name of each picture.
Write the letter that stands for the **middle** sound to complete the word.

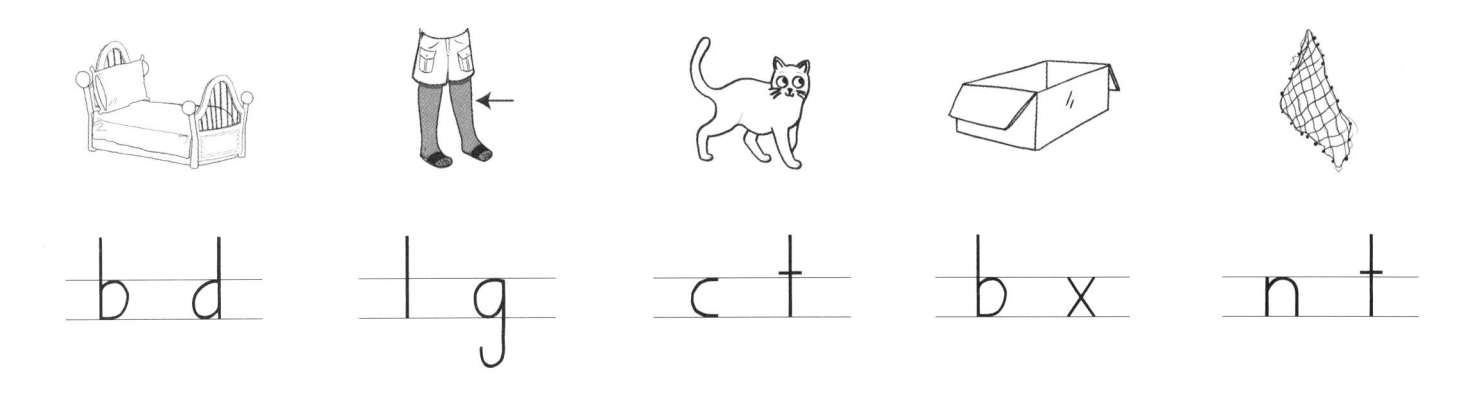

b___d   l___g   c___t   b___x   n___t

Look around. Find names that start with capital **E** and things that start with lowercase **e**.
Write the words.

Dax and the Dolphin Dd

Understanding the Story: Setting

(Circle) the picture that shows where the story takes place.

Where is Dax in the story? Write about the place and draw a picture.

Dd Dax and the Dolphin

dolphin

Practice the Letter Dd

Say the letter name and the sound it stands for. Then, trace and write capital **D** and lowercase **d**.

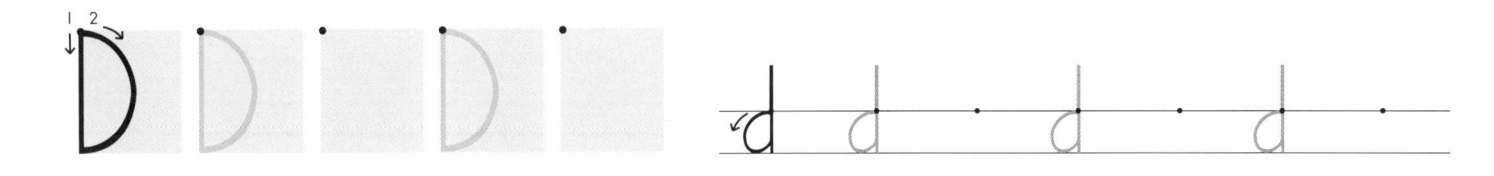

Say the name of each picture.
Write the letter that stands for the **beginning** sound to complete the word.

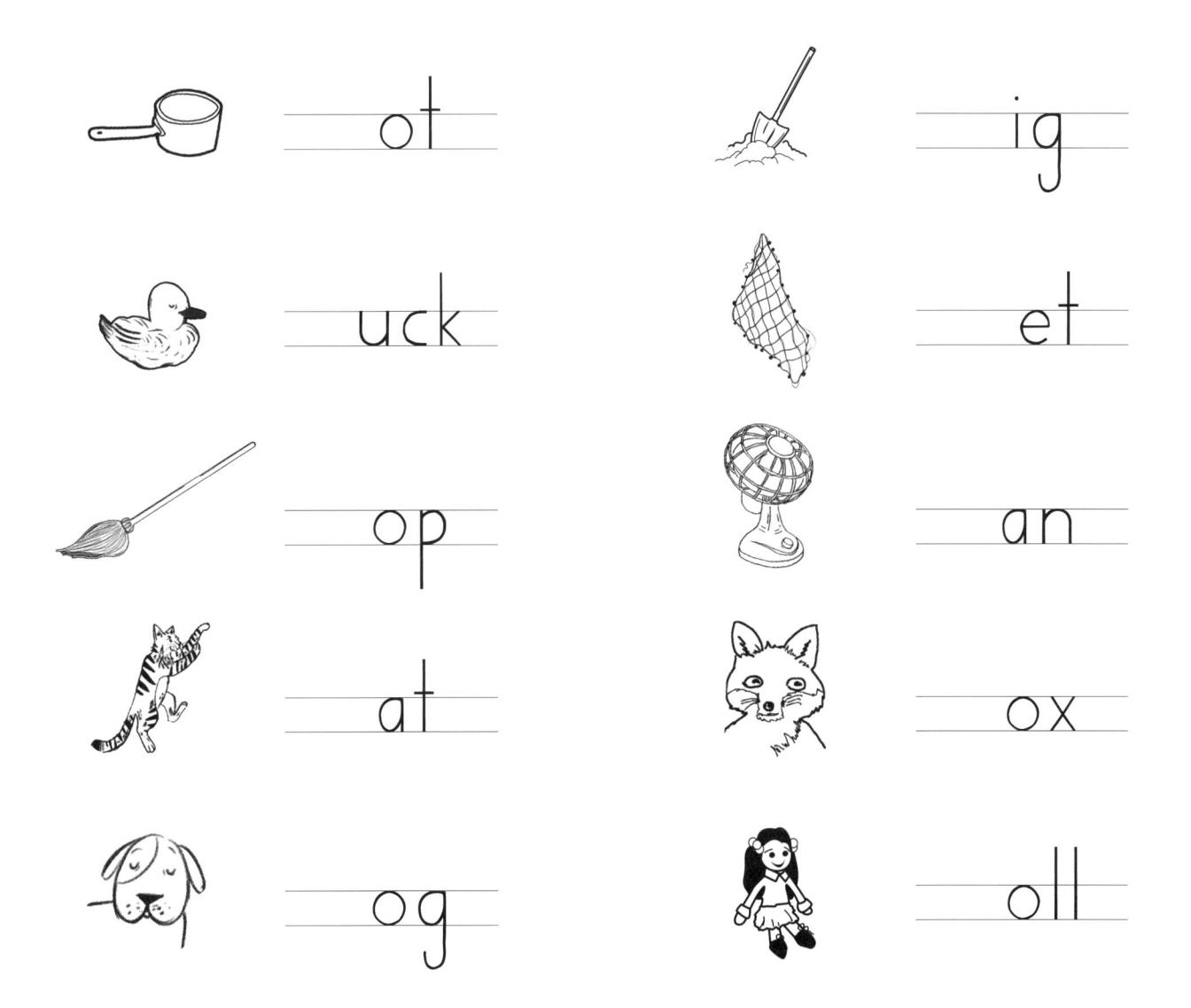

_ot

_uck

_op

_at

_og

_ig

_et

_an

_ox

_oll

Cora and the Coconut   Cc

Understanding the Story: Events

Think about what happens in the story. The middle of the story is filled in. Now, draw and write about what happens in the beginning and end.

Beginning

Middle

Cora holds up a cat.

End

Cc Cora and the Coconut

coconut

Practice the Letter Cc

Say the letter name and the sound it stands for. Then, trace and write capital **C** and lowercase **c**.

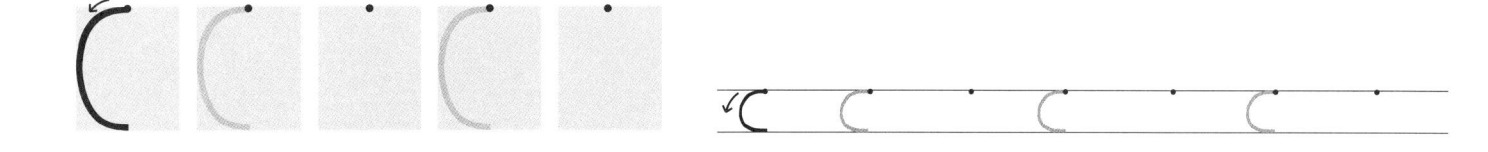

Say the name of each picture.
Write the letter that stands for the **beginning** sound to complete the word.

_at   _ox   _up   _ar   _ed   _ips

Look around. Find names that start with capital **C** and things that start with lowercase **c**.
Write the words.

Ben and the Big Bagels   Bb

Understanding the Story: Setting

Circle the picture that shows where the story takes place.

Where is Ben in the story? Write about the place and draw a picture.

© 2022 Learning Without Tears — A–Z for Mat Man® and Me: Practice for Developing Readers - **Meaning Making**   9

Bb — Ben and the Big Bagels

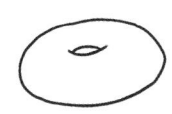

bagel

Practice the Letter Bb

Say the letter name and the sound it stands for. Then, trace and write capital **B** and lowercase **b**.

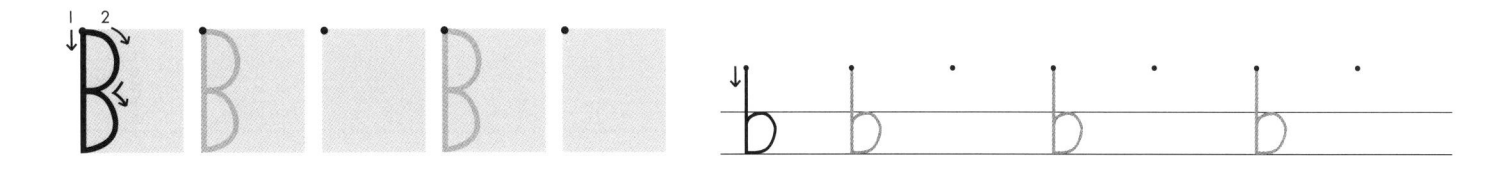

Say the name of each picture.
Write the letter that stands for the **beginning** sound to complete the word.

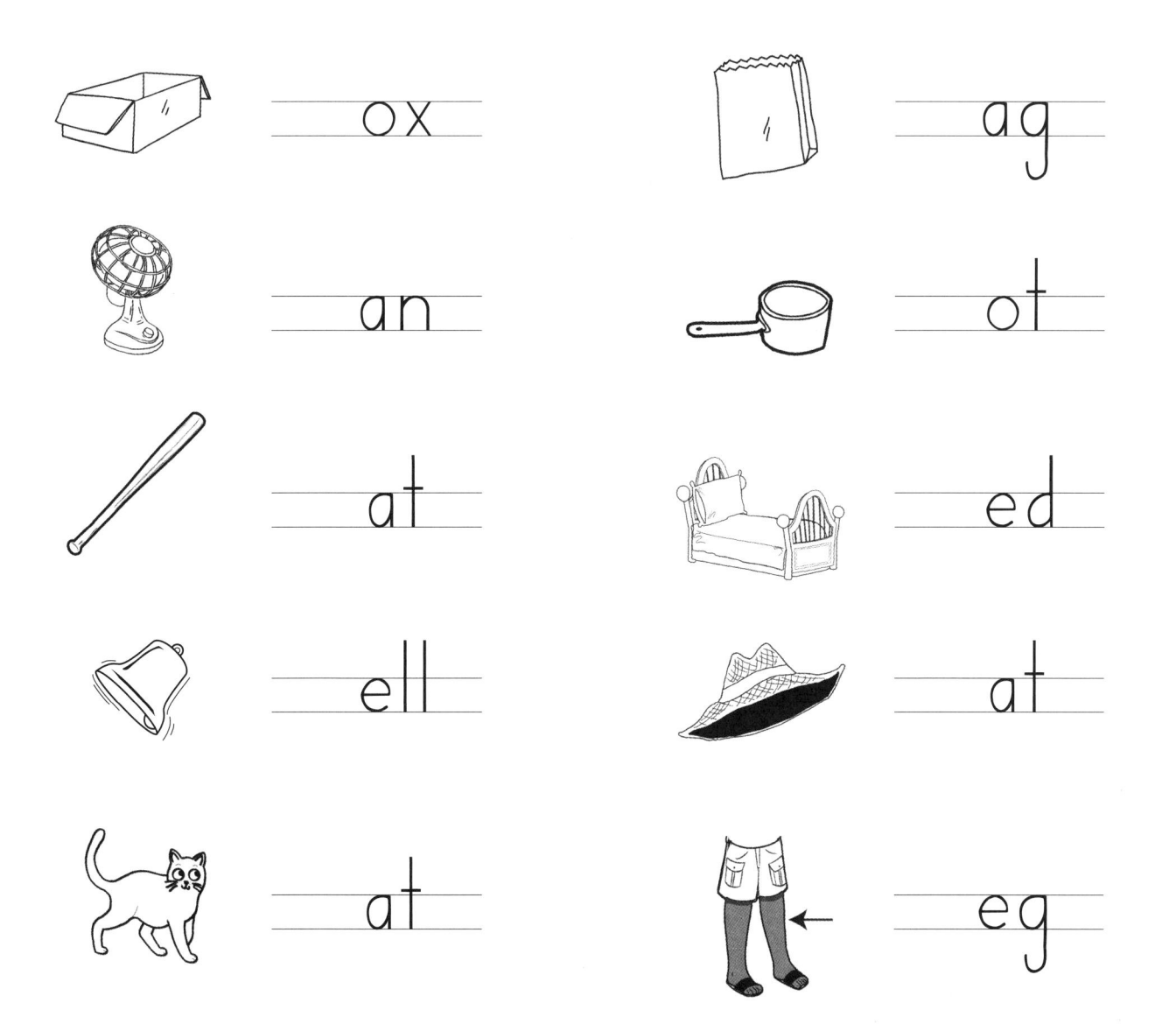

_ox

_ag

_an

_ot

_at

_ed

_ell

_at

_at

_eg

8 A–Z for Mat Man® and Me: Practice for Developing Readers - Letter Learning

© 2022 Learning Without Tears

Ally and the Apple   Aa

Understanding the Story: Events

Think about what happens in the story. The middle of the story is filled in. Now, draw and write about what happens in the beginning and end.

Beginning

Middle

Ally asks for help.

End

© 2022 Learning Without Tears   *A–Z for Mat Man® and Me: Practice for Developing Readers* - **Meaning Making**   7

Aa Ally and the Apple

apple

Practice the Letter Aa

Say the letter name and the sound it stands for. Then, trace and write capital **A** and lowercase **a**.

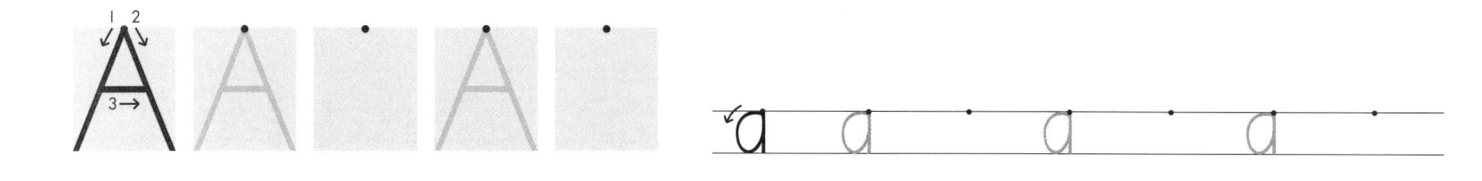

Say the name of each picture.
Write the letter that stands for the **middle** sound to complete the word.

_ck h_t p_t f_n c_t r_g

Think of two things that start with the same beginning sound as **apple**. Draw them.

6 A–Z for Mat Man® and Me: Practice for Developing Readers - **Letter Learning** © 2022 Learning Without Tears

Mat Man® and the Great Alphabet Parade

The First Letter in Your Name

First, ⟨circle⟩ the letter your first name starts with. Then, underline the letter your last name starts with.

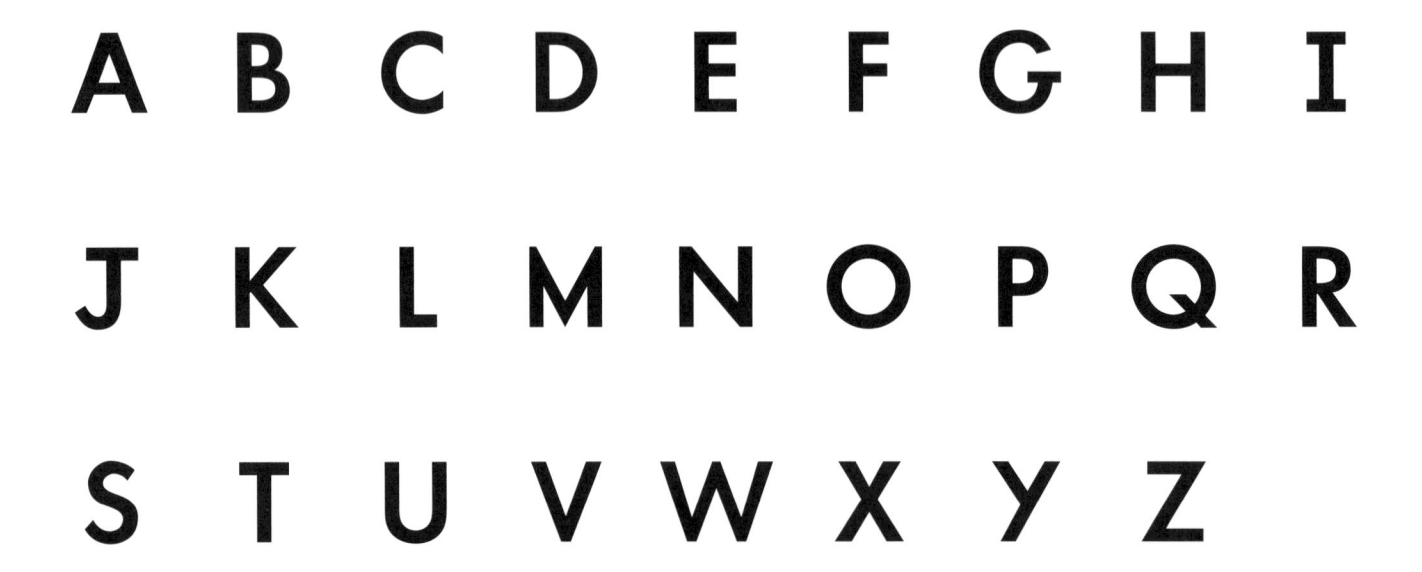

A B C D E F G H I

J K L M N O P Q R

S T U V W X Y Z

Draw a picture of something from the parade that starts with the same letter your first name starts with. Then, draw a picture of something that starts with the first letter in your last name.

© 2022 Learning Without Tears   A–Z for Mat Man® and Me: Practice for Developing Readers   5

Mat Man® and the Great Alphabet Parade

Sing the Alphabet Song

Help Mat Man sing the ABC song! Underline each letter as we sing it. The **a** is done for you. Then, color the pictures.

a b c d e f g

h i j k l m n o p

q r s

t u v

w x

y and z

TABLE OF CONTENTS

Sing the Alphabet Song 4

The First Letter in Your Name 5

Letter Aa: *Ally and the Apple*
Practice the Letter **Aa** 6
Understanding the Story: Events 7

Letter Bb: *Ben and the Big Bagels*
Practice the Letter **Bb** 8
Understanding the Story: Setting 9

Letter Cc: *Cora and the Coconut*
Practice the Letter **Cc** 10
Understanding the Story: Events 11

Letter Dd: *Dax and the Dolphin*
Practice the Letter **Dd** 12
Understanding the Story: Setting 13

Letter Ee: *Emma and Her Elephant*
Practice the Letter **Ee** 14
Understanding the Story: Character 15

Letter Ff: *Feng, Finn, and the Fan*
Practice the Letter **Ff** 16
Understanding the Story: Events 17

Letter Gg: *Gabby and Her Goat*
Practice the Letter **Gg** 18
Understanding the Story: Events 19

Letter Hh: *Hana Has a Hammer*
Practice the Letter **Hh** 20
Understanding the Story: Events 21

Letter Ii: *Ikiaq and the Igloo*
Practice the Letter **Ii** 22
Understanding the Story: Setting 23

Letter Jj: *Jana, Jen, and the Jellyfish*
Practice the Letter **Jj** 24
Understanding the Story: Character 25

Letter Kk: *Kaya and the Kite*
Practice the Letter **Kk** 26
Understanding the Story: Setting 27

Letter Ll: *Lola and the Lock*
Practice the Letter **Ll** 28
Understanding the Story: Events 29

Letter Mm: *Mac and the Magnificent Masks*
Practice the Letter **Mm** 30
Understanding the Story: Events 31

Letter Nn: *Nell and the Nest*
Practice the Letter **Nn** 32
Understanding the Story: Setting 33

Letter Oo: *Oz and the Octopus*
Practice the Letter **Oo** 34
Understanding the Story: Events 35

Letter Pp: *Paco and the Piano*
Practice the Letter **Pp** 36
Understanding the Story: Character 37

Letter Qq: *Quinn and the Quilt*
Practice the Letter **Qq** 38
Understanding the Story: Events 39

Letter Rr: *Rex and the Rake*
Practice the Letter **Rr** 40
Understanding the Story: Character 41

Letter Ss: *Sam in the Sun*
Practice the Letter **Ss** 42
Understanding the Story: Setting 43

Letter Tt: *Tere and the Tomato*
Practice the Letter **Tt** 44
Understanding the Story: Character 45

Letter Uu: *Umberto and the Umbrella*
Practice the Letter **Uu** 46
Understanding the Story: Events 47

Letter Vv: *Vic, Val, and the Vacuum*
Practice the Letter **Vv** 48
Understanding the Story: Character 49

Letter Ww: *Wes and the Watermelon*
Practice the Letter **Ww** 50
Understanding the Story: Setting 51

Letter Xx: *Xavier Gets an X-ray*
Practice the Letter **Xx** 52
Understanding the Story: Setting 53

Letter Yy: *Yolanda and the Yo-Yo*
Practice the Letter **Yy** 54
Understanding the Story: Events 55

Letter Zz: *Zack and His Zipper*
Practice the Letter **Zz** 56
Understanding the Story: Character 57

Letter Check 1 58

Letter Check 2 60

Letter Check 3 62

Letter Review 64

LEARNING
Without Tears®

8001 MacArthur Blvd.
Cabin John, MD 20818
LWTears.com | 888.983.8409

Art Director: Shannon Rutledge
Graphic Designer: Sammie Simon
Curriculum Designers: Adam Berkin, Nicole Iorio, Cari Meister, Casey Schultz

Copyright © 2022 Learning Without Tears
First Edition
ISBN: 978-1-954728-42-4
23456789RRD232221
Printed in Dongguan, China

The contents of this consumable workbook are protected by US copyright law. If a workbook has been purchased for a child, the author and Learning Without Tears give limited permission to copy pages for additional practice or homework for that child. No copied pages from this book can be given to another person without written permission from Learning Without Tears.

A-Z for Mat Man® and Me

Practice for Developing Readers

LEARNING Without Tears®

Letter Review

Letter Review

Say the name for each picture. Circle the letter that stands for its **beginning** sound. Write the lowercase letter on the double lines.

1. m / p / s
2. s / w / m
3. c / n / b
4. r / p / b
5. e / r / m
6. t / w / v
7. a / p / u
8. r / f / l

64 *A–Z for Mat Man® and Me: Practice for Developing Readers* © 2022 Learning Without Tears

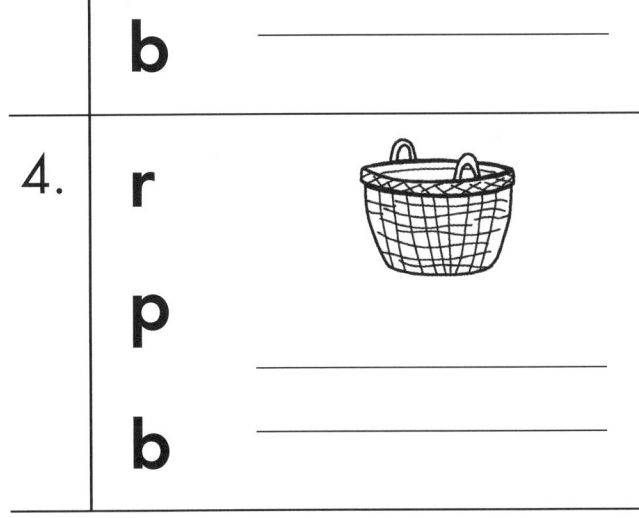

Letter Check 3

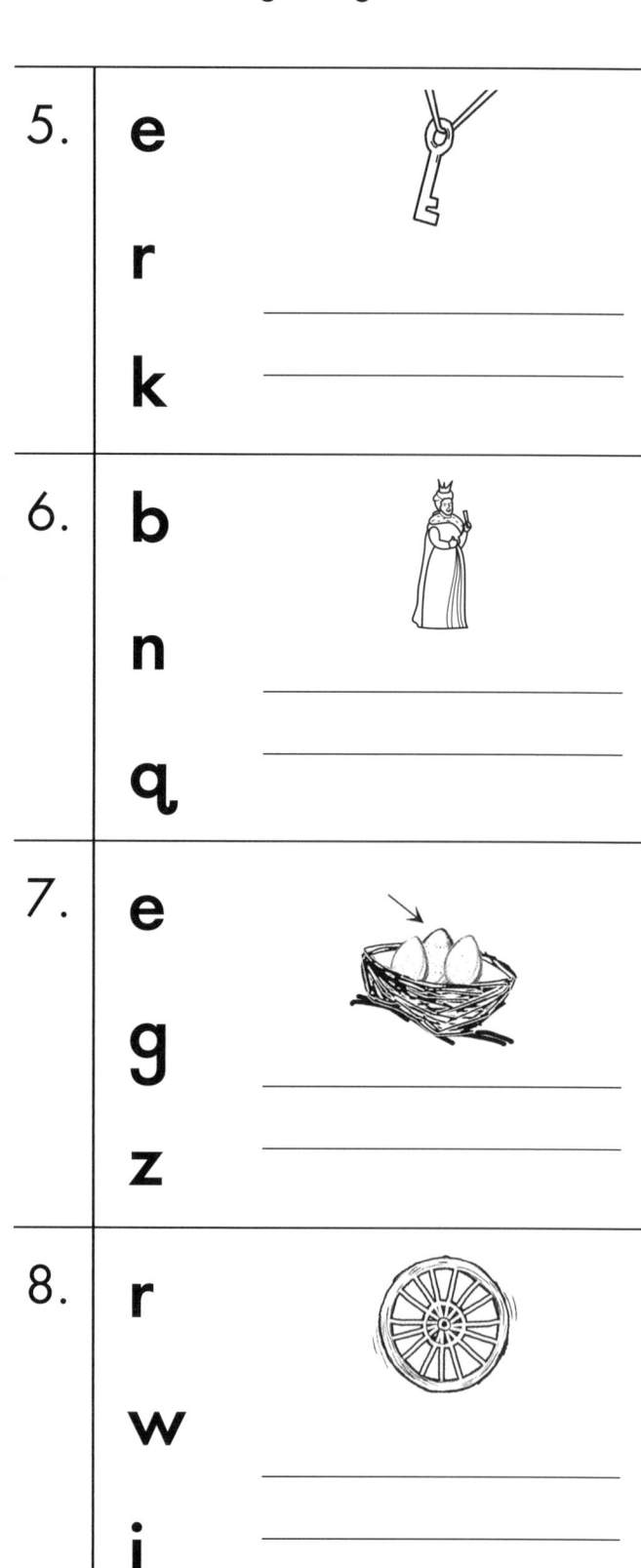

Letter Check 3, Part B

Say the name for each picture. ⓒircle the letter that stands for its **beginning** sound.
Write the lowercase letter on the double lines.

1. x
   k
   a

2. s
   j
   t

3. k
   t
   f

4. y
   j
   s

5. e
   r
   k

6. b
   n
   q

7. e
   g
   z

8. r
   w
   i

Letter Check 3

Letter Check 3, Part A

Say the name for each picture. Ⓒircle the letter that stands for its **beginning** sound. Write the lowercase letter on the double lines.

1. j / s / v

2. y / k / a

3. i / d / u

4. j / s / p

5. w / f / n

6. d / q / e

7. g / p / o

8. q / i / l

62   *A–Z for Mat Man and Me: Practice for Developing Readers*   © 2022 Learning Without Tears

Letter Check 2

Letter Check 2, Part B

Say the name for each picture. Circle the letter that stands for its **beginning** sound.
Write the lowercase letter on the double lines.

1. r
   l
   g

2. c
   p
   v

3. n
   f
   l

4. m
   b
   e

5. m
   d
   z

6. h
   l
   w

7. i
   d
   o

8. f
   g
   j

Letter Check 2

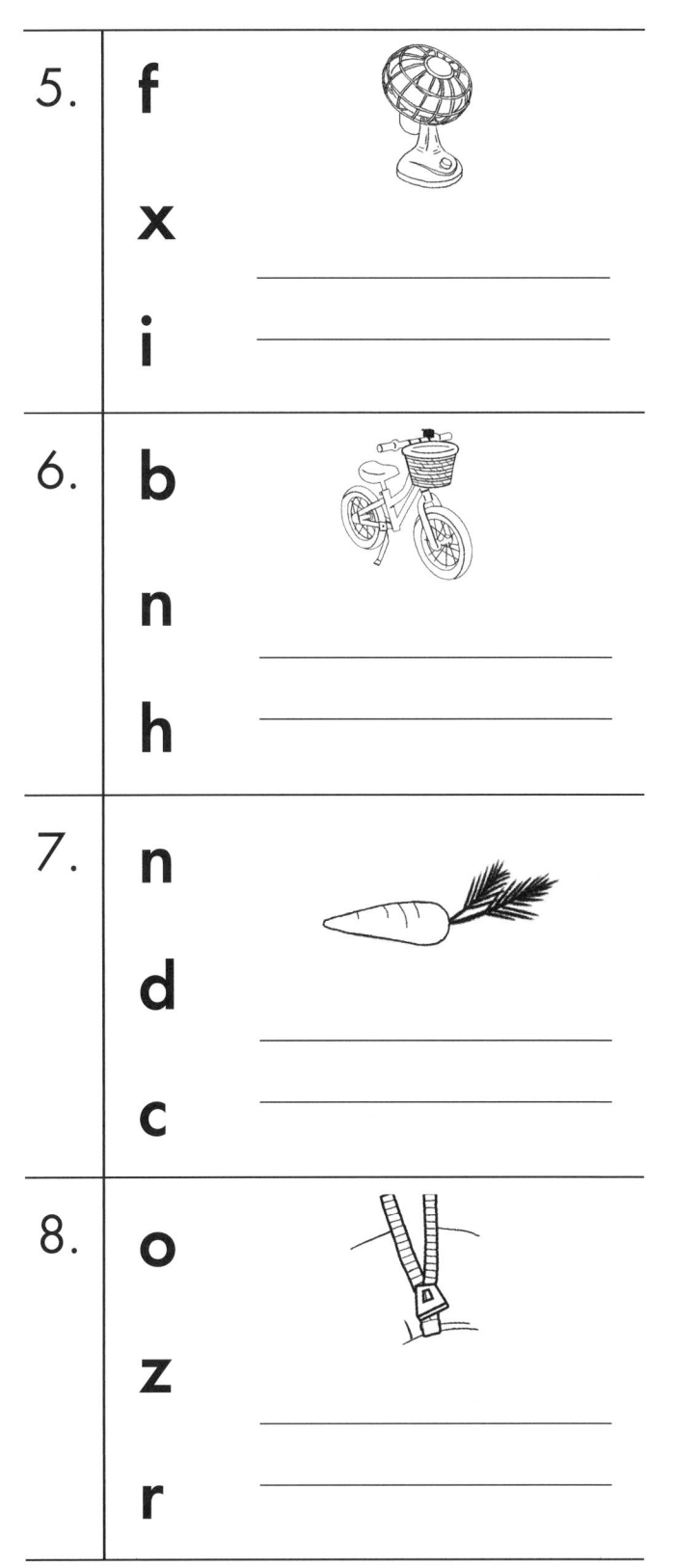

Letter Check 2, Part A

Say the name for each picture. Circle the letter that stands for its **beginning** sound. Write the lowercase letter on the double lines.

1. l
   d
   k

2. p
   h
   b

3. g
   w
   s

4. z
   t
   l

5. f
   x
   i

6. b
   n
   h

7. n
   d
   c

8. o
   z
   r

Letter Check 1

Letter Check 1, Part B

Say the name for each picture. Circle the letter that stands for its **beginning** sound. Write the lowercase letter on the double lines.

1.	s r l		5.	a v m
2.	i y p		6.	b v a
3.	p n g		7.	t n r
4.	k s r		8.	t q p

© 2022 Learning Without Tears — A–Z for Mat Man® and Me: Practice for Developing Readers

Letter Check 1

Letter Check 1, Part A

Say the name for each picture. ⓒircle the letter that stands for its **beginning** sound. Write the lowercase letter on the double lines.

1.	m p a		5.	g r m	
2.	s p t		6.	t s v	
3.	i n b		7.	a b u	
4.	r d p		8.	r o i	

58   A–Z for Mat Man® and Me: Practice for Developing Readers   © 2022 Learning Without Tears

Zack and His Zipper **Zz**

Understanding the Story: Characters

Think about what Zack does and how he feels. When does Zack feel mad? Draw and write about it.

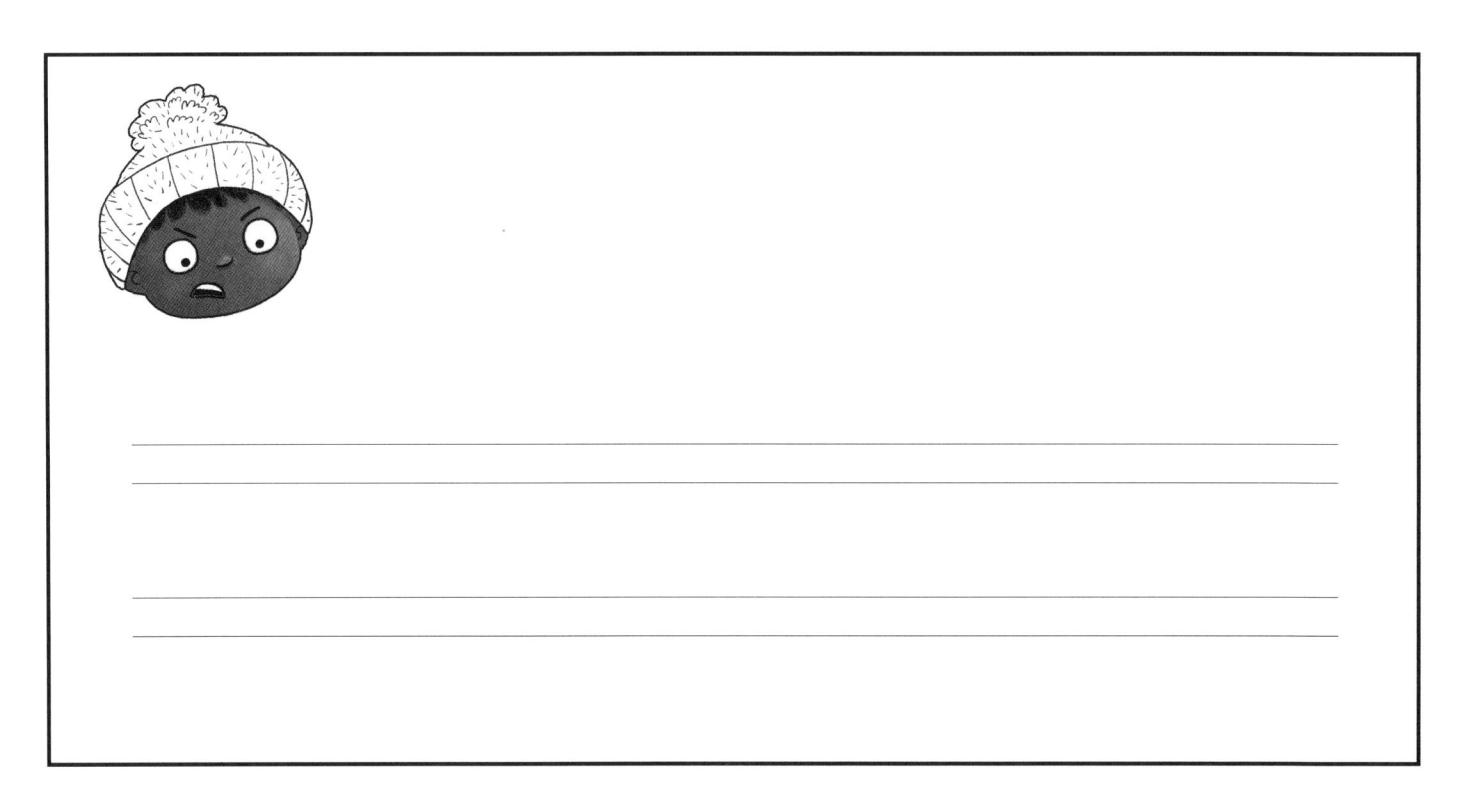

When does Zack feel happy in the story? Draw and write.

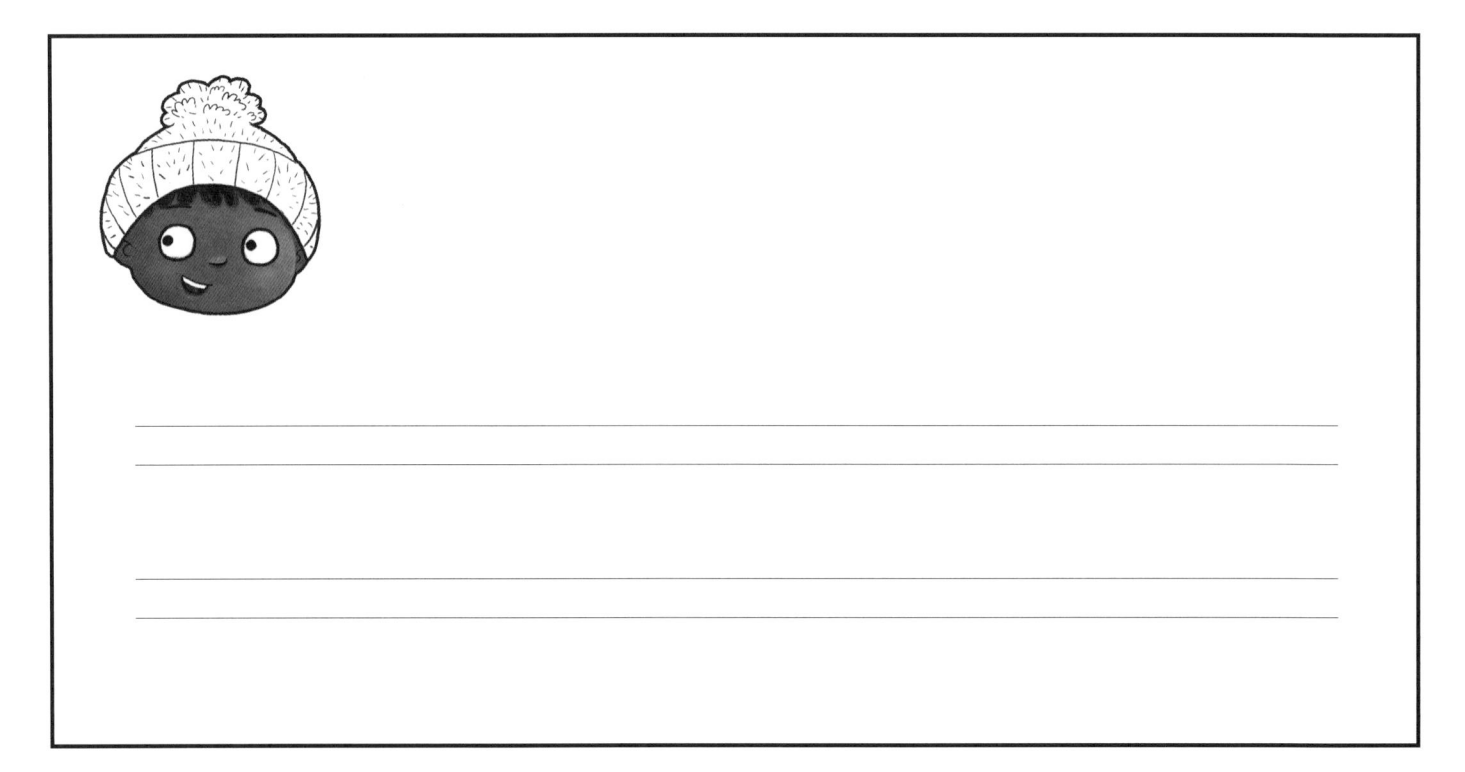

© 2022 Learning Without Tears — *A–Z for Mat Man® and Me: Practice for Developing Readers* - **Meaning Making**

Zz Zack and His Zipper

zipper

Practice the Letter Zz

Say the letter name and the sound it stands for. Then, trace and write capital **Z** and lowercase **z**.

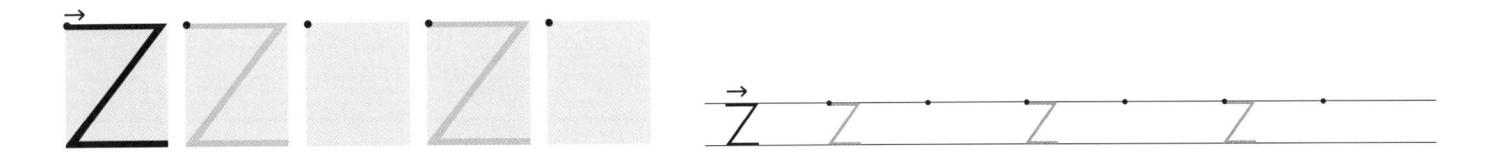

Read as much as you can. Then, circle every capital **Z** and lowercase **z** you see.

Liz zips up her coat.

It is a size too big.

It keeps out the breeze.

Liz and Zoe get to the zoo!

They look at a zebra.

Think of two things that start with the same beginning sound as **zipper**. Draw them.

Practice the Letter Yy

Understanding the Story: Events

Think about what happens in the story. The middle of the story is filled in. Now, draw and write about what happens in the beginning and end.

Beginning

Middle

Yaz does not trade back.

End

Yy Practice the Letter Yy

yo-yo

Practice the Letter Yy

Say the letter name and the sound it stands for. Then, trace and write capital **Y** and lowercase **y**.

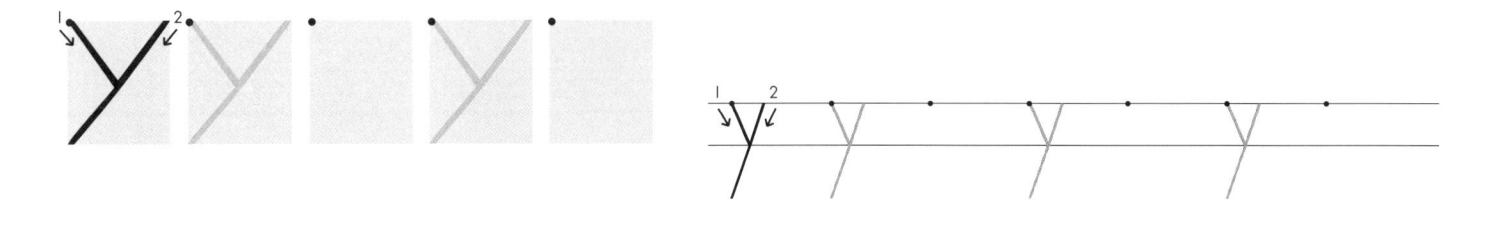

Read as much as you can. Then, circle every capital **Y** and lowercase **y** you see.

Yams are hot.

Yum! Cy says yes.

Cy gets a lot.

Jay says no.

Why yams? Yuck!

Jay gets a yogurt.

Think of two things that start with the same beginning sound as **yo-yo**. Draw them.

Xavier Gets an X-ray **Xx**

Understanding the Story: Setting

Where is Xavier in the story? Draw and write about three place where you see Xavier.

Xx Xavier Gets an X-ray

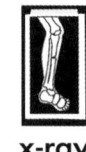

x-ray

Practice the Letter Xx

Say the letter name and the sound it stands for. Then, trace and write capital **X** and lowercase **x**.

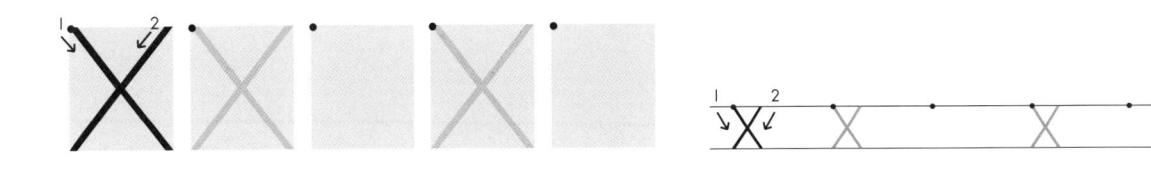

Say the name of each picture.
Write the letter that stands for the **ending** sound to complete the word.

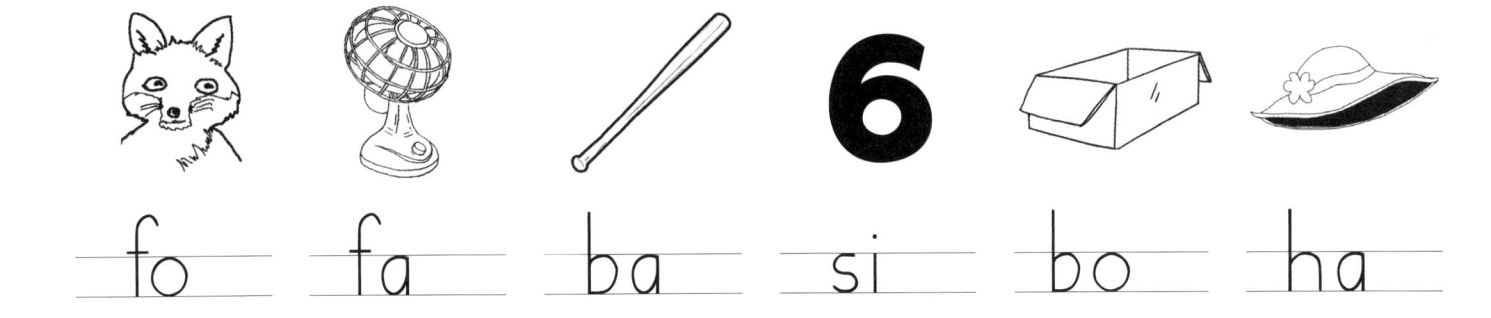

fo___   fa___   ba___   si___   bo___   ha___

Look around. Find names and words that have an **x** in them. Write the words.

Wes and the Watermelon   Ww

Understanding the Story: Setting

Circle the picture that shows where the story takes place.

Where is Wes in the story? Write about the place and draw a picture.

Ww Wes and the Watermelon

watermelon

Practice the Letter Ww

Say the letter name and the sound it stands for. Then, trace and write capital **W** and lowercase **w**.

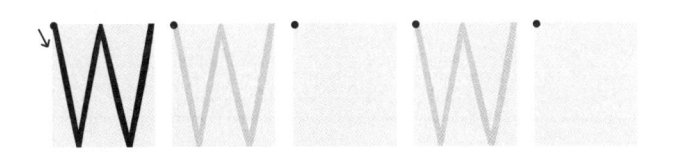

W W W   W W W W

Read as much you can. Then, circle every capital **W** and lowercase **w** you see.

Will has to win.

Wu has to win, too.

Who will win the swim race?

Will swims a lap.

Wu swims a lap.

They tap the wall. Tie!

Think of two things that start with the same beginning sound as **watermelon**. Draw them.

Vic, Val, and the Vacuum Vv

Understanding the Story: Characters

Think about what Val does and how she feels. When does Val feel mad? Draw and write about it.

When does Val feel happy and thankful in the story? Draw and write.

49

Vv Vic, Val, and the Vacuum

vacuum

Practice the Letter Vv

Say the letter name and the sound it stands for. Then, trace and write capital **V** and lowercase **v**.

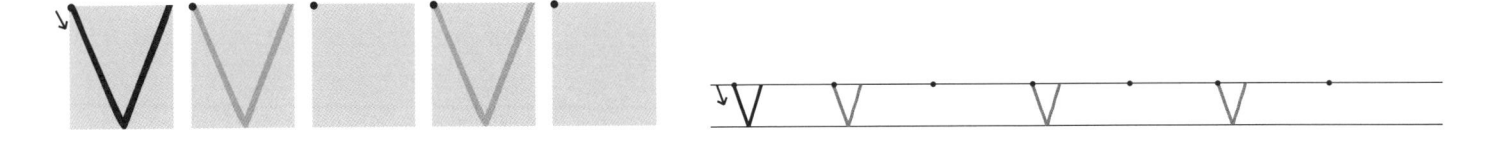

Say the name of each picture.
Write the letter that stands for the **beginning** sound to complete the word.

___ase   ___at   ___an   ___og   ___op   ___ug

Think of two things that start with the same beginning sound as **vacuum**. Draw them.

Umberto and the Umbrella Uu

Understanding the Story: Events

What does Umberto do in the story? Draw three things Umberto uses to try to stay dry.

Uu — Umberto and the Umbrella

umbrella

Practice the Letter Uu

Say the letter name and the sound it stands for. Then, trace and write capital **U** and lowercase **u**.

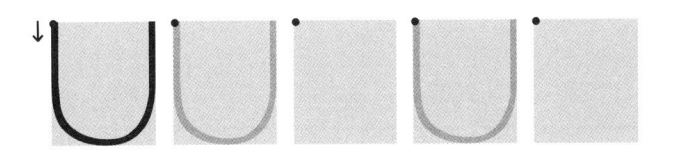

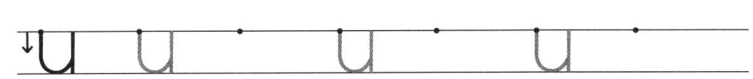

Say the name of each picture.
Write the letter that stands for the **middle** sound to complete the word.

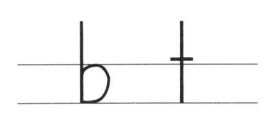

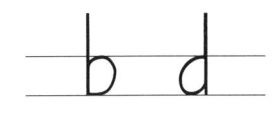

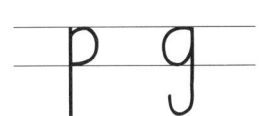

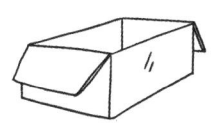

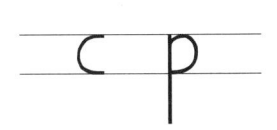

r _ cks

b _ t

s _ n

d _ ck

n _ ts

b _ d

p _ g

b _ x

c _ p

r _ g

46 A–Z for Mat Man® and Me: Practice for Developing Readers - Letter Learning © 2022 Learning Without Tears

Tere and the Tomato — Tt

Understanding the Story: Characters

Think about what Tere does and how she feels in the story. When does Tere feel worried? Draw and write about it.

When does Tere feel happy in the story? Draw and write about it.

© 2022 Learning Without Tears — A–Z for Mat Man® and Me: Practice for Developing Readers - Meaning Making

Tt Tere and the Tomato

tomato

Practice the Letter Tt

Say the letter name and the sound it stands for. Then, trace and write capital **T** and lowercase **t**.

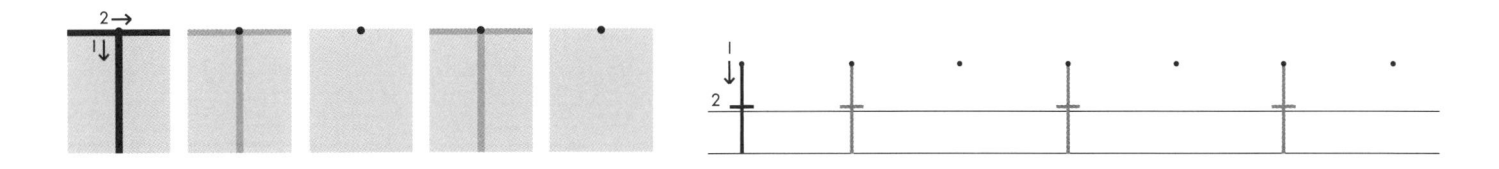

Say the name of each picture.
Write the letter that stands for the **beginning** sound to complete the word.

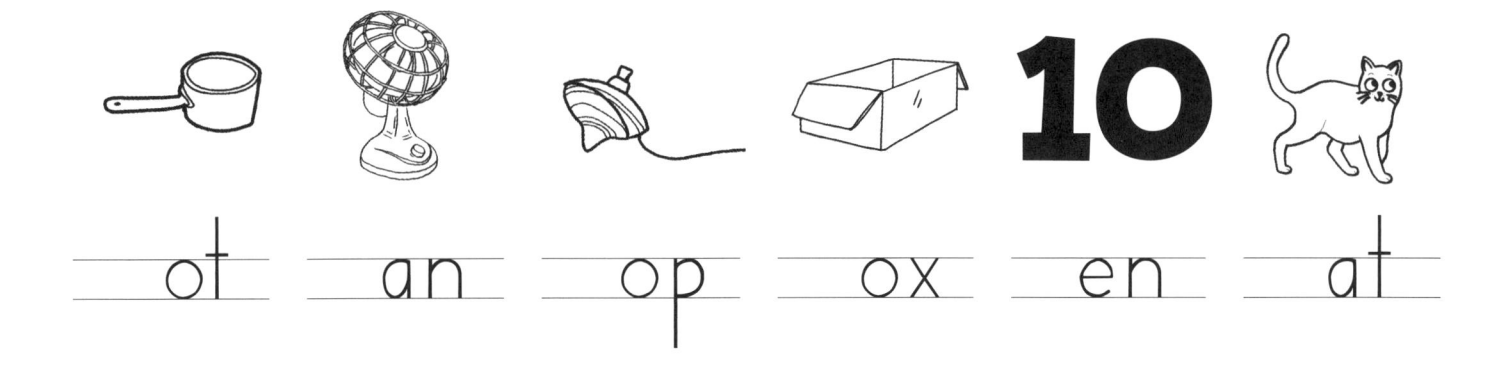

___ot   ___an   ___op   ___ox   ___en   ___at

Look around. Find names that start with capital **T** and things that start with lowercase **t**.
Write the words.

Sam in the Sun — Ss

Understanding the Story: Setting

Circle the picture that shows where the story takes place.

Where is Sam in the story? Write about the place and draw a picture.

© 2022 Learning Without Tears — A–Z for Mat Man® and Me: Practice for Developing Readers - Meaning Making

Ss Sam in the Sun

sun

Practice the Letter **Ss**

Say the letter name and the sound it stands for. Then, trace and write capital **S** and lowercase **s**.

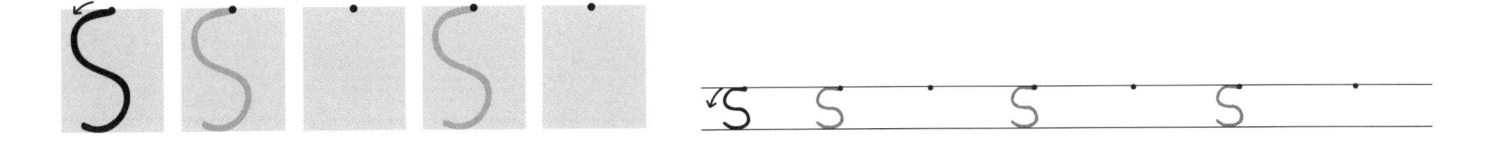

Say the name of each picture.
Write the letter that stands for the **beginning** sound to complete the word.

_at   _un   _ink   _og   _ix   _an

Think of two things that start with the same beginning sound as **sun**. Draw them.

Rex and the Rake Rr

Understanding the Story: Characters

Think about what Rex does and how he feels.
When does Rex feel confused about something in the story? Write and draw about it.

When does Rex feel upset and frustrated in the story? Write and draw about it.

© 2022 Learning Without Tears — A–Z for Mat Man® and Me: Practice for Developing Readers - **Meaning Making**

Rr Rex and the Rake

rake

Practice the Letter **Rr**

Say the letter name and the sound it stands for. Then, trace and write capital **R** and lowercase **r**.

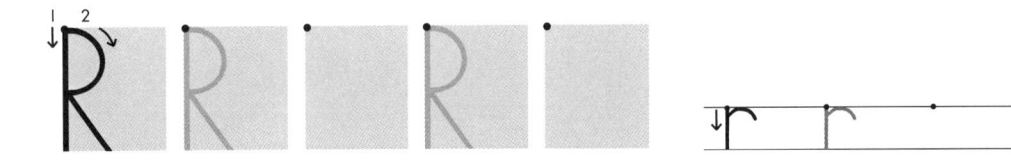

Say the name of each picture.
Write the letter that stands for the **beginning** sound to complete the word.

___oof ___an ___ocks ___un ___ug ___ips

Look around. Find names that start with capital **R** and things that start with lowercase **r**.
Write the words.

Quinn and the Quilt   Qq

Understanding the Story: Events

Think about what happens in the story. The middle of the story is filled in. Now, draw and write about what happens in the beginning and end.

Beginning

_____
_____
_____
_____

Middle

"Dad!"

The quilt gets wet.

End

_____
_____
_____
_____

| Qq | Quinn and the Quilt

quilt

Practice the Letter Qq

Say the letter name and the sound it stands for. Then, trace and write capital **Q** and lowercase **q**.

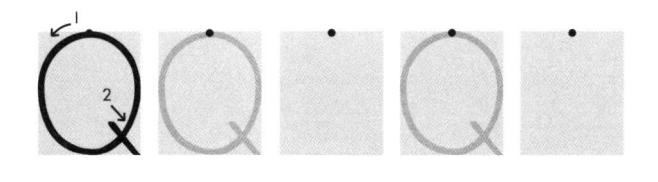

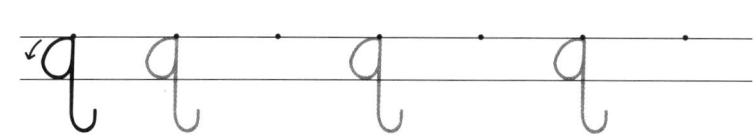

Read as much as you can. Then, circle every capital **Q** and lowercase **q** you see.

Monique has a duck.

Quack! Quack! Quack!

It is not quiet.

Raquan will get it.

Raquan can not.

The duck is quick!

Think of two things that start with the same beginning sound as **quilt**. Draw them.

Paco and the Piano Pp

Understanding the Story: Setting

Circle the picture that shows where the story takes place.

Write and draw about where Paco goes in the story.

Pp Paco and the Piano

piano

Practice the Letter Pp

Say the letter name and the sound it stands for. Then, trace and write capital **P** and lowercase **p**.

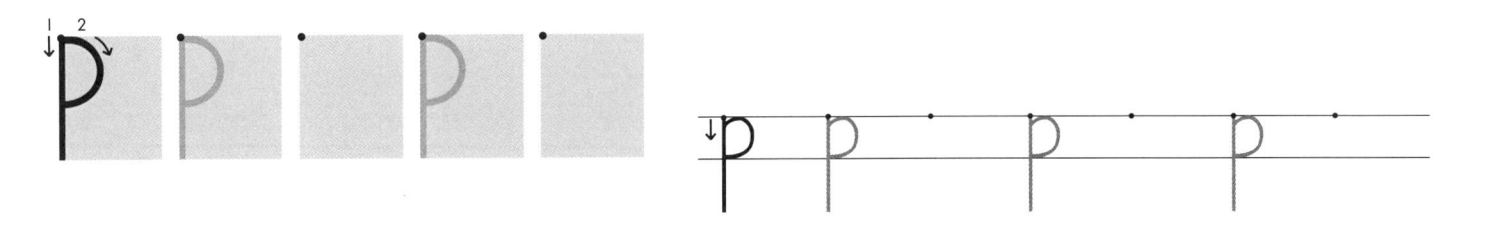

Say the name of each picture.
Write the letter that stands for the **beginning** sound to complete the word.

___ot   ___at   ___up   ___ig   ___ug   ___an

Look around. Find names that start with capital **P** and things that start with lowercase **p**.
Write the words.

Oz and the Octopus Oo

Understanding the Story: Events

Think about what happens in the story. The middle of the story is filled in. Now, draw and write about what happens in the beginning and end.

Beginning

Middle

The octopus is on the tank.

End

Oo   Oz and the Octopus

octopus

Practice the Letter Oo

Say the letter name and the sound it stands for. Then, trace and write capital **O** and lowercase **o**.

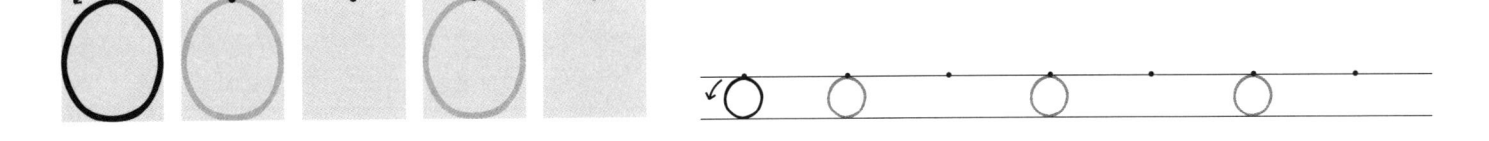

Say the name of each picture.
Write the letter that stands for the **middle** sound to complete the word.

f _ sh   m _ p

p _ t   l _ g

f _ n   d _ g

b _ d   c _ t

f _ x   b _ x

34   A–Z for Mat Man® and Me: Practice for Developing Readers - Letter Learning   © 2022 Learning Without Tears

Nell and the Nest Nn

Understanding the Story: Setting

Circle the picture that shows where the story takes place.

Write and draw about the place where Nell is and why it is important to what happens in the story.

© 2022 Learning Without Tears — A–Z for Mat Man® and Me: Practice for Developing Readers - **Meaning Making**

Nn Nell and the Nest

nest

Practice the Letter Nn

Say the letter name and the sound it stands for. Then, trace and write capital **N** and lowercase **n**.

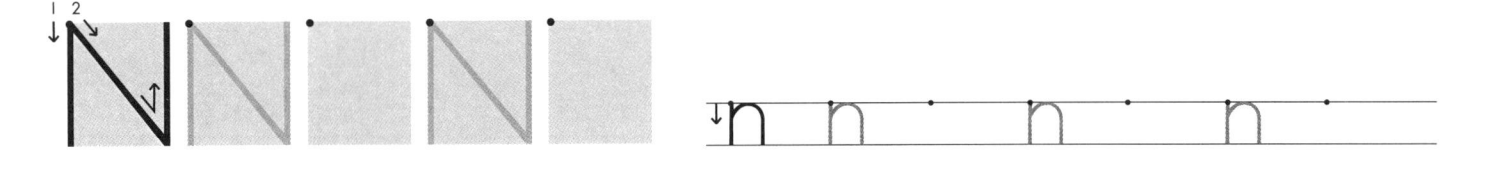

Say the name of each picture.
Write the letter that stands for the **beginning** sound to complete the word.

___ox ___at ___uts ___et ___ggs ___am

Think of two things that start with the same beginning sound as **nest**. Draw them.

Mac and the Magnificent Masks Mm

Understanding the Story: Events

Think about what happens in the story. The middle of the story is filled in. Now, draw and write about what happens in the beginning and end.

Beginning

Middle

Marcos tosses markers.

End

© 2022 Learning Without Tears — A–Z for Mat Man® and Me: Practice for Developing Readers - **Meaning Making**

Mm Mac and the Magnificent Masks

mask

Practice the Letter Mm

Say the letter name and the sound it stands for. Then, trace and write capital **M** and lowercase **m**.

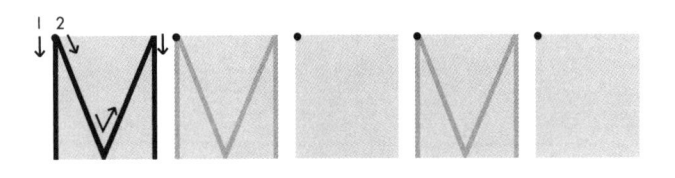

Say the name of each picture.
Write the letter that stands for the beginning sound to complete the word.

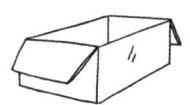

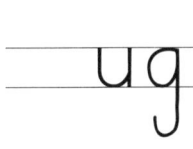

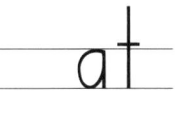

___op   ___ox   ___ug   ___at   ___ed   ___ick

Look around. Find names that start with capital **M** and things that start with lowercase **m**.
Write the words.

Lola and the Lock Ll

Understanding the Story: Events
Where does Lola look for her lock? Draw and write about three places where Lola looks.

Ll Lola and the Lock

lock

Practice the Letter Ll

Say the letter name and the sound it stands for. Then, trace and write capital **L** and lowercase **l**.

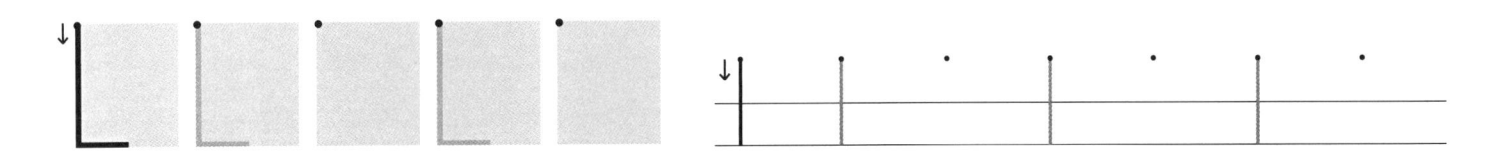

Say the name of each picture.
Write the letter that stands for the **beginning** sound to complete the word.

_eg   _un   _og   _ick   _ock   _og

Think of two things that start with the same beginning sound as **lock**. Draw them.

28 A–Z for Mat Man® and Me: Practice for Developing Readers - Letter Learning   © 2022 Learning Without Tears

Kaya and the Kayak Kk

Understanding the Story: Setting

Circle the picture that shows where the story takes place.

Where is Kaya in the story? Write about the place and draw a picture.

Kk Kaya and the Kayak

kayak

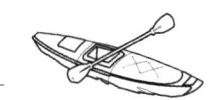

Practice the Letter Kk

Say the letter name and the sound it stands for. Then, trace and write capital **K** and lowercase **k**.

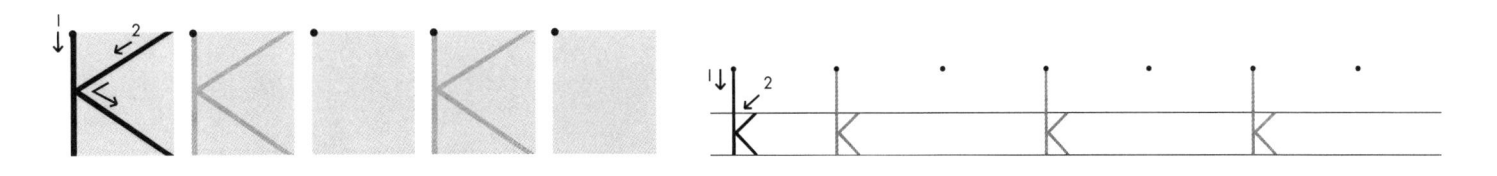

Say the name of each picture.
Write the letter that stands for the **beginning** sound to complete the word.

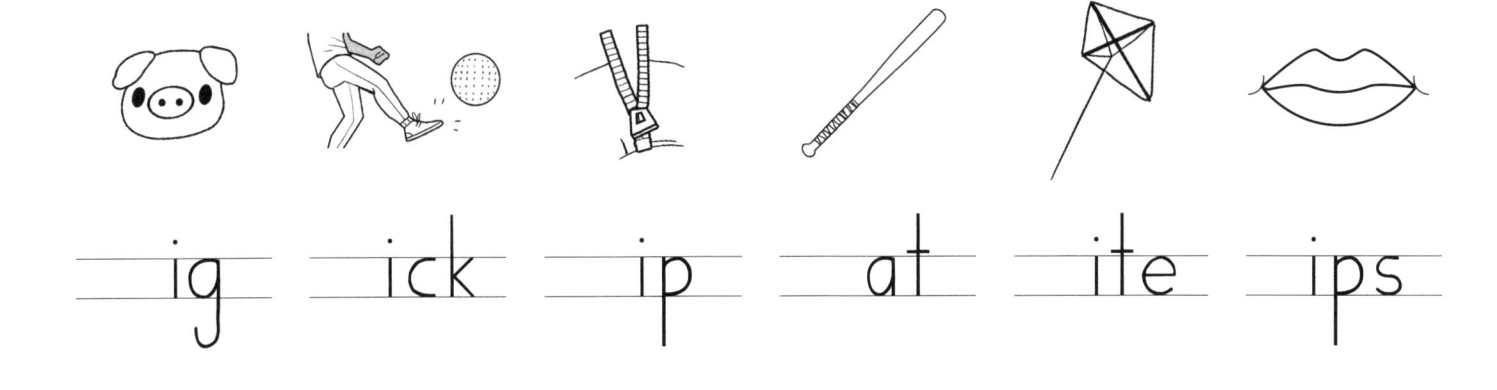

_ig _ick _ip _at _ite _ips

Look around. Find names that start with capital **K** and things that start with lowercase **k**.
Write the words.

26 A–Z for Mat Man® and Me: Practice for Developing Readers - **Letter Learning** © 2022 Learning Without Tears

Jana, Jen, and the Jellyfish **Jj**

Understanding the Story: Character

Find the two main characters in the story. (Circle) two pictures.

Write about something the characters do in the story and draw a picture.

Jana, Jen, and the Jellyfish

© 2022 Learning Without Tears — A–Z for Mat Man® and Me: Practice for Developing Readers - **Meaning Making** 25

Jj Jana, Jen, and the Jellyfish

jellyfish

Practice the Letter Jj

Say the letter name and the sound it stands for. Then, trace and write capital **J** and lowercase **j**.

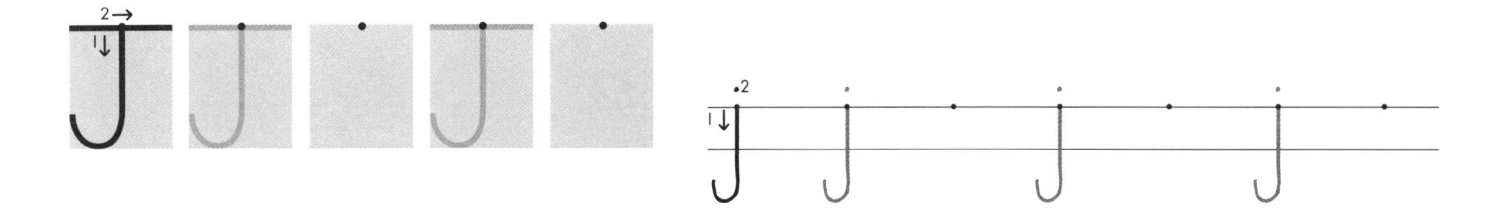

Say the name of each picture.
Write the letter that stands for the **beginning** sound to complete the word.

___un ___an ___am ___ox ___eep ___at

Think of two things that start with the same beginning sound as **jellyfish**. Draw them.

Ikiaq and the Igloo Ii

Understanding the Story: Setting

Circle the picture that shows where the story takes place.

Write about a place from the story and draw a picture.

Ii Ikiaq and the Igloo

igloo

Practice the Letter Ii

Say the letter name and the sound it stands for. Then, trace and write capital **I** and lowercase **i**.

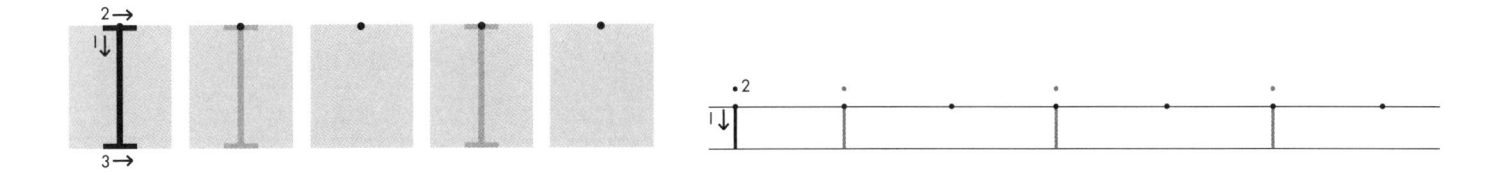

Say the name of each picture.
Write the letter that stands for the **middle** sound to complete the word.

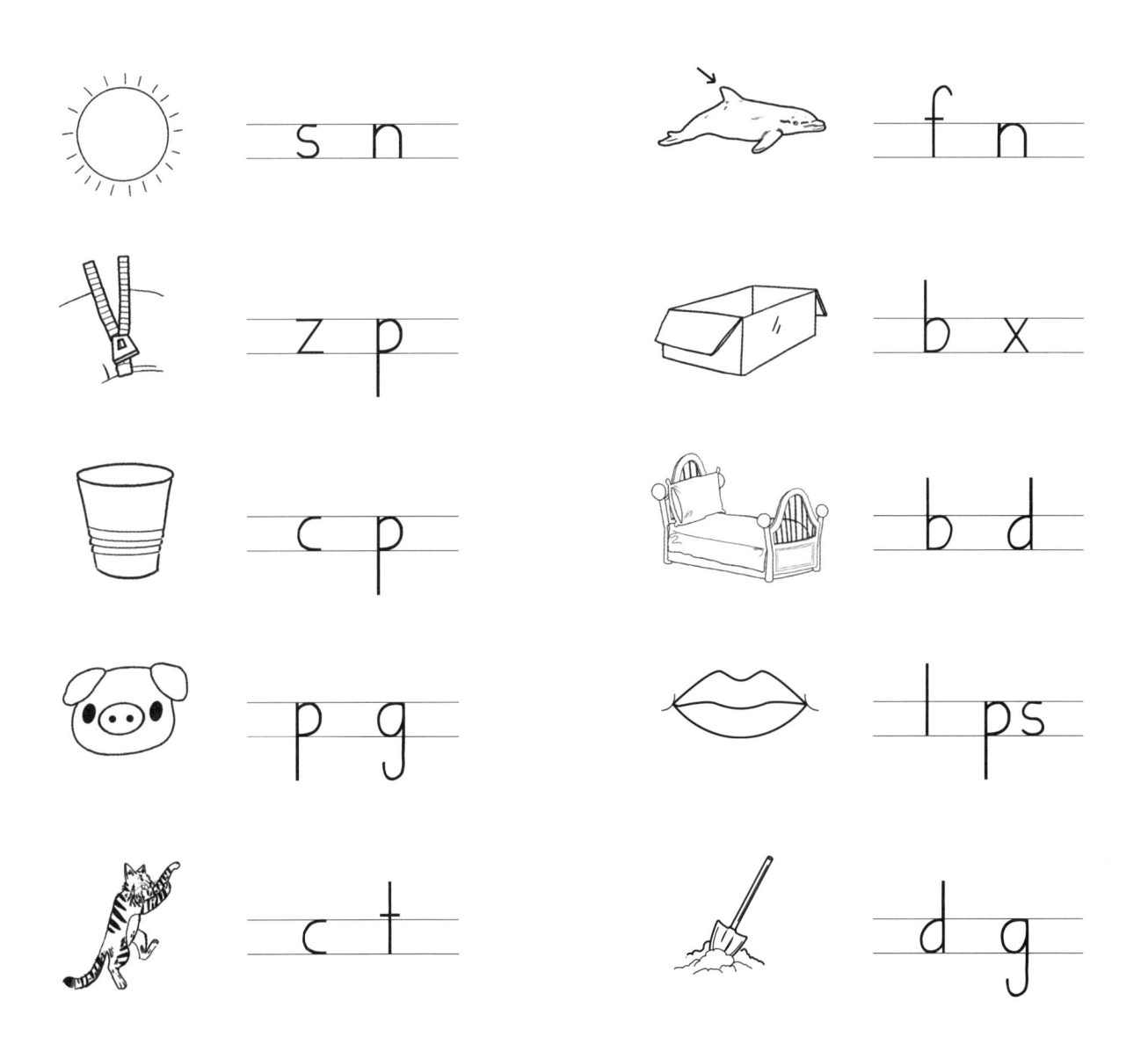

s _ n   f _ n

z _ p   b _ x

c _ p   b _ d

p _ g   l _ ps

c _ t   d _ g

22 *A–Z for Mat Man® and Me: Practice for Developing Readers - Letter Learning*   © 2022 Learning Without Tears

Hana has a Hammer Hh

Understanding the Story: Characters

Which animals get out in the story? Draw three that Hana has to chase. Write the names.

Hh Hana has a Hammer

hammer

Practice the Letter Hh

Say the letter name and the sound it stands for. Then, trace and write capital **H** and lowercase **h**.

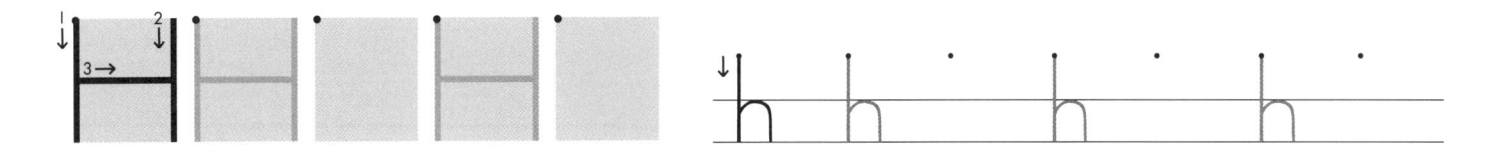

Say the name of each picture.
Write the letter that stands for the **beginning** sound to complete the word.

___ox ___en ___at ___eg ___og ___ig

Look around. Find names that start with capital **H** and things that start with lowercase **h**.
Write the words.

20 A–Z for Mat Man® and Me: Practice for Developing Readers - Letter Learning © 2022 Learning Without Tears

Gabby and Her Goat Gg

Understanding the Story: Events

What does Gus do in the story? Draw and write three things Gus gets.

Gg Gabby and Her Goat

goat

Practice the Letter Gg

Say the letter name and the sound it stands for. Then, trace and write capital **G** and lowercase **g**.

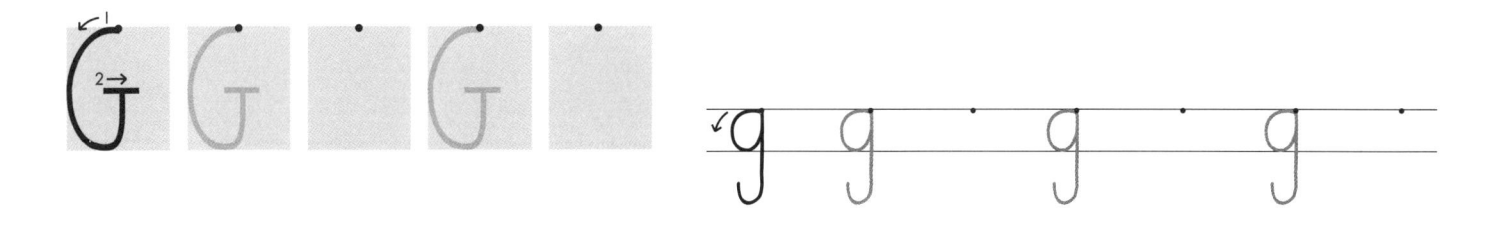

Say the name of each picture.
Write the letter that stands for the **ending** sound to complete the word.

ba___   mo___   do___   pi___   po___   ru___

Look around. Find names that start with capital **G** and things that start with lowercase **g**.
Write the words.

Feng, Finn, and the Fan | Ff

Understanding the Story: Events

Think about what happens in the story. The middle of the story is filled in. Now, draw and write about what happens in the beginning and end.

Beginning

Middle

Feng and Finn fight.

End

Ff Feng, Finn, and the Fan

fan

Practice the Letter **Ff**

Say the letter name and the sound it stands for. Then, trace and write capital **F** and lowercase **f**.

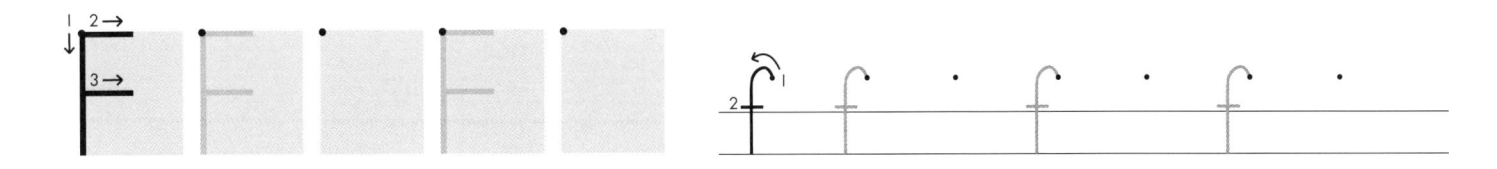

Say the name of each picture.
Write the letter that stands for the **beginning** sound to complete the word.

_at   _an   _ox   _in   _ox   _am

Think of two things that start with the same beginning sound as **fan**. Draw them.

Emma and the Elephant Ee

Understanding the Story: Characters

Think about what Emma does and how she feels. When does Emma feel sad? Draw and write about it.

When does Emma feel happy in the story? Draw and write about it.

Ee Cora and the Coconut

elephant

Practice the Letter Ee

Say the letter name and the sound it stands for. Then, trace and write capital **E** and lowercase **e**.

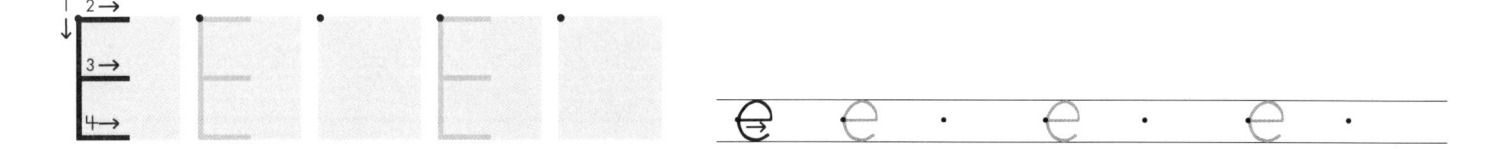

Say the name of each picture.
Write the letter that stands for the **middle** sound to complete the word.

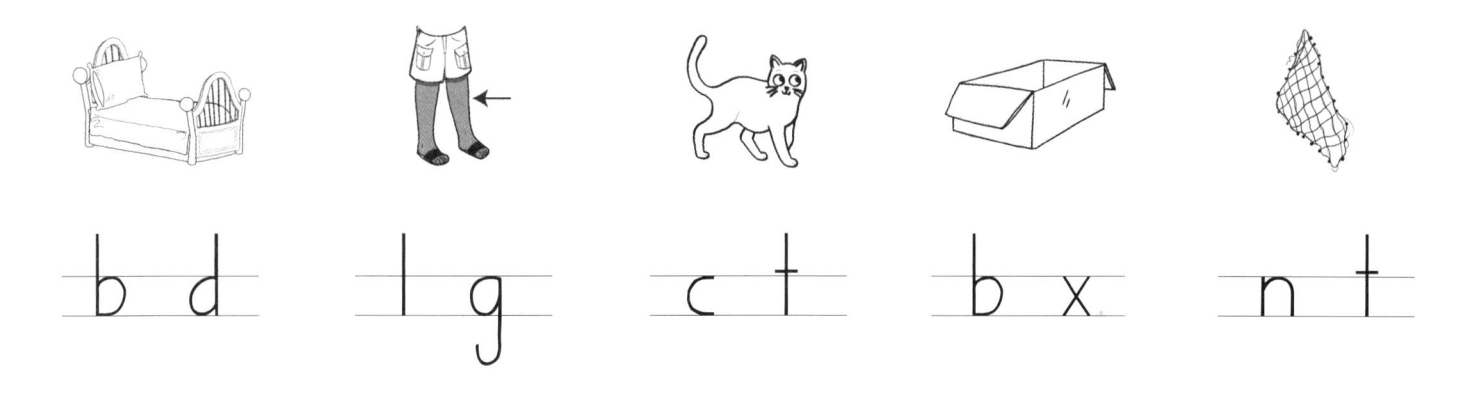

b__d l__g c__t b__x n__t

Look around. Find names that start with capital **E** and things that start with lowercase **e**. Write the words.

14 A–Z for Mat Man® and Me: Practice for Developing Readers - Letter Learning © 2022 Learning Without Tears

Dax and the Dolphin — **Dd**

Understanding the Story: Setting

Circle the picture that shows where the story takes place.

Where is Dax in the story? Write about the place and draw a picture.

Dd Dax and the Dolphin

dolphin

Practice the Letter Dd

Say the letter name and the sound it stands for. Then, trace and write capital **D** and lowercase **d**.

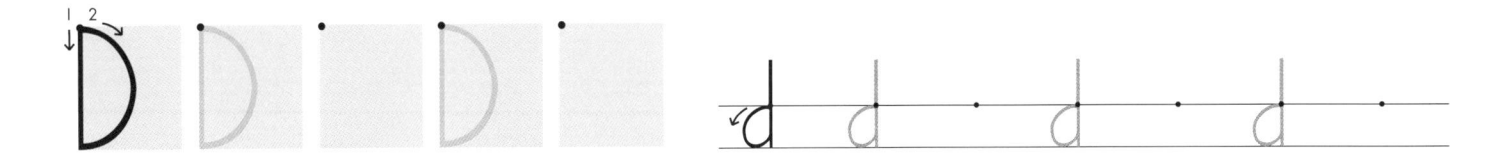

Say the name of each picture.
Write the letter that stands for the **beginning** sound to complete the word.

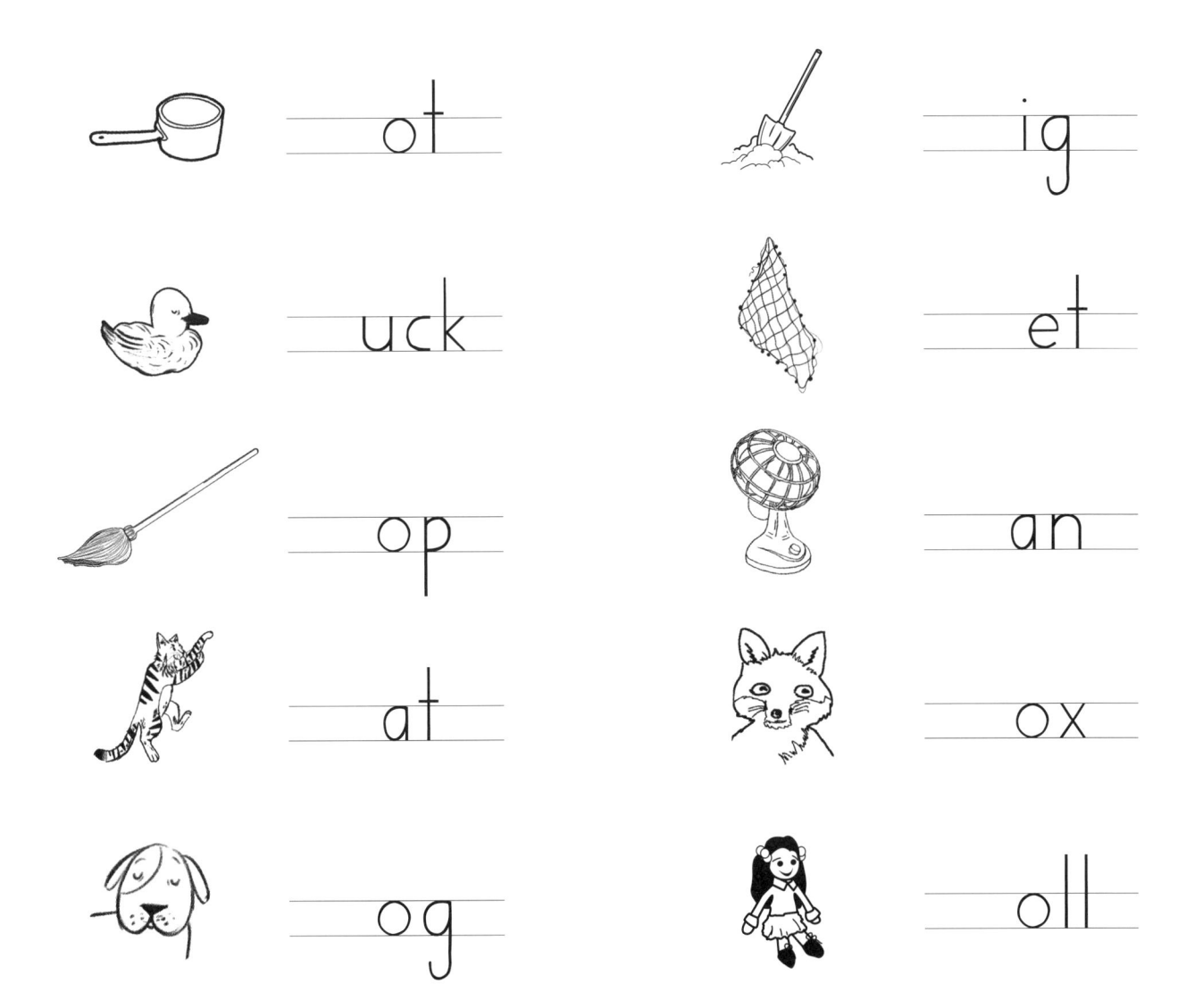

_ot

_uck

_op

_at

_og

_ig

_et

_an

_ox

_oll

Cora and the Coconut   Cc

Understanding the Story: Events

Think about what happens in the story. The middle of the story is filled in. Now, draw and write about what happens in the beginning and end.

Beginning

Middle

Cora holds up a cat.

End

© 2022 Learning Without Tears — A–Z for Mat Man® and Me: Practice for Developing Readers - **Meaning Making**

Cc Cora and the Coconut

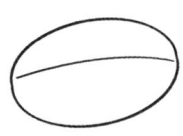

coconut

Practice the Letter Cc

Say the letter name and the sound it stands for. Then, trace and write capital **C** and lowercase **c**.

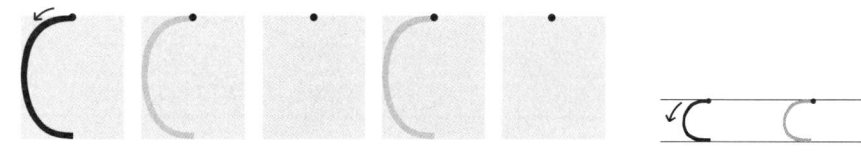

Say the name of each picture.
Write the letter that stands for the **beginning** sound to complete the word.

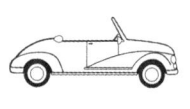

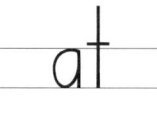

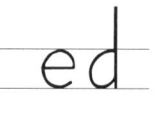

___at   ___ox   ___up   ___ar   ___ed   ___ips

Look around. Find names that start with capital **C** and things that start with lowercase **c**. Write the words.

Ben and the Big Bagels   Bb

Understanding the Story: Setting

Circle the picture that shows where the story takes place.

Where is Ben in the story? Write about the place and draw a picture.

Bb Ben and the Big Bagels

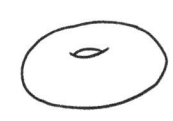

bagel

Practice the Letter Bb

Say the letter name and the sound it stands for. Then, trace and write capital **B** and lowercase **b**.

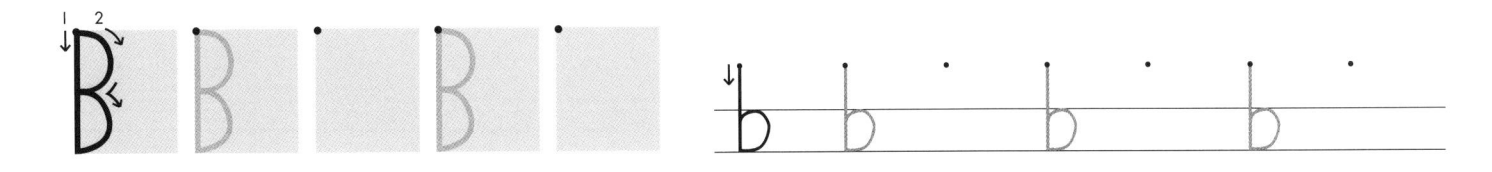

Say the name of each picture.
Write the letter that stands for the **beginning** sound to complete the word.

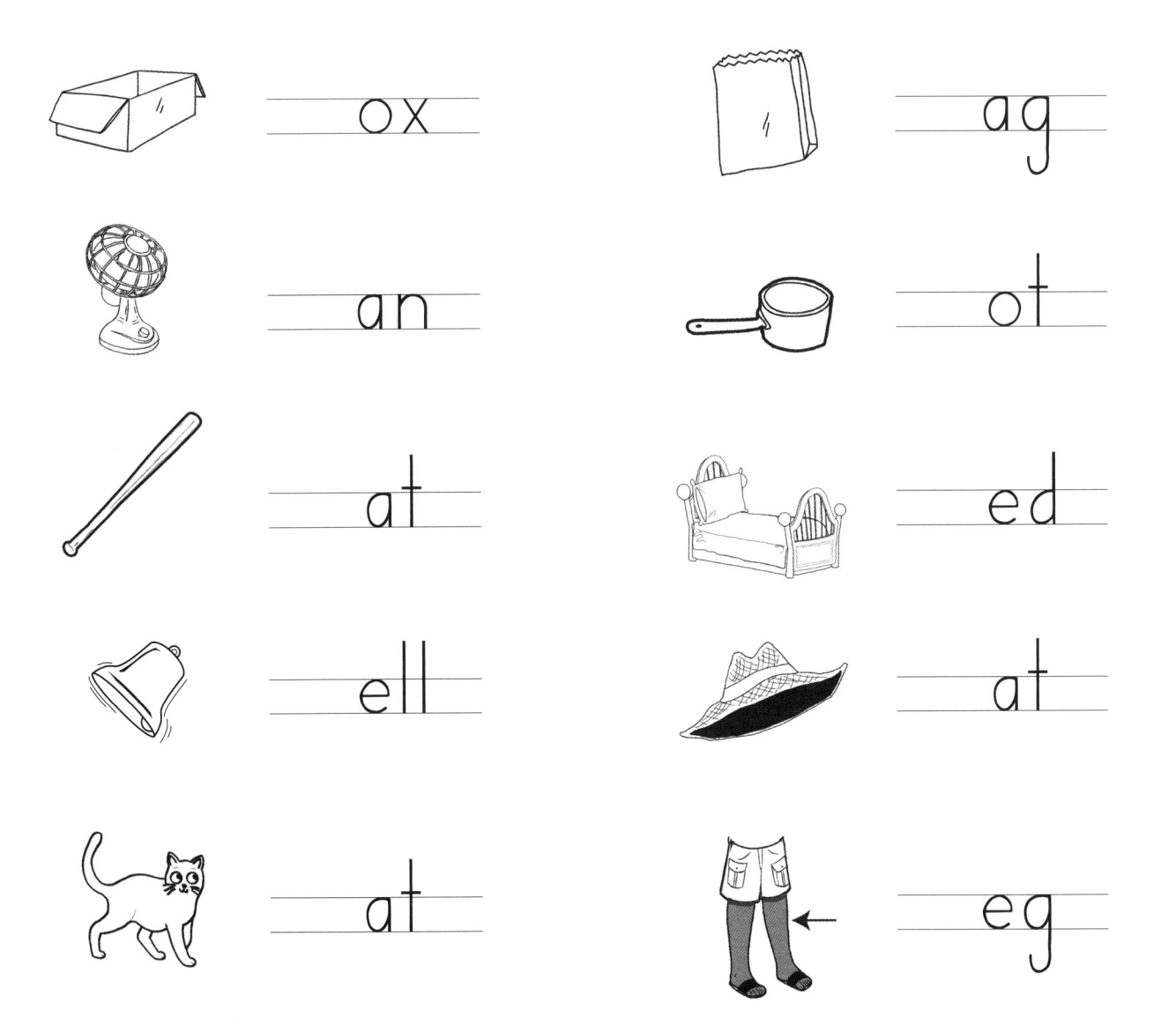

_ox   _ag

_an   _ot

_at   _ed

_ell   _at

_at   _eg

8   A–Z for Mat Man® and Me: Practice for Developing Readers - Letter Learning   © 2022 Learning Without Tears

Ally and the Apple   Aa

Understanding the Story: Events

Think about what happens in the story. The middle of the story is filled in. Now, draw and write about what happens in the beginning and end.

Beginning

Middle

Ally asks for help.

End

Aa Ally and the Apple

apple

Practice the Letter Aa

Say the letter name and the sound it stands for. Then, trace and write capital **A** and lowercase **a**.

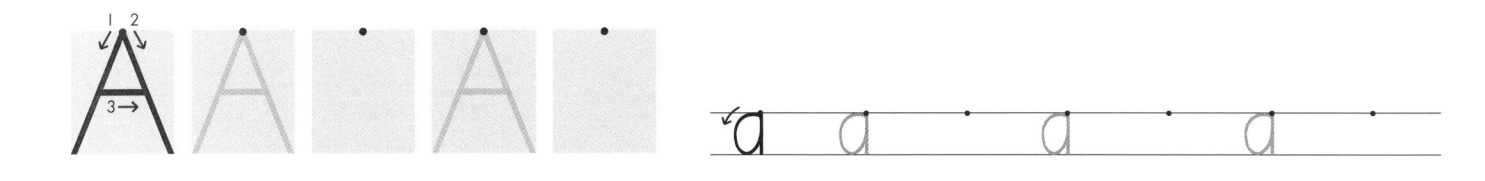

Say the name of each picture.
Write the letter that stands for the **middle** sound to complete the word.

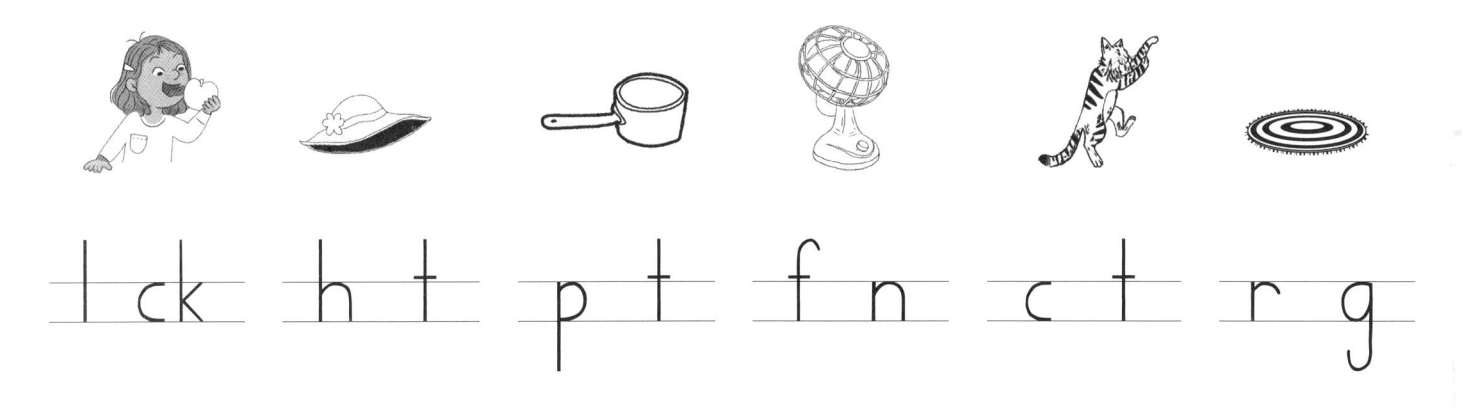

l_ck   h_t   p_t   f_n   c_t   r_g

Think of two things that start with the same beginning sound as **apple**. Draw them.

---

6   A–Z for Mat Man® and Me: Practice for Developing Readers - Letter Learning   © 2022 Learning Without Tears

Mat Man® and the Great Alphabet Parade

The First Letter in Your Name

First, circle the letter your first name starts with. Then, underline the letter your last name starts with.

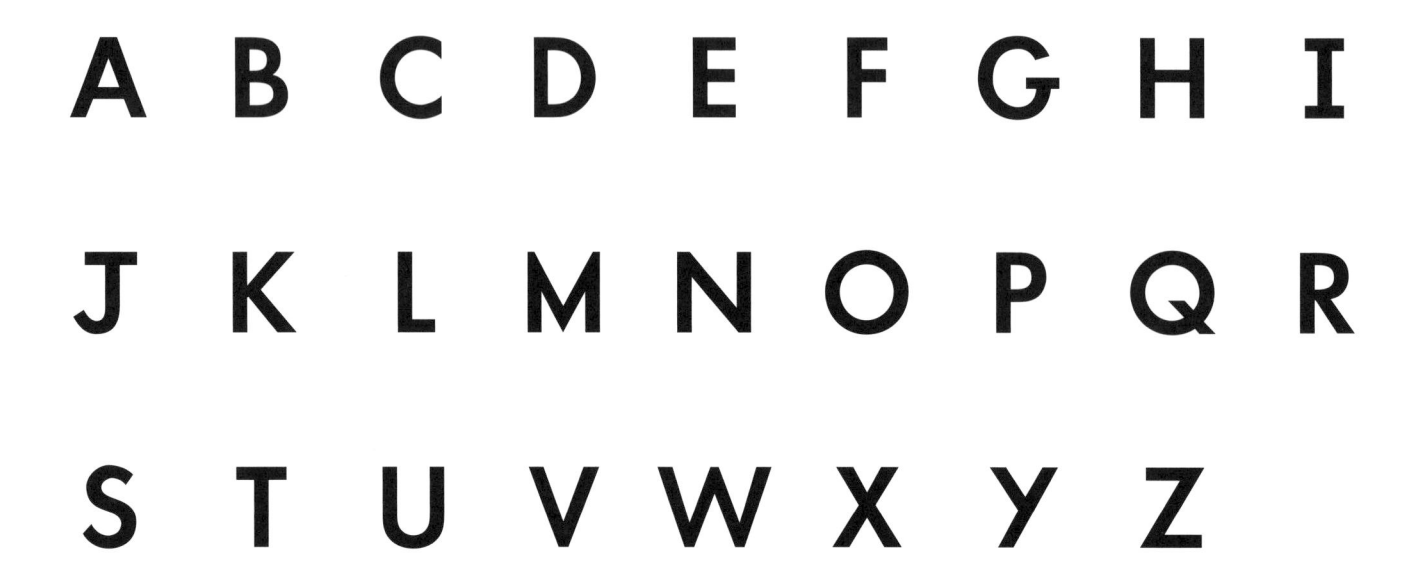

A B C D E F G H I
J K L M N O P Q R
S T U V W X Y Z

Draw a picture of something from the parade that starts with the same letter your first name starts with. Then, draw a picture of something that starts with the first letter in your last name.

Mat Man® and the Great Alphabet Parade

Sing the Alphabet Song

Help Mat Man sing the ABC song! Underline each letter as we sing it. The **a** is done for you. Then, color the pictures.

a b c d e f g

h i j k l m n o p

q r s

t u v

w x

y and z

TABLE OF CONTENTS

Sing the Alphabet Song 4

The First Letter in Your Name 5

Letter Aa: *Ally and the Apple*
  Practice the Letter **Aa** 6
  Understanding the Story: Events 7

Letter Bb: *Ben and the Big Bagels*
  Practice the Letter **Bb** 8
  Understanding the Story: Setting 9

Letter Cc: *Cora and the Coconut*
  Practice the Letter **Cc** 10
  Understanding the Story: Events 11

Letter Dd: *Dax and the Dolphin*
  Practice the Letter **Dd** 12
  Understanding the Story: Setting 13

Letter Ee: *Emma and Her Elephant*
  Practice the Letter **Ee** 14
  Understanding the Story: Character 15

Letter Ff: *Feng, Finn, and the Fan*
  Practice the Letter **Ff** 16
  Understanding the Story: Events 17

Letter Gg: *Gabby and Her Goat*
  Practice the Letter **Gg** 18
  Understanding the Story: Events 19

Letter Hh: *Hana Has a Hammer*
  Practice the Letter **Hh** 20
  Understanding the Story: Events 21

Letter Ii: *Ikiaq and the Igloo*
  Practice the Letter **Ii** 22
  Understanding the Story: Setting 23

Letter Jj: *Jana, Jen, and the Jellyfish*
  Practice the Letter **Jj** 24
  Understanding the Story: Character 25

Letter Kk: *Kaya and the Kite*
  Practice the Letter **Kk** 26
  Understanding the Story: Setting 27

Letter Ll: *Lola and the Lock*
  Practice the Letter **Ll** 28
  Understanding the Story: Events 29

Letter Mm: *Mac and the Magnificent Masks*
  Practice the Letter **Mm** 30
  Understanding the Story: Events 31

Letter Nn: *Nell and the Nest*
  Practice the Letter **Nn** 32
  Understanding the Story: Setting 33

Letter Oo: *Oz and the Octopus*
  Practice the Letter **Oo** 34
  Understanding the Story: Events 35

Letter Pp: *Paco and the Piano*
  Practice the Letter **Pp** 36
  Understanding the Story: Character 37

Letter Qq: *Quinn and the Quilt*
  Practice the Letter **Qq** 38
  Understanding the Story: Events 39

Letter Rr: *Rex and the Rake*
  Practice the Letter **Rr** 40
  Understanding the Story: Character 41

Letter Ss: *Sam in the Sun*
  Practice the Letter **Ss** 42
  Understanding the Story: Setting 43

Letter Tt: *Tere and the Tomato*
  Practice the Letter **Tt** 44
  Understanding the Story: Character 45

Letter Uu: *Umberto and the Umbrella*
  Practice the Letter **Uu** 46
  Understanding the Story: Events 47

Letter Vv: *Vic, Val, and the Vacuum*
  Practice the Letter **Vv** 48
  Understanding the Story: Character 49

Letter Ww: *Wes and the Watermelon*
  Practice the Letter **Ww** 50
  Understanding the Story: Setting 51

Letter Xx: *Xavier Gets an X-ray*
  Practice the Letter **Xx** 52
  Understanding the Story: Setting 53

Letter Yy: *Yolanda and the Yo-Yo*
  Practice the Letter **Yy** 54
  Understanding the Story: Events 55

Letter Zz: *Zack and His Zipper*
  Practice the Letter **Zz** 56
  Understanding the Story: Character 57

Letter Check 1 58

Letter Check 2 60

Letter Check 3 62

Letter Review 64

LEARNING
Without Tears®

8001 MacArthur Blvd.
Cabin John, MD 20818
LWTears.com | 888.983.8409

Art Director: Shannon Rutledge
Graphic Designer: Sammie Simon
Curriculum Designers: Adam Berkin, Nicole Iorio, Cari Meister, Casey Schultz

Copyright © 2022 Learning Without Tears
First Edition
ISBN: 978-1-954728-42-4
23456789RRD232221
Printed in Dongguan, China

The contents of this consumable workbook are protected by US copyright law. If a workbook has been purchased for a child, the author and Learning Without Tears give limited permission to copy pages for additional practice or homework for that child. No copied pages from this book can be given to another person without written permission from Learning Without Tears.

A-Z for Mat Man® and Me

Practice for Developing Readers

LEARNING Without Tears®

Letter Review

Letter Review

Say the name for each picture. Circle the letter that stands for its **beginning** sound.
Write the lowercase letter on the double lines.

1. m
   p
   s

2. s
   w
   m

3. c
   n
   b

4. r
   p
   b

5. e
   r
   m

6. t
   w
   v

7. a
   p
   u

8. r
   f
   l

Letter Check 3

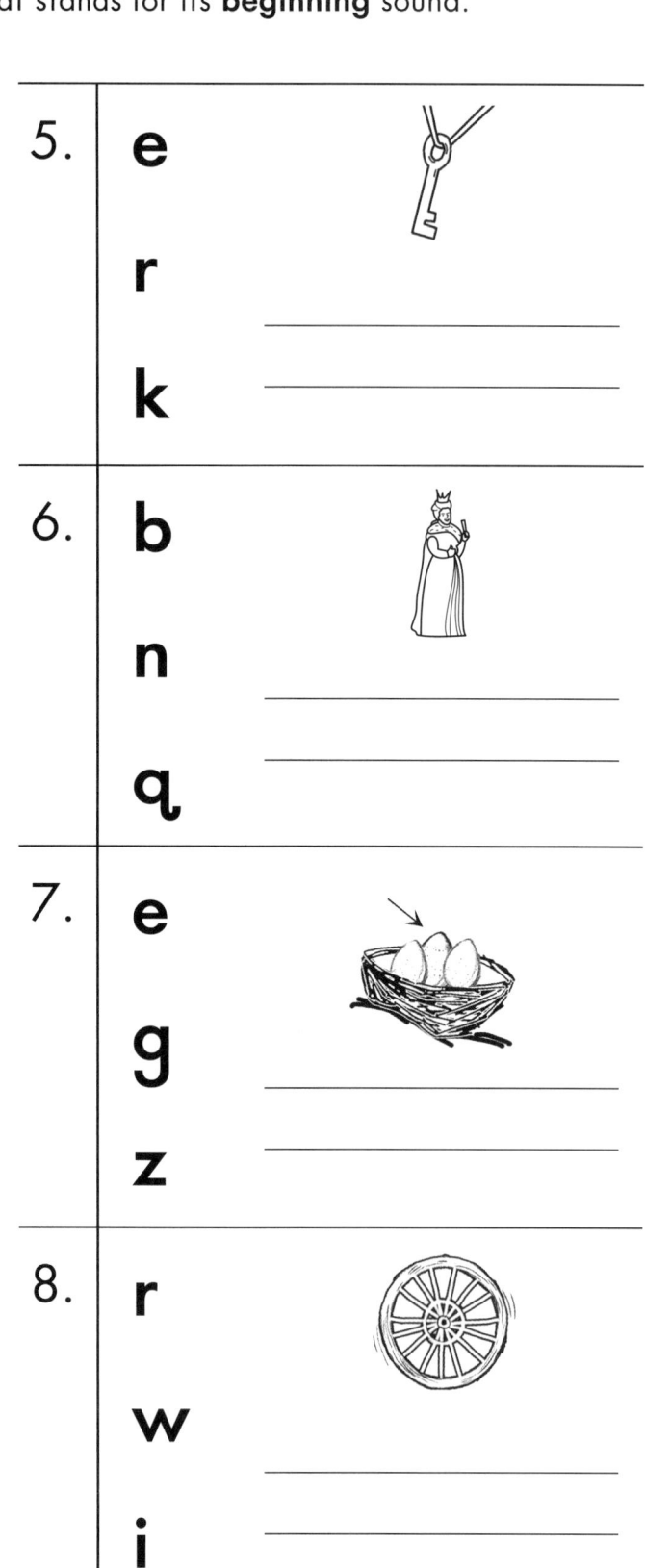

Letter Check 3, Part B

Say the name for each picture. ⓒircle the letter that stands for its **beginning** sound. Write the lowercase letter on the double lines.

1. x / k / a

2. s / j / t

3. k / t / f

4. y / j / s

5. e / r / k

6. b / n / q

7. e / g / z

8. r / w / i

Letter Check 3

Letter Check 3, Part A

Say the name for each picture. Circle the letter that stands for its **beginning** sound. Write the lowercase letter on the double lines.

1. j / s / v

2. y / k / a

3. i / d / u

4. j / s / p

5. w / f / n

6. d / q / e

7. g / p / o

8. q / i / l

62 *A–Z for Mat Man® and Me: Practice for Developing Readers* © 2022 Learning Without Tears

Letter Check 2

Letter Check 2, Part B

Say the name for each picture. Circle the letter that stands for its **beginning** sound. Write the lowercase letter on the double lines.

1. r / l / g

2. c / p / v

3. n / f / l

4. m / b / e

5. m / d / z

6. h / l / w

7. i / d / o

8. f / g / j

© 2022 Learning Without Tears

Letter Check 2

Letter Check 2, Part A

Say the name for each picture. Ⓒircle the letter that stands for its **beginning** sound.
Write the lowercase letter on the double lines.

1. l
   d
   k

2. p
   h
   b

3. g
   w
   s

4. z
   t
   l

5. f
   x
   i

6. b
   n
   h

7. n
   d
   c

8. o
   z
   r

60 A–Z for Mat Man and Me: Practice for Developing Readers © 2022 Learning Without Tears

Letter Check 1

Letter Check 1, Part B

Say the name for each picture. Circle the letter that stands for its **beginning** sound. Write the lowercase letter on the double lines.

1. s / r / l

2. i / y / p

3. p / n / g

4. k / s / r

5. a / v / m

6. b / v / a

7. t / n / r

8. t / q / p

Letter Check 1

Letter Check 1, Part A

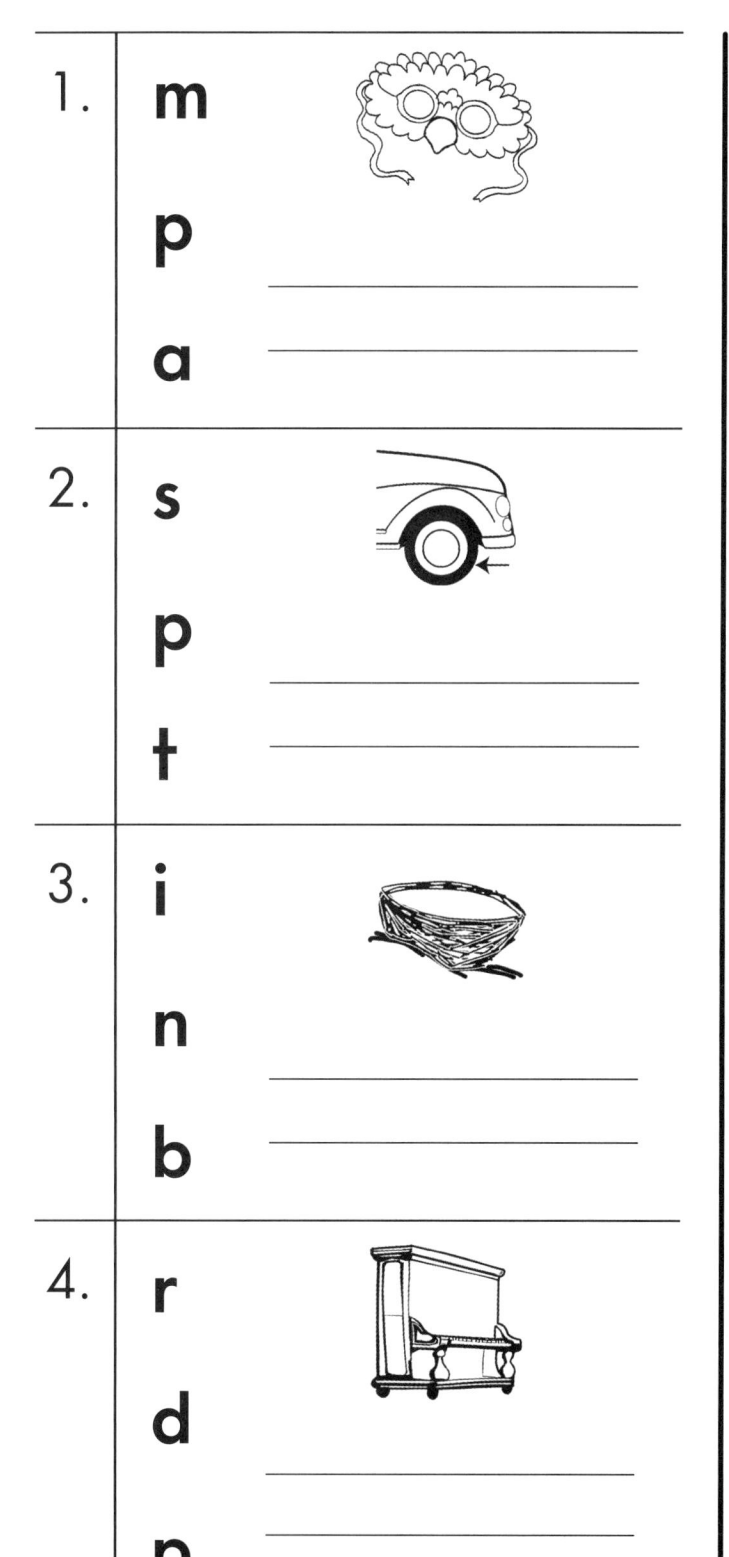

Say the name for each picture. (Circle) the letter that stands for its **beginning** sound.
Write the lowercase letter on the double lines.

1.	m p a		5.	g r m	
2.	s p t		6.	t s v	
3.	i n b		7.	a b u	
4.	r d p		8.	r o i	

58   A–Z for Mat Man® and Me: Practice for Developing Readers

Zack and His Zipper Zz

Understanding the Story: Characters

Think about what Zack does and how he feels. When does Zack feel mad? Draw and write about it.

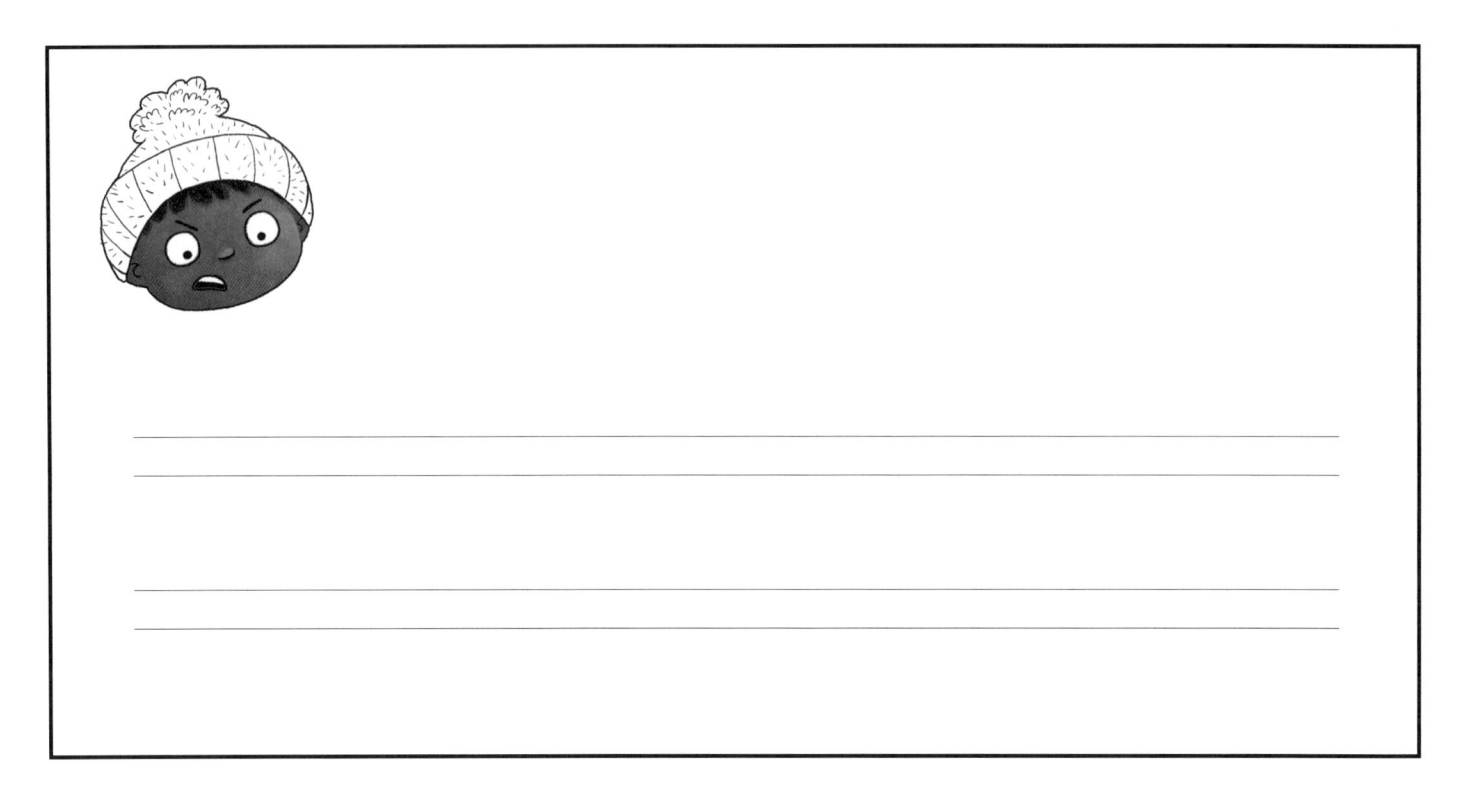

When does Zack feel happy in the story? Draw and write.

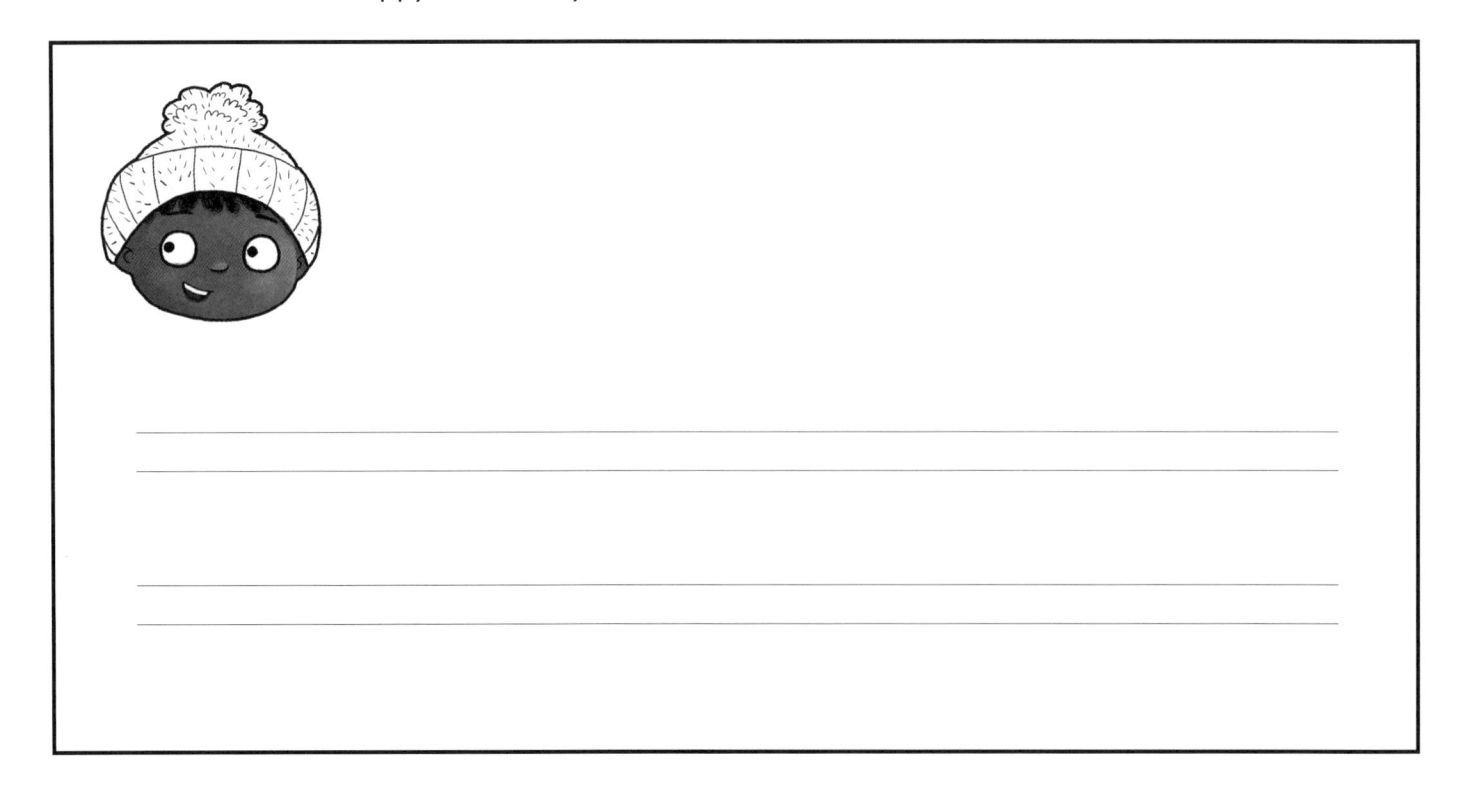

© 2022 Learning Without Tears — A–Z for Mat Man® and Me: Practice for Developing Readers - **Meaning Making**

Zz Zack and His Zipper

zipper

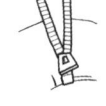

Practice the Letter Zz

Say the letter name and the sound it stands for. Then, trace and write capital **Z** and lowercase **z**.

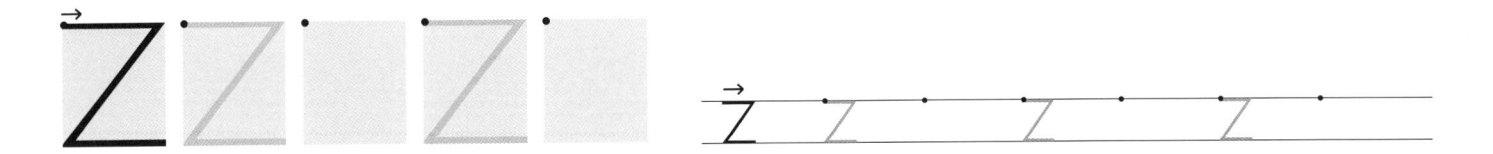

Read as much as you can. Then, circle every capital **Z** and lowercase **z** you see.

Liz zips up her coat.

It is a size too big.

It keeps out the breeze.

Liz and Zoe get to the zoo!

They look at a zebra.

Think of two things that start with the same beginning sound as **zipper**. Draw them.

Practice the Letter Yy

Understanding the Story: Events

Think about what happens in the story. The middle of the story is filled in. Now, draw and write about what happens in the beginning and end.

Beginning

Middle

Yaz does not trade back.

End

© 2022 Learning Without Tears — A–Z for Mat Man® and Me: Practice for Developing Readers - Meaning Making

Yy Practice the Letter Yy

Practice the Letter Yy

Say the letter name and the sound it stands for. Then, trace and write capital **Y** and lowercase **y**.

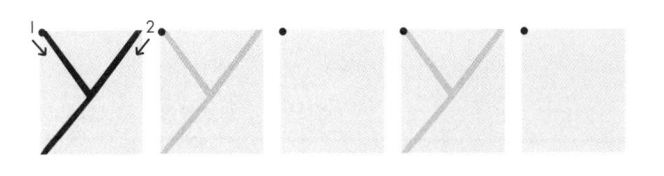

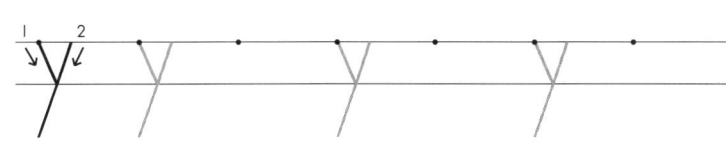

yo-yo

Read as much as you can. Then, (circle) every capital **Y** and lowercase **y** you see.

Yams are hot.

Yum! Cy says yes.

Cy gets a lot.

Jay says no.

Why yams? Yuck!

Jay gets a yogurt.

Think of two things that start with the same beginning sound as **yo-yo**. Draw them.

Xavier Gets an X-ray Xx

Understanding the Story: Setting

Where is Xavier in the story? Draw and write about three place where you see Xavier.

53

Xx Xavier Gets an X-ray

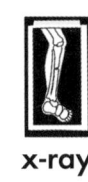

x-ray

Practice the Letter Xx

Say the letter name and the sound it stands for. Then, trace and write capital **X** and lowercase **x**.

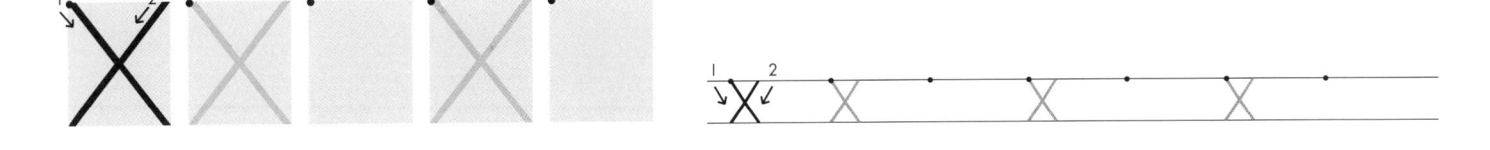

Say the name of each picture.
Write the letter that stands for the **ending** sound to complete the word.

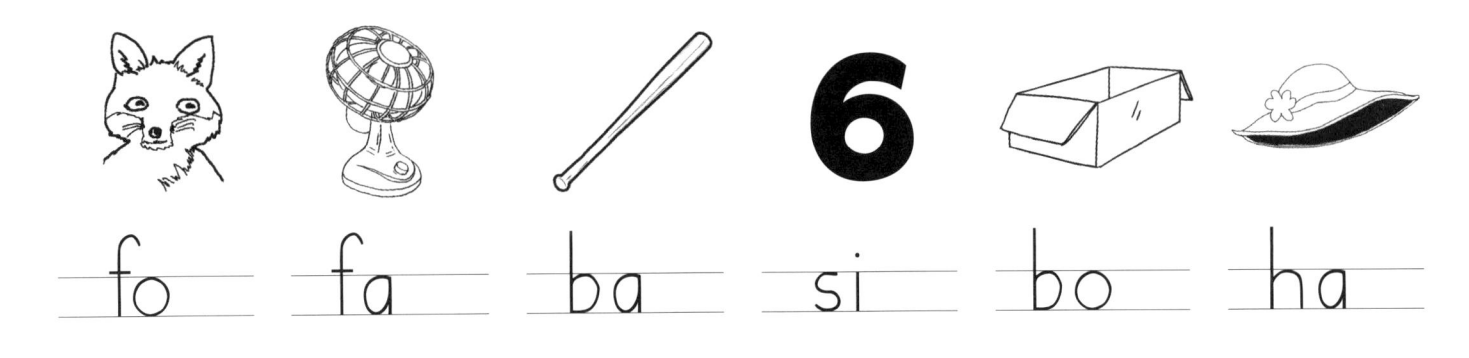

fo___   fa___   ba___   si___   bo___   ha___

Look around. Find names and words that have an **x** in them. Write the words.

52 A–Z for Mat Man® and Me: Practice for Developing Readers - Letter Learning   © 2022 Learning Without Tears

Wes and the Watermelon Ww

Understanding the Story: Setting

Circle the picture that shows where the story takes place.

Where is Wes in the story? Write about the place and draw a picture.

Ww — Wes and the Watermelon

watermelon

Practice the Letter Ww

Say the letter name and the sound it stands for. Then, trace and write capital **W** and lowercase **w**.

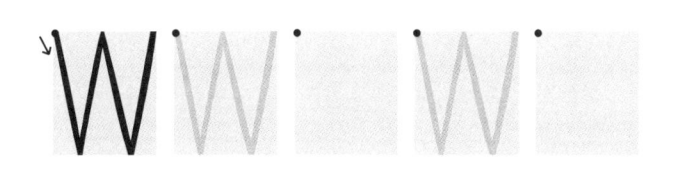

Read as much as you can. Then, circle every capital **W** and lowercase **w** you see.

Will has to win.

Wu has to win, too.

Who will win the swim race?

Will swims a lap.

Wu swims a lap.

They tap the wall. Tie!

Think of two things that start with the same beginning sound as **watermelon**. Draw them.

Vic, Val, and the Vacuum   Vv

Understanding the Story: Characters

Think about what Val does and how she feels. When does Val feel mad? Draw and write about it.

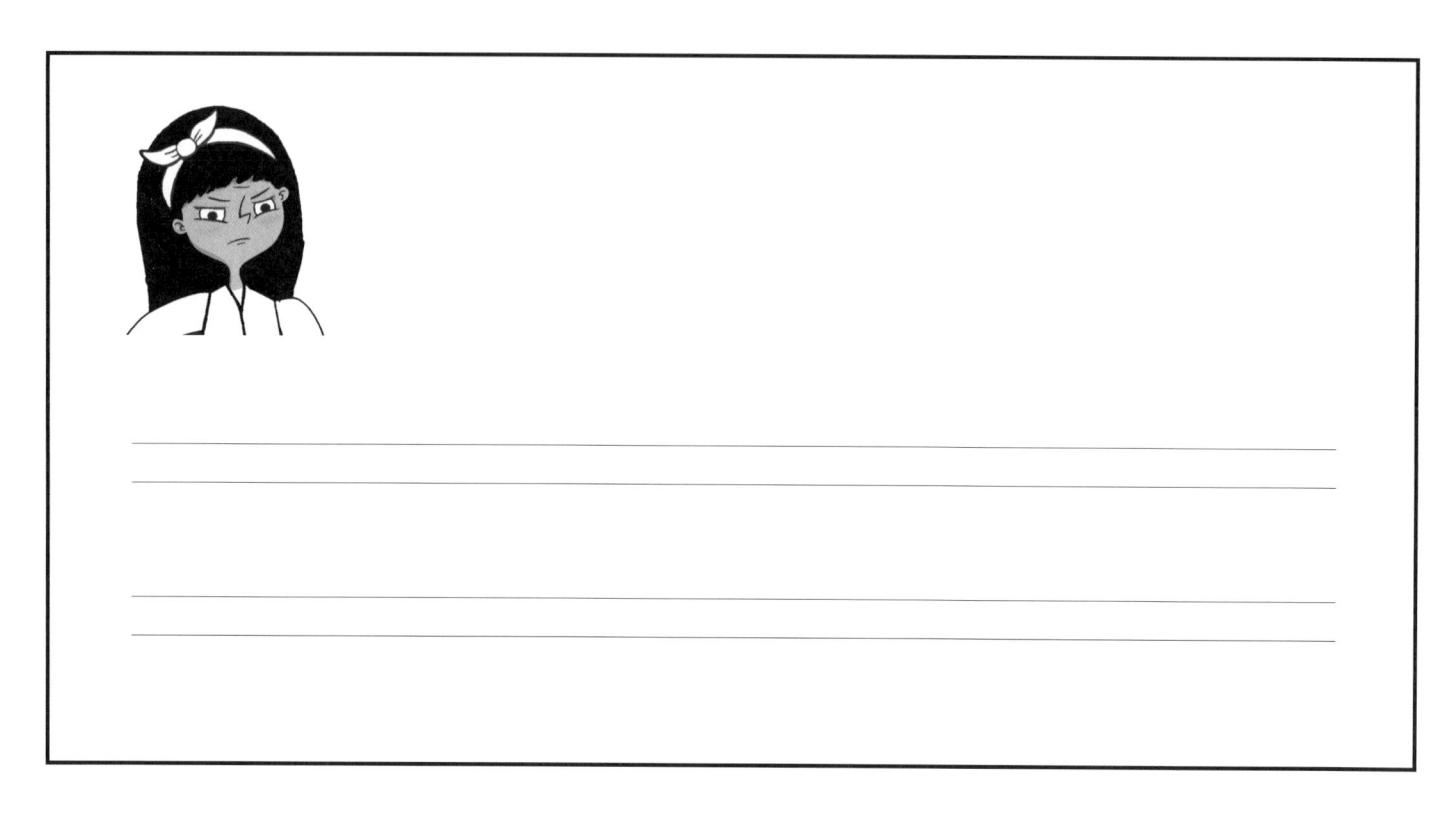

When does Val feel happy and thankful in the story? Draw and write.

Vv Vic, Val, and the Vacuum

vacuum

Practice the Letter Vv

Say the letter name and the sound it stands for. Then, trace and write capital **V** and lowercase **v**.

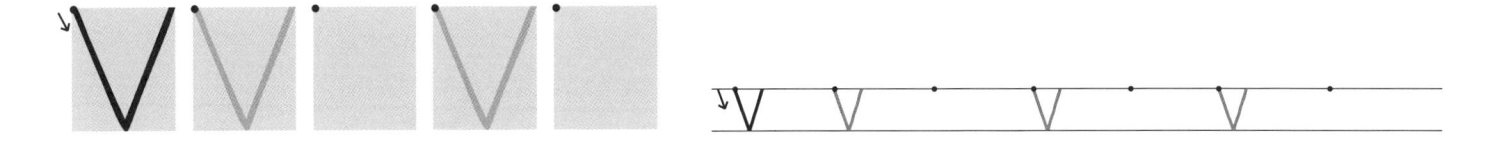

Say the name of each picture.
Write the letter that stands for the **beginning** sound to complete the word.

___ase   ___at   ___an   ___og   ___op   ___ug

Think of two things that start with the same beginning sound as **vacuum**. Draw them.

48 A–Z for Mat Man® and Me: Practice for Developing Readers - **Letter Learning**   © 2022 Learning Without Tears

Umberto and the Umbrella Uu

Understanding the Story: Events

What does Umberto do in the story? Draw three things Umberto uses to try to stay dry.

Uu | Umberto and the Umbrella

umbrella

Practice the Letter **Uu**

Say the letter name and the sound it stands for. Then, trace and write capital **U** and lowercase **u**.

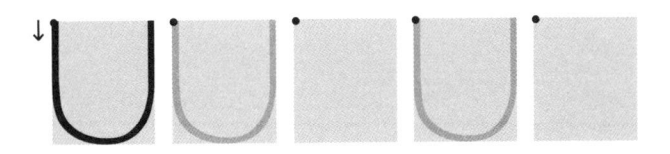

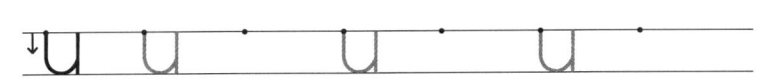

Say the name of each picture.
Write the letter that stands for the **middle** sound to complete the word.

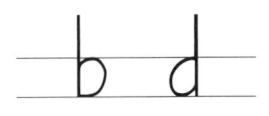

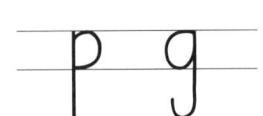

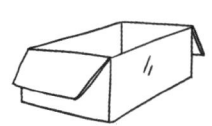

r _ cks

b _ t

s _ n

d _ ck

n _ ts

b _ d

p _ g

b _ x

c _ p

r _ g

46 A–Z for Mat Man® and Me: Practice for Developing Readers - Letter Learning © 2022 Learning Without Tears

Tere and the Tomato Tt

Understanding the Story: Characters

Think about what Tere does and how she feels in the story. When does Tere feel worried? Draw and write about it.

When does Tere feel happy in the story? Draw and write about it.

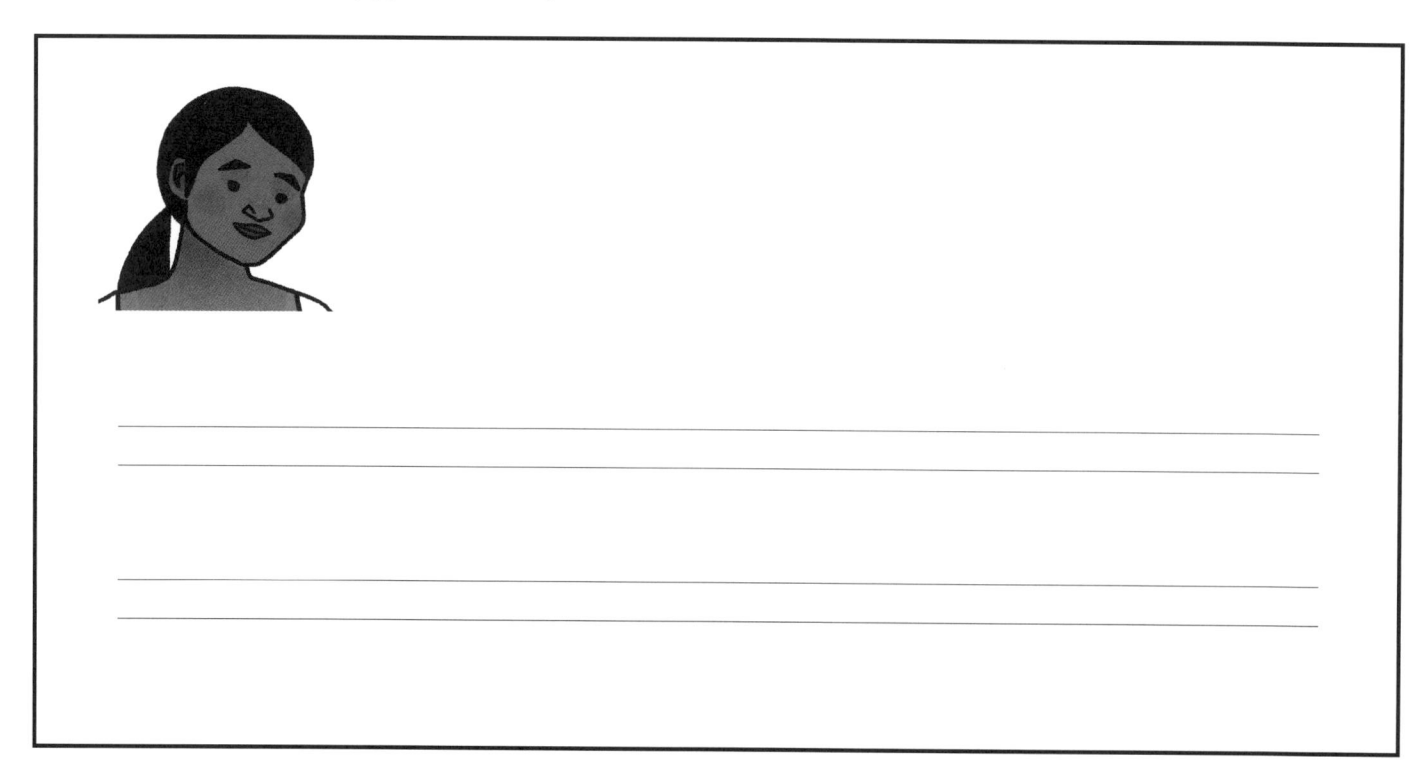

Tt Tere and the Tomato

tomato

Practice the Letter Tt

Say the letter name and the sound it stands for. Then, trace and write capital **T** and lowercase **t**.

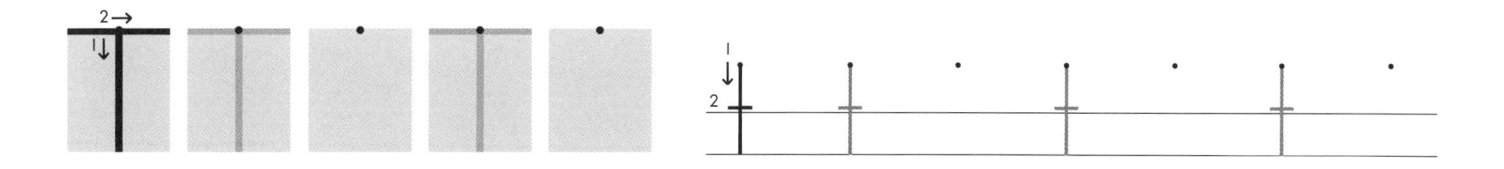

Say the name of each picture.
Write the letter that stands for the **beginning** sound to complete the word.

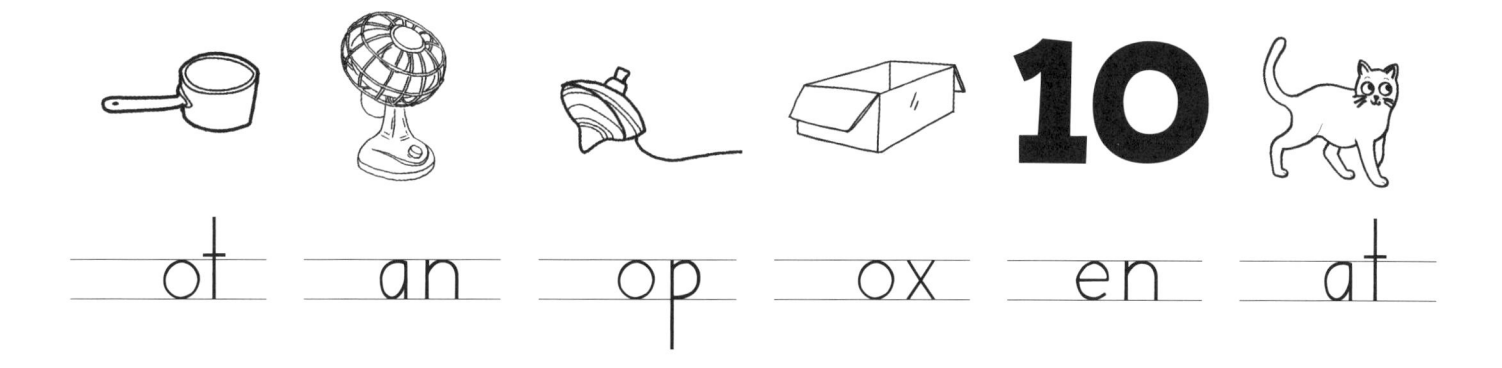

_ot   _an   _op   _ox   _en   _at

Look around. Find names that start with capital **T** and things that start with lowercase **t**.
Write the words.

Sam in the Sun | **Ss**

Understanding the Story: Setting

Circle the picture that shows where the story takes place.

Where is Sam in the story? Write about the place and draw a picture.

Ss Sam in the Sun

sun

Practice the Letter Ss

Say the letter name and the sound it stands for. Then, trace and write capital **S** and lowercase **s**.

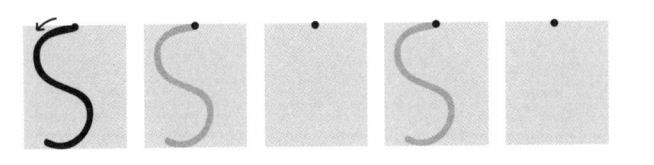

Say the name of each picture.
Write the letter that stands for the **beginning** sound to complete the word.

___at   ___un   ___ink   ___og   ___ix   ___an

Think of two things that start with the same beginning sound as **sun**. Draw them.

Rex and the Rake   Rr

Understanding the Story: Characters

Think about what Rex does and how he feels.
When does Rex feel confused about something in the story? Write and draw about it.

When does Rex feel upset and frustrated in the story? Write and draw about it.

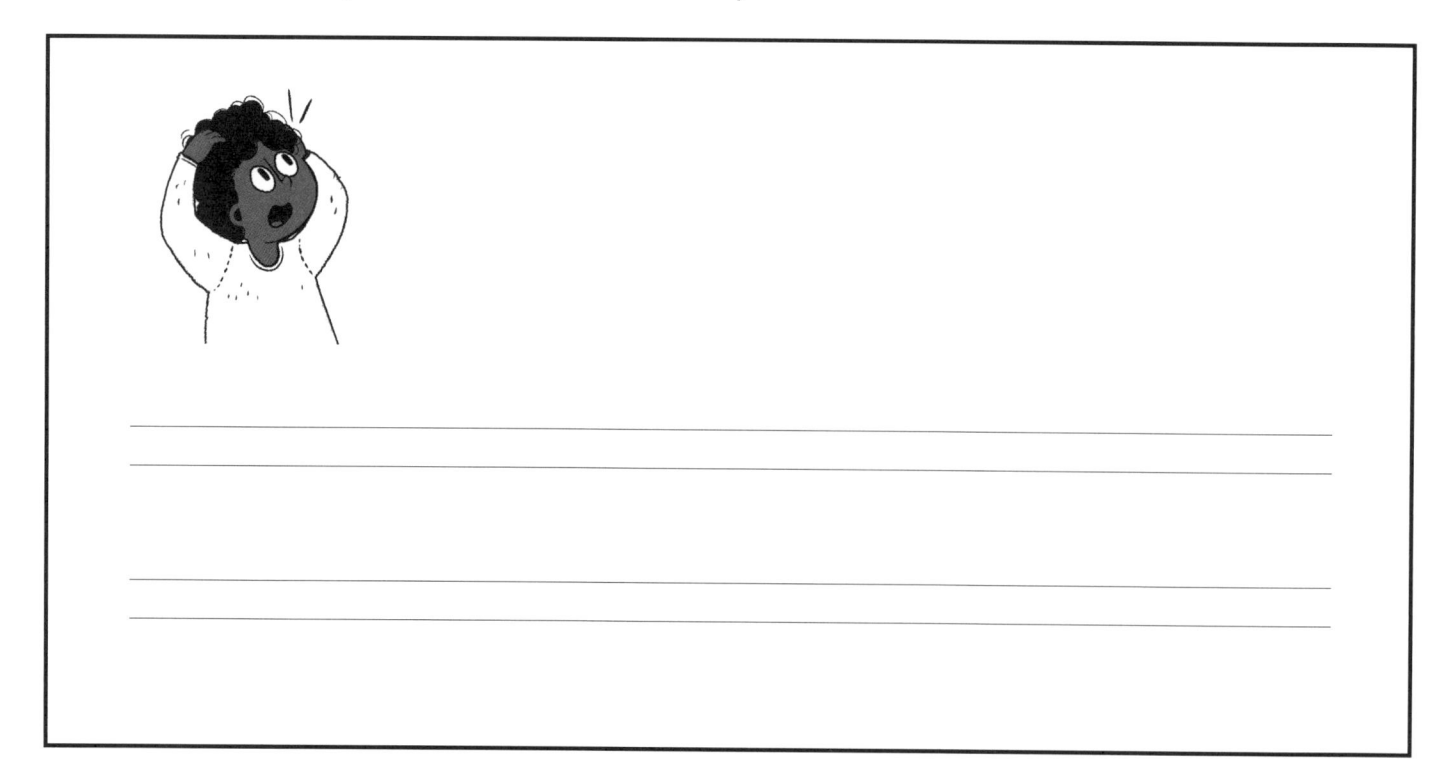

© 2022 Learning Without Tears   A–Z for Mat Man® and Me: Practice for Developing Readers - **Meaning Making**   41

Rr Rex and the Rake

rake

Practice the Letter **Rr**

Say the letter name and the sound it stands for. Then, trace and write capital **R** and lowercase **r**.

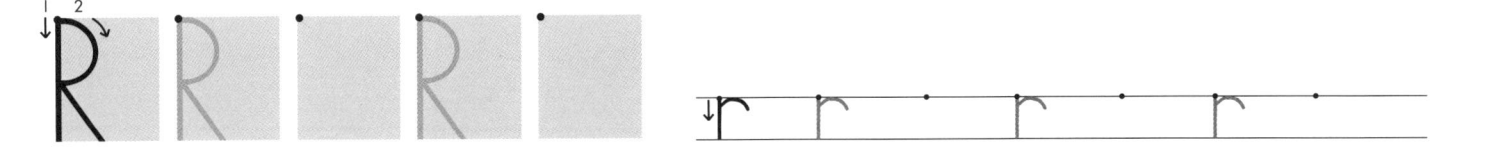

Say the name of each picture.
Write the letter that stands for the **beginning** sound to complete the word.

___oof ___an ___ocks ___un ___ug ___ips

Look around. Find names that start with capital **R** and things that start with lowercase **r**.
Write the words.

Quinn and the Quilt Qq

Understanding the Story: Events

Think about what happens in the story. The middle of the story is filled in. Now, draw and write about what happens in the beginning and end.

Beginning

Middle

"Dad!"

The quilt gets wet.

End

Qq Quinn and the Quilt

quilt

Practice the Letter Qq

Say the letter name and the sound it stands for. Then, trace and write capital Q and lowercase q.

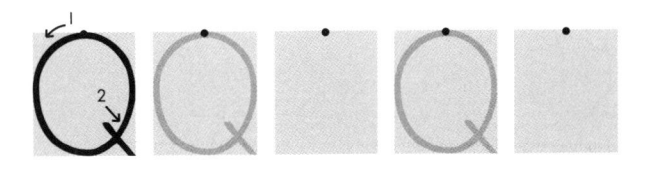

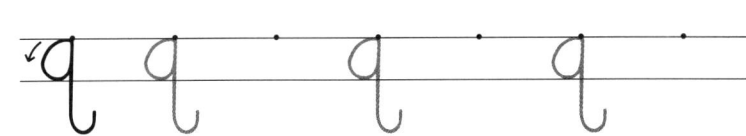

Read as much as you can. Then, circle every capital Q and lowercase q you see.

Monique has a duck.

Quack! Quack! Quack!

It is not quiet.

Raquan will get it.

Raquan can not.

The duck is quick!

Think of two things that start with the same beginning sound as **quilt**. Draw them.

Paco and the Piano Pp

Understanding the Story: Setting

Circle the picture that shows where the story takes place.

Write and draw about where Paco goes in the story.

Pp   Paco and the Piano

piano

Practice the Letter **Pp**

Say the letter name and the sound it stands for. Then, trace and write capital **P** and lowercase **p**.

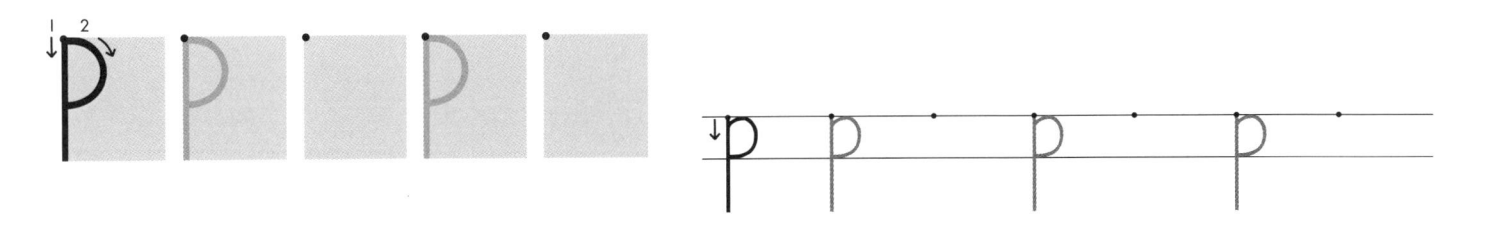

Say the name of each picture.
Write the letter that stands for the **beginning** sound to complete the word.

___ot   ___at   ___up   ___ig   ___ug   ___an

Look around. Find names that start with capital **P** and things that start with lowercase **p**.
Write the words.

Oz and the Octopus Oo

Understanding the Story: Events

Think about what happens in the story. The middle of the story is filled in. Now, draw and write about what happens in the beginning and end.

Beginning

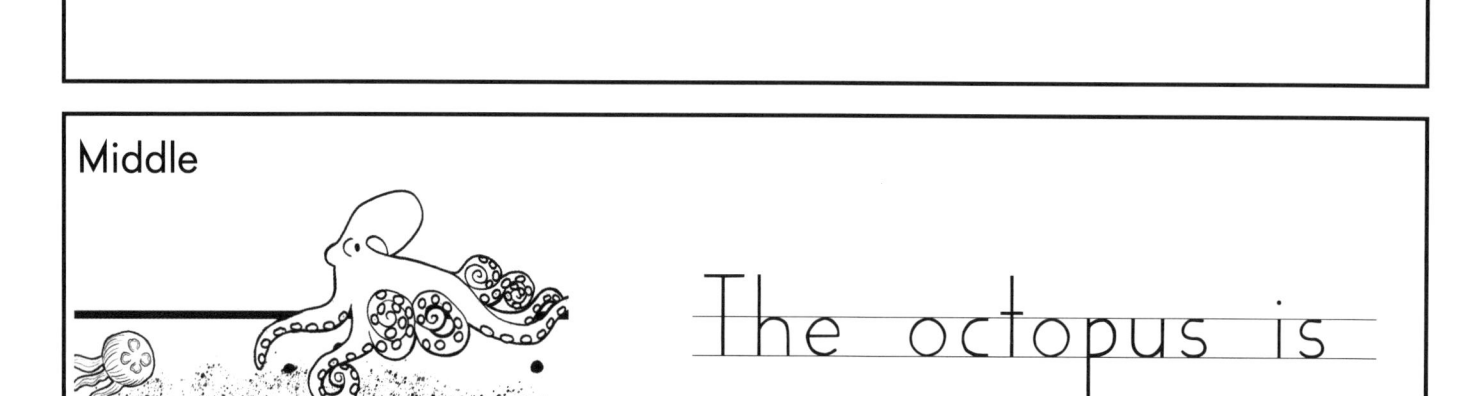

Middle

The octopus is on the tank.

End

© 2022 Learning Without Tears — A–Z for Mat Man® and Me: Practice for Developing Readers - **Meaning Making** — 35

Oo   Oz and the Octopus

octopus

Practice the Letter Oo

Say the letter name and the sound it stands for. Then, trace and write capital **O** and lowercase **o**.

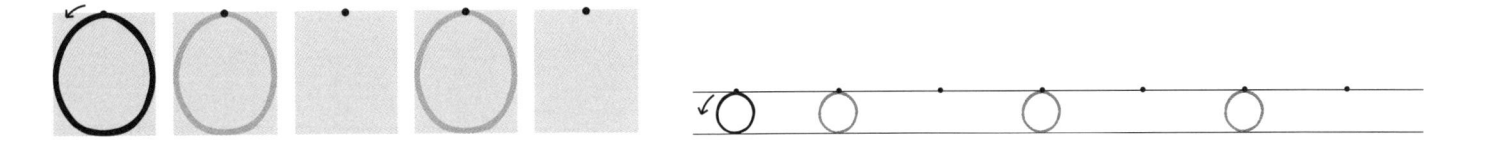

Say the name of each picture.
Write the letter that stands for the **middle** sound to complete the word.

f _ sh   m _ p

p _ t   l _ g

f _ n   d _ g

b _ d   c _ t

f _ x   b _ x

Nell and the Nest Nn

Understanding the Story: Setting

Circle the picture that shows where the story takes place.

Write and draw about the place where Nell is and why it is important to what happens in the story.

Nn Nell and the Nest

nest

Practice the Letter **Nn**

Say the letter name and the sound it stands for. Then, trace and write capital **N** and lowercase **n**.

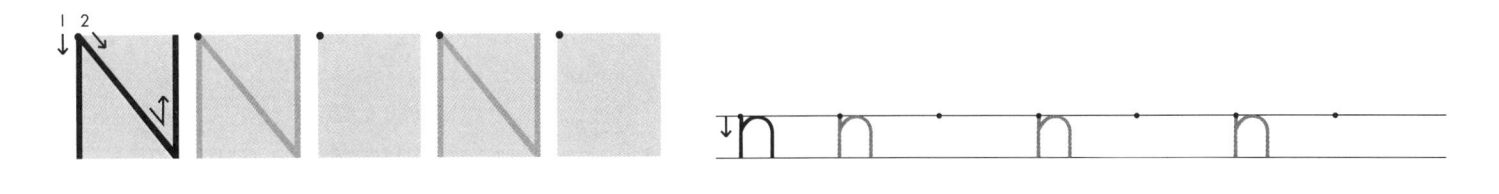

Say the name of each picture.
Write the letter that stands for the **beginning** sound to complete the word.

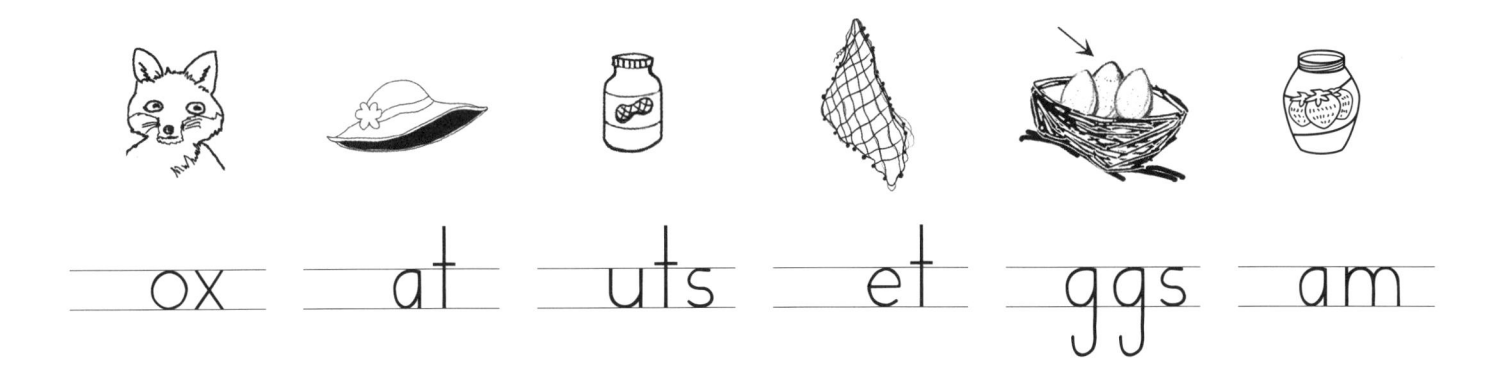

__ox   __at   __uts   __et   __ggs   __am

Think of two things that start with the same beginning sound as **nest**. Draw them.

32   A–Z for Mat Man® and Me: Practice for Developing Readers - **Letter Learning**   © 2022 Learning Without Tears

Mac and the Magnificent Masks

Understanding the Story: Events

Think about what happens in the story. The middle of the story is filled in. Now, draw and write about what happens in the beginning and end.

Beginning

Middle

Marcos tosses markers.

End

Mm Mac and the Magnificent Masks

mask

Practice the Letter Mm

Say the letter name and the sound it stands for. Then, trace and write capital **M** and lowercase **m**.

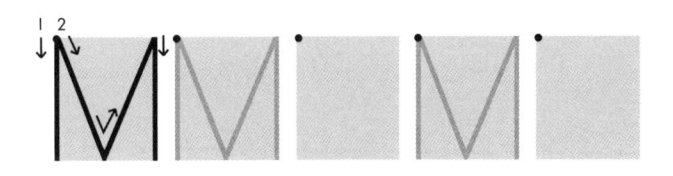

M M M   m m m m

Say the name of each picture.
Write the letter that stands for the beginning sound to complete the word.

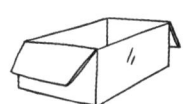

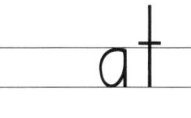

___op   ___ox   ___ug   ___at   ___ed   ___ick

Look around. Find names that start with capital **M** and things that start with lowercase **m**.
Write the words.

Lola and the Lock — Ll

Understanding the Story: Events
Where does Lola look for her lock? Draw and write about three places where Lola looks.

Ll Lola and the Lock

lock

Practice the Letter Ll

Say the letter name and the sound it stands for. Then, trace and write capital **L** and lowercase **l**.

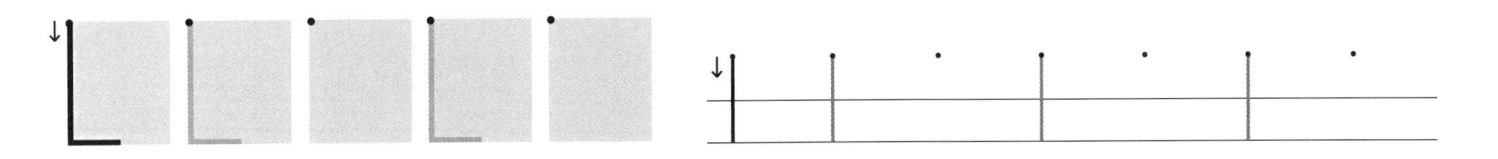

Say the name of each picture.
Write the letter that stands for the **beginning** sound to complete the word.

_eg   _un   _og   _ick   _ock   _og

Think of two things that start with the same beginning sound as **lock**. Draw them.

Kaya and the Kayak Kk

Understanding the Story: Setting
Circle the picture that shows where the story takes place.

Where is Kaya in the story? Write about the place and draw a picture.

Kk Kaya and the Kayak

kayak

Practice the Letter Kk

Say the letter name and the sound it stands for. Then, trace and write capital **K** and lowercase **k**.

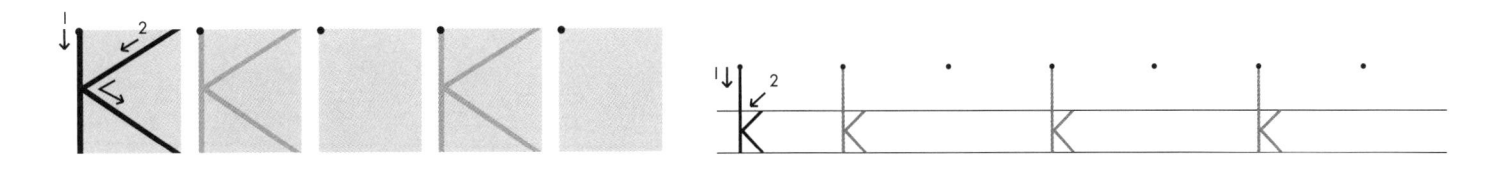

Say the name of each picture.
Write the letter that stands for the **beginning** sound to complete the word.

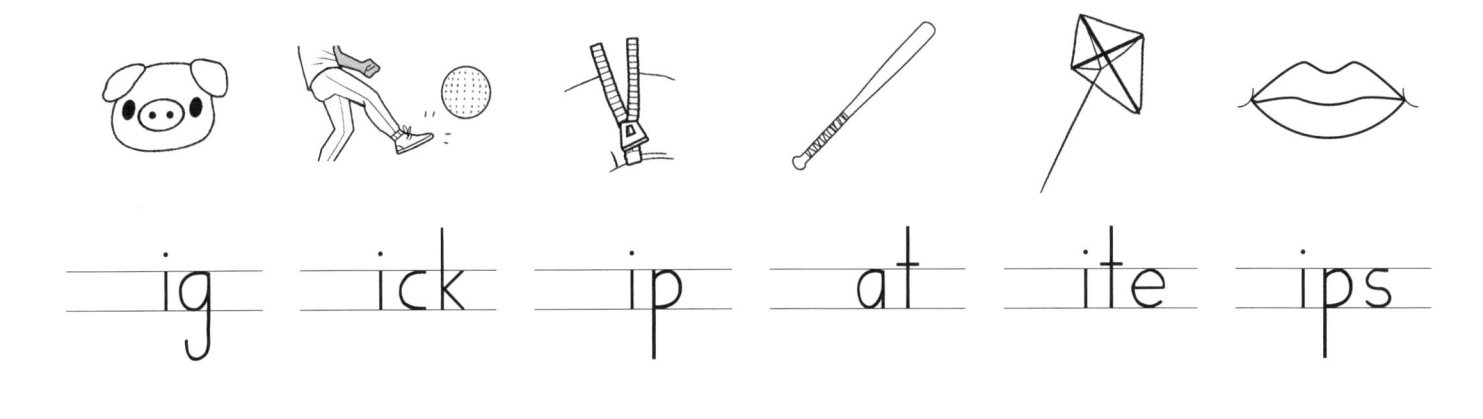

___ig   ___ick   ___ip   ___at   ___ite   ___ips

Look around. Find names that start with capital **K** and things that start with lowercase **k**.
Write the words.

Jana, Jen, and the Jellyfish   Jj

Understanding the Story: Character

Find the two main characters in the story. Circle two pictures.

Write about something the characters do in the story and draw a picture.

Jj Jana, Jen, and the Jellyfish

jellyfish

Practice the Letter Jj

Say the letter name and the sound it stands for. Then, trace and write capital **J** and lowercase **j**.

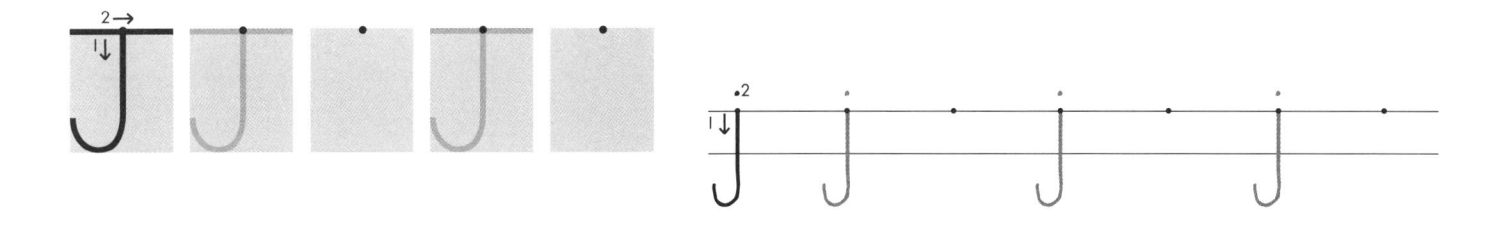

Say the name of each picture.
Write the letter that stands for the **beginning** sound to complete the word.

___un ___an ___am ___ox ___eep ___at

Think of two things that start with the same beginning sound as **jellyfish**. Draw them.

24   A–Z for Mat Man® and Me: Practice for Developing Readers - **Letter Learning**   © 2022 Learning Without Tears

Ikiaq and the Igloo Ii

Understanding the Story: Setting

Circle the picture that shows where the story takes place.

Write about a place from the story and draw a picture.

Ii Ikiaq and the Igloo

igloo

Practice the Letter Ii

Say the letter name and the sound it stands for. Then, trace and write capital **I** and lowercase **i**.

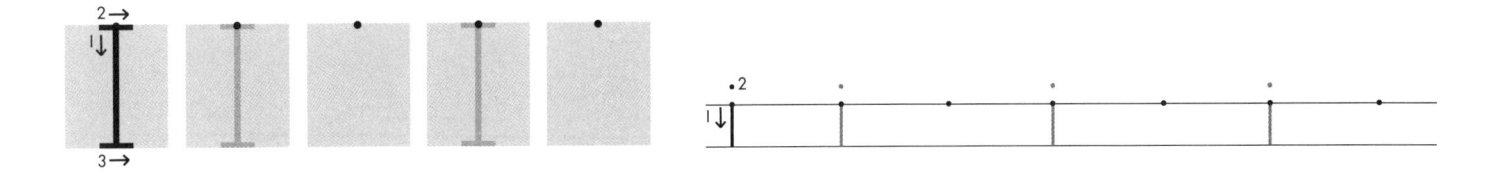

Say the name of each picture.
Write the letter that stands for the **middle** sound to complete the word.

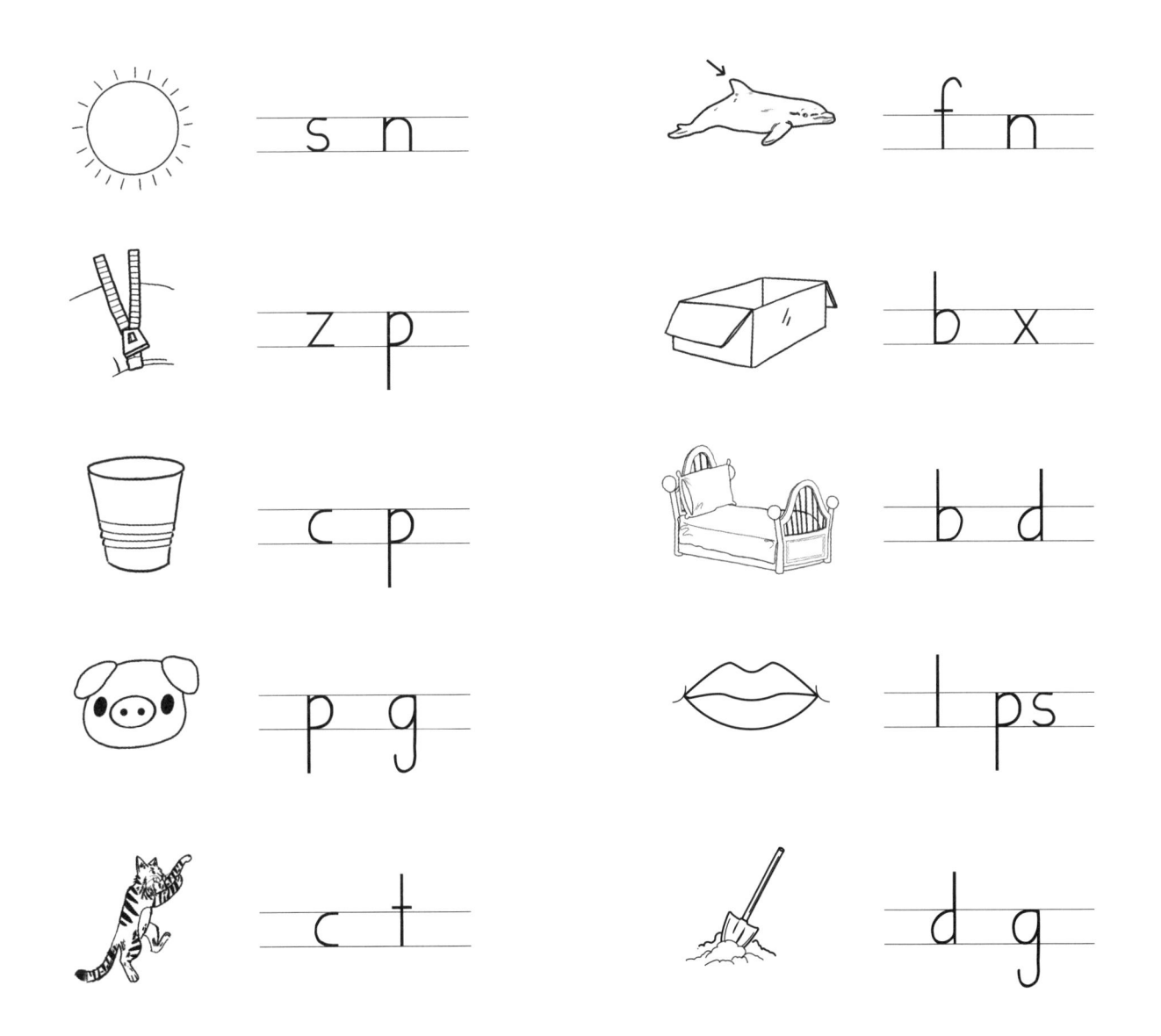

s _ n   f _ n

z _ p   b _ x

c _ p   b _ d

p _ g   l _ ps

c _ t   d _ g

Hana has a Hammer   Hh

Understanding the Story: Characters

Which animals get out in the story? Draw three that Hana has to chase. Write the names.

© 2022 Learning Without Tears — A–Z for Mat Man® and Me: Practice for Developing Readers - **Meaning Making**

Hh Hana has a Hammer

hammer

Practice the Letter Hh

Say the letter name and the sound it stands for. Then, trace and write capital **H** and lowercase **h**.

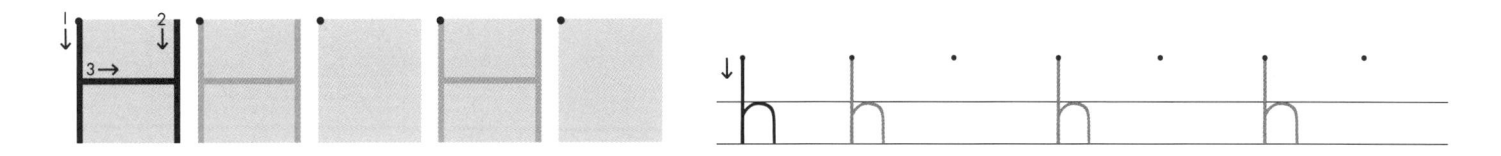

Say the name of each picture.
Write the letter that stands for the **beginning** sound to complete the word.

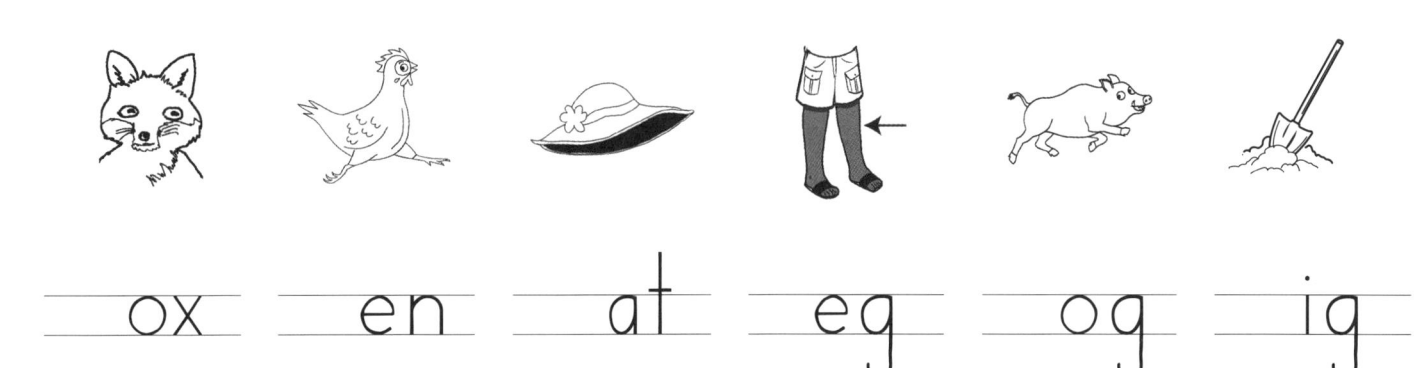

___ ox   ___ en   ___ at   ___ eg   ___ og   ___ ig

Look around. Find names that start with capital **H** and things that start with lowercase **h**.
Write the words.

Gabby and Her Goat

Gg

Understanding the Story: Events

What does Gus do in the story? Draw and write three things Gus gets.

Gg Gabby and Her Goat

goat

Practice the Letter Gg

Say the letter name and the sound it stands for. Then, trace and write capital **G** and lowercase **g**.

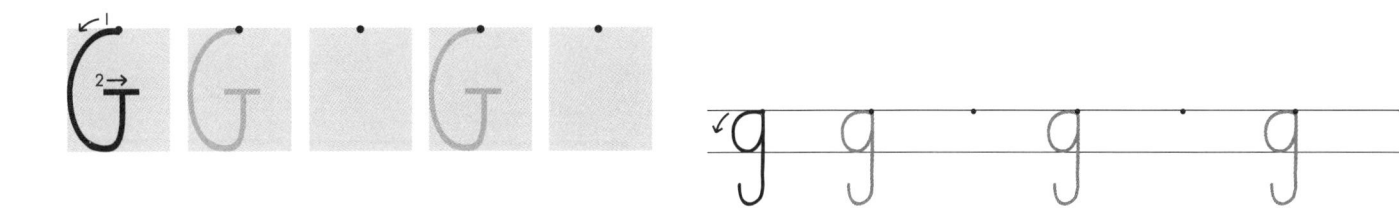

Say the name of each picture.
Write the letter that stands for the **ending** sound to complete the word.

ba___   mo___   do___   pi___   po___   ru___

Look around. Find names that start with capital **G** and things that start with lowercase **g**.
Write the words.

Feng, Finn, and the Fan Ff

Understanding the Story: Events

Think about what happens in the story. The middle of the story is filled in. Now, draw and write about what happens in the beginning and end.

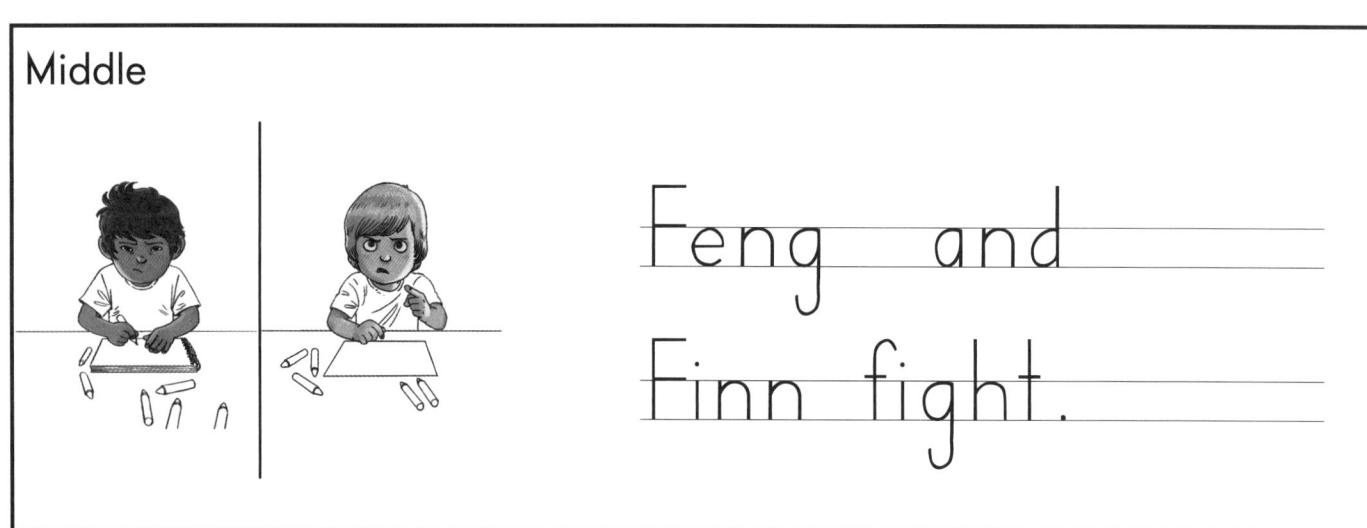

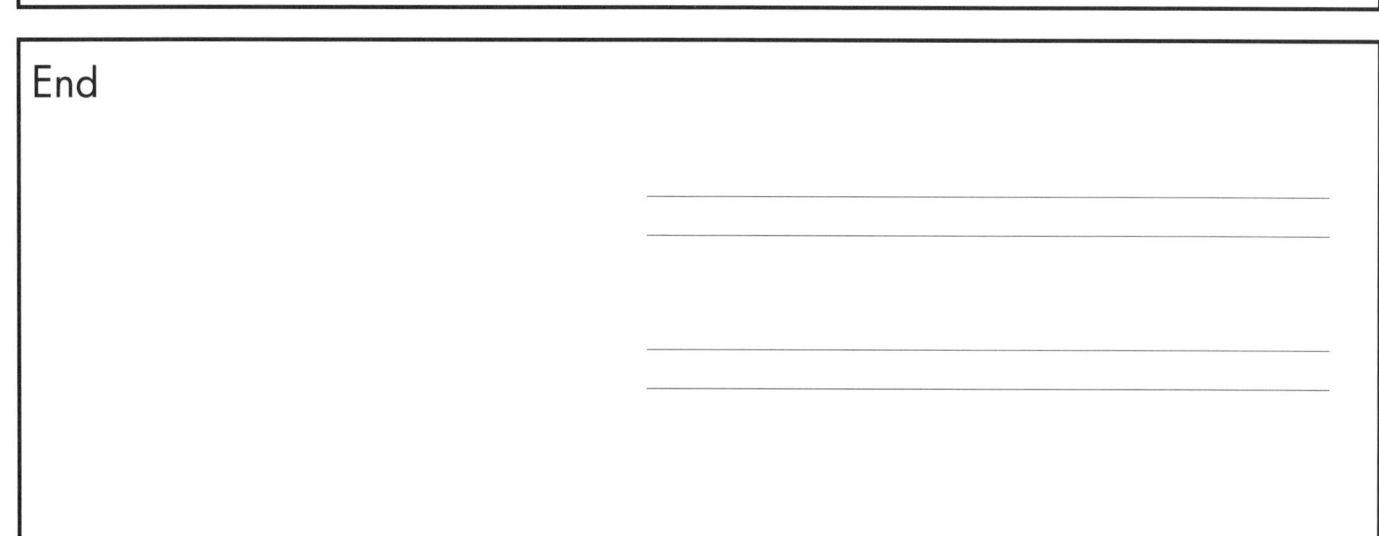

Beginning

Middle

Feng and
Finn fight.

End

© 2022 Learning Without Tears — A–Z for Mat Man® and Me: Practice for Developing Readers - **Meaning Making**

Ff — Feng, Finn, and the Fan

fan

Practice the Letter Ff

Say the letter name and the sound it stands for. Then, trace and write capital **F** and lowercase **f**.

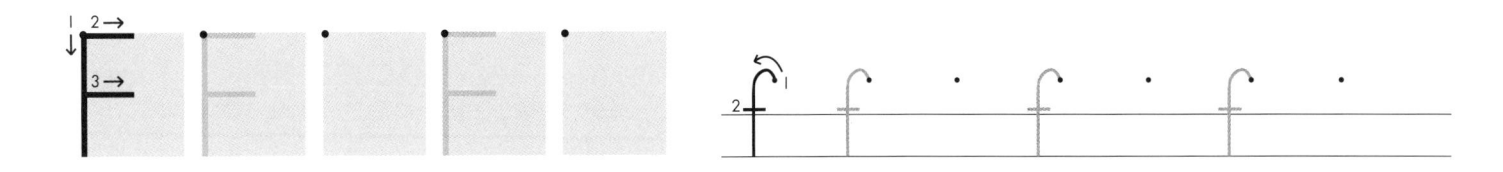

Say the name of each picture.
Write the letter that stands for the **beginning** sound to complete the word.

___at   ___an   ___ox   ___in   ___ox   ___am

Think of two things that start with the same beginning sound as **fan**. Draw them.

Emma and the Elephant Ee

Understanding the Story: Characters

Think about what Emma does and how she feels. When does Emma feel sad? Draw and write about it.

When does Emma feel happy in the story? Draw and write about it.

© 2022 Learning Without Tears — A–Z for Mat Man® and Me: Practice for Developing Readers - **Meaning Making** 15

Ee Cora and the Coconut

elephant

Practice the Letter Ee

Say the letter name and the sound it stands for. Then, trace and write capital **E** and lowercase **e**.

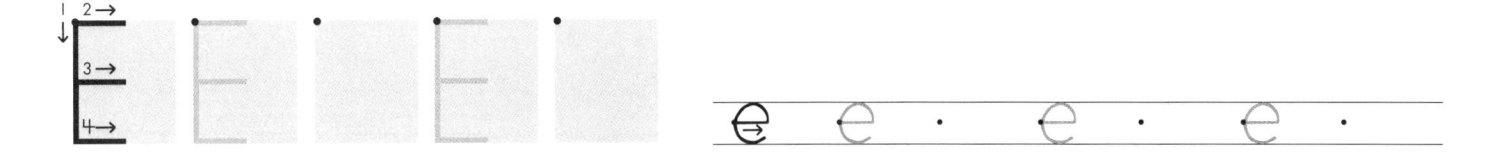

Say the name of each picture.
Write the letter that stands for the **middle** sound to complete the word.

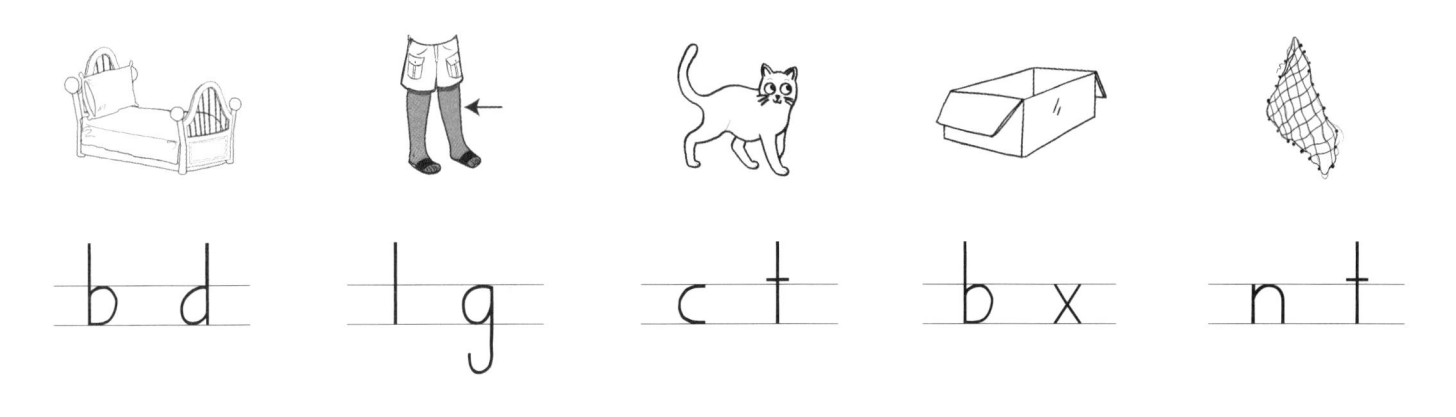

b_d   l_g   c_t   b_x   n_t

Look around. Find names that start with capital **E** and things that start with lowercase **e**.
Write the words.

Dax and the Dolphin Dd

Understanding the Story: Setting

Circle the picture that shows where the story takes place.

Where is Dax in the story? Write about the place and draw a picture.

Dd Dax and the Dolphin

dolphin

Practice the Letter Dd

Say the letter name and the sound it stands for. Then, trace and write capital **D** and lowercase **d**.

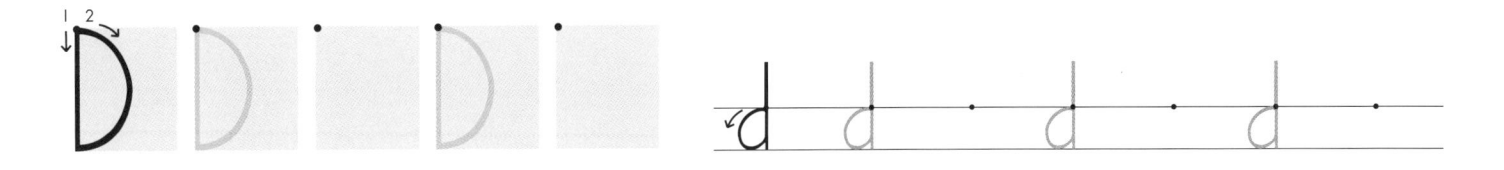

Say the name of each picture.
Write the letter that stands for the **beginning** sound to complete the word.

_ot

_ig

_uck

_et

_op

_an

_at

_ox

_og

_oll

12 A–Z for Mat Man® and Me: Practice for Developing Readers - Letter Learning

© 2022 Learning Without Tears

Cora and the Coconut Cc

Understanding the Story: Events

Think about what happens in the story. The middle of the story is filled in. Now, draw and write about what happens in the beginning and end.

Beginning

Middle

Cora holds up a cat.

End

© 2022 Learning Without Tears — A–Z for Mat Man® and Me: Practice for Developing Readers - **Meaning Making** — 11

Cc Cora and the Coconut

coconut

Practice the Letter Cc

Say the letter name and the sound it stands for. Then, trace and write capital **C** and lowercase **c**.

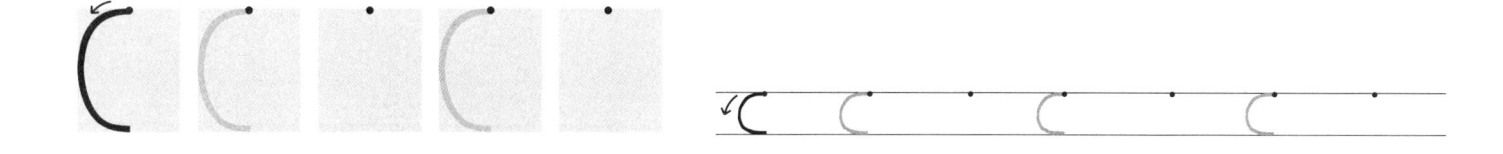

Say the name of each picture.
Write the letter that stands for the **beginning** sound to complete the word.

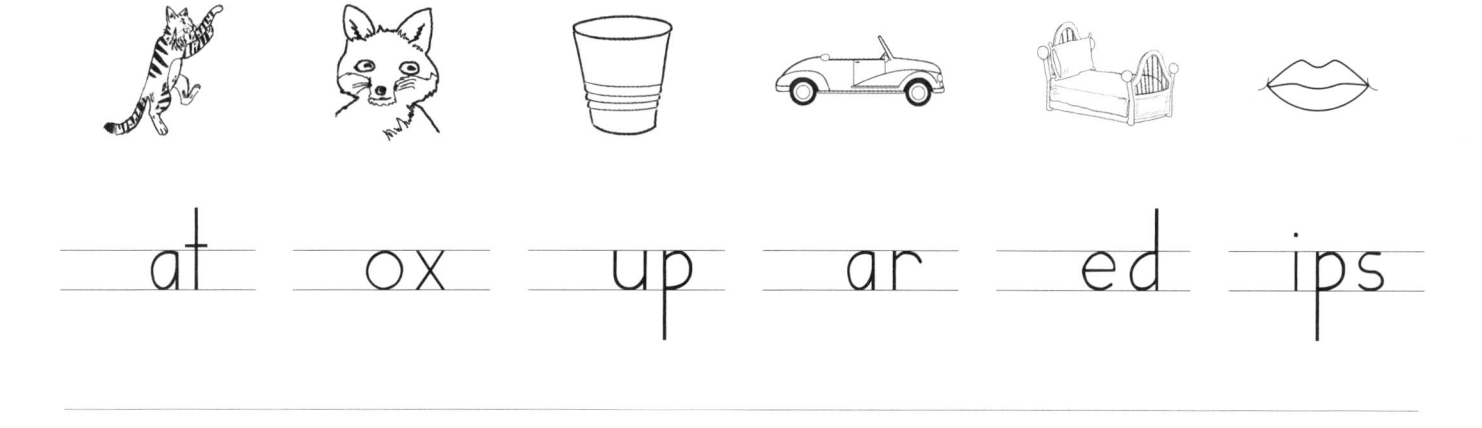

___at ___ox ___up ___ar ___ed ___ips

Look around. Find names that start with capital **C** and things that start with lowercase **c**.
Write the words.

Ben and the Big Bagels Bb

Understanding the Story: Setting

Circle the picture that shows where the story takes place.

Where is Ben in the story? Write about the place and draw a picture.

Bb Ben and the Big Bagels

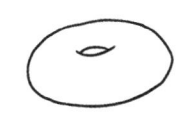

bagel

Practice the Letter **Bb**

Say the letter name and the sound it stands for. Then, trace and write capital **B** and lowercase **b**.

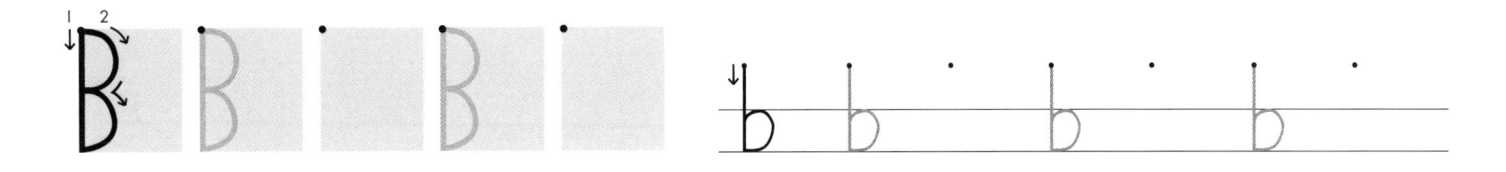

B B B B   b b b b b

Say the name of each picture.
Write the letter that stands for the **beginning** sound to complete the word.

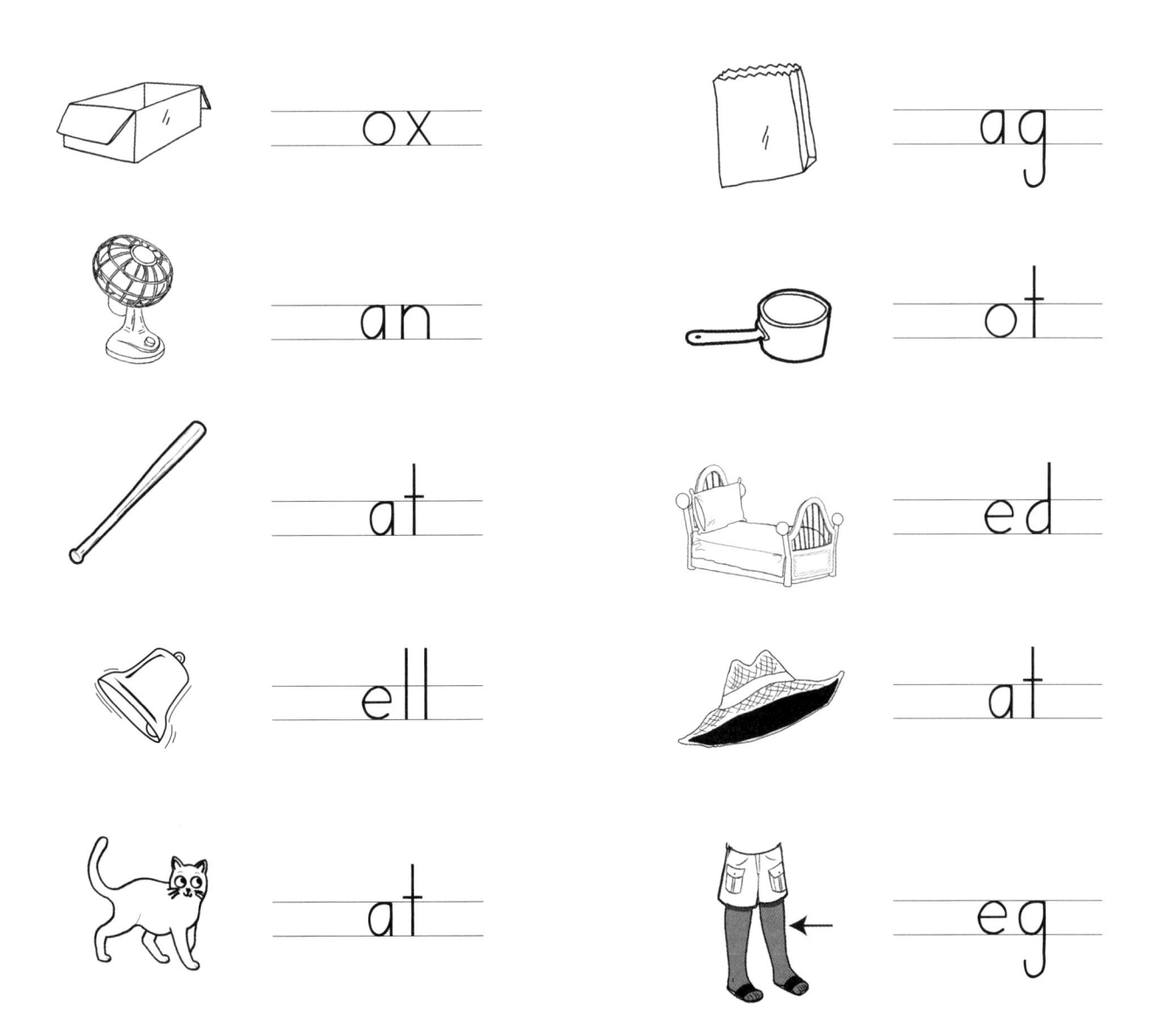

_ox   _ag

_an   _ot

_at   _ed

_ell   _at

_at   _eg

8   A–Z for Mat Man® and Me: Practice for Developing Readers - Letter Learning   © 2022 Learning Without Tears

Ally and the Apple   Aa

Understanding the Story: Events

Think about what happens in the story. The middle of the story is filled in. Now, draw and write about what happens in the beginning and end.

Beginning

Middle

Ally asks for help.

End

Aa Ally and the Apple

apple

Practice the Letter **Aa**

Say the letter name and the sound it stands for. Then, trace and write capital **A** and lowercase **a**.

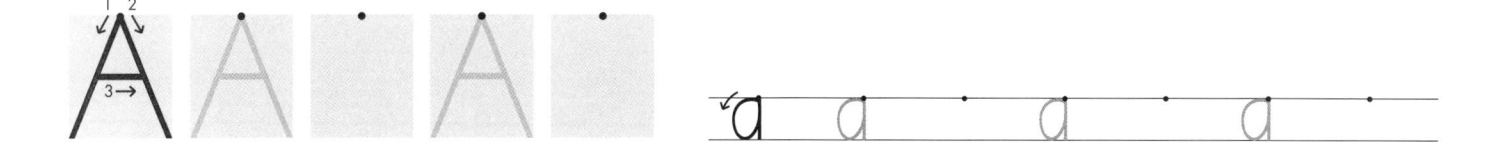

Say the name of each picture.
Write the letter that stands for the **middle** sound to complete the word.

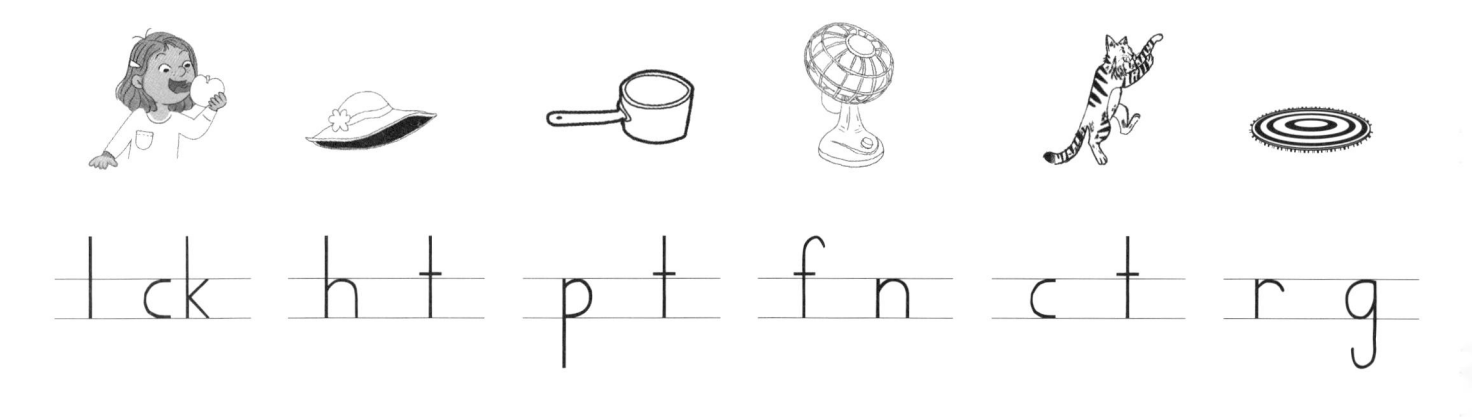

t _ ck   h _ t   p _ t   f _ n   c _ t   r _ g

Think of two things that start with the same beginning sound as **apple**. Draw them.

6 A–Z for Mat Man® and Me: Practice for Developing Readers - Letter Learning   © 2022 Learning Without Tears

Mat Man® and the Great Alphabet Parade

The First Letter in Your Name

First, ⬭circle⬯ the letter your first name starts with. Then, underline the letter your last name starts with.

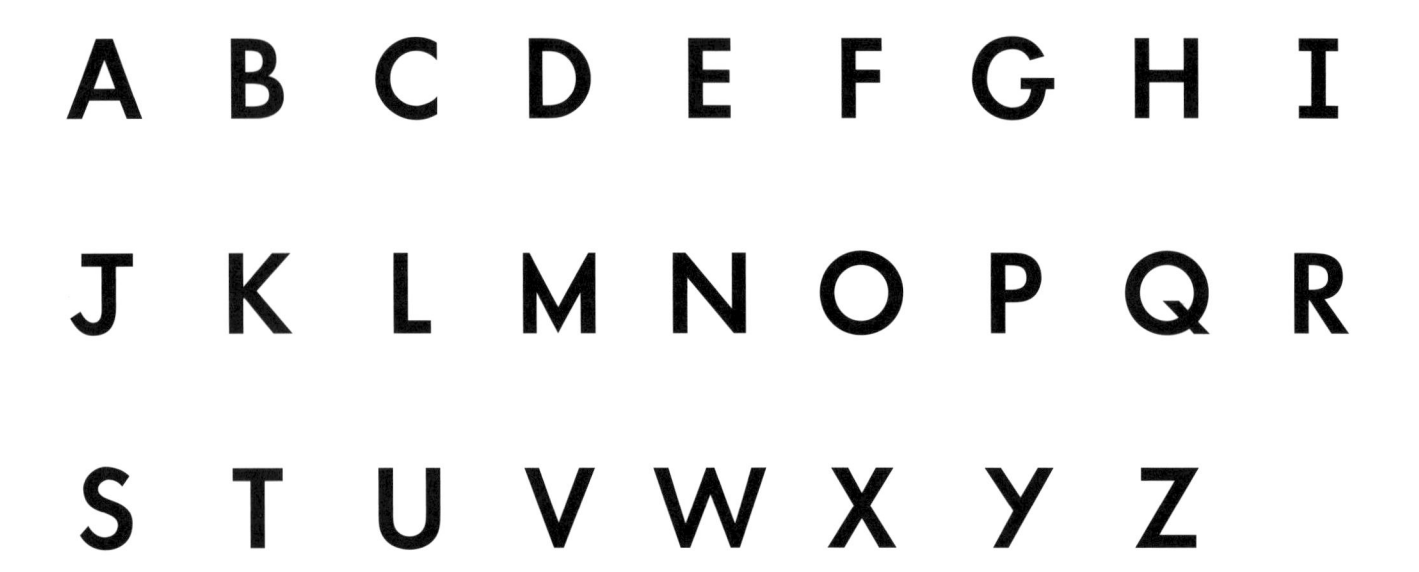

A B C D E F G H I

J K L M N O P Q R

S T U V W X Y Z

Draw a picture of something from the parade that starts with the same letter your first name starts with. Then, draw a picture of something that starts with the first letter in your last name.

© 2022 Learning Without Tears

A–Z for Mat Man® and Me: Practice for Developing Readers

Mat Man® and the Great Alphabet Parade

Sing the Alphabet Song

Help Mat Man sing the ABC song! Underline each letter as we sing it. The **a** is done for you. Then, color the pictures.

a b c d e f g

h i j k l m n o p

q r s

t u v

w x

y and z

TABLE OF CONTENTS

Sing the Alphabet Song 4

The First Letter in Your Name 5

Letter Aa: *Ally and the Apple*
Practice the Letter **Aa**..6
Understanding the Story: Events 7

Letter Bb: *Ben and the Big Bagels*
Practice the Letter **Bb**..8
Understanding the Story: Setting 9

Letter Cc: *Cora and the Coconut*
Practice the Letter **Cc**..10
Understanding the Story: Events 11

Letter Dd: *Dax and the Dolphin*
Practice the Letter **Dd**..12
Understanding the Story: Setting 13

Letter Ee: *Emma and Her Elephant*
Practice the Letter **Ee**..14
Understanding the Story: Character 15

Letter Ff: *Feng, Finn, and the Fan*
Practice the Letter **Ff**..16
Understanding the Story: Events 17

Letter Gg: *Gabby and Her Goat*
Practice the Letter **Gg**..18
Understanding the Story: Events 19

Letter Hh: *Hana Has a Hammer*
Practice the Letter **Hh**..20
Understanding the Story: Events 21

Letter Ii: *Ikiaq and the Igloo*
Practice the Letter **Ii**..22
Understanding the Story: Setting 23

Letter Jj: *Jana, Jen, and the Jellyfish*
Practice the Letter **Jj**..24
Understanding the Story: Character 25

Letter Kk: *Kaya and the Kite*
Practice the Letter **Kk**..26
Understanding the Story: Setting 27

Letter Ll: *Lola and the Lock*
Practice the Letter **Ll**..28
Understanding the Story: Events 29

Letter Mm: *Mac and the Magnificent Masks*
Practice the Letter **Mm**..30
Understanding the Story: Events 31

Letter Nn: *Nell and the Nest*
Practice the Letter **Nn**..32
Understanding the Story: Setting 33

Letter Oo: *Oz and the Octopus*
Practice the Letter **Oo**..34
Understanding the Story: Events 35

Letter Pp: *Paco and the Piano*
Practice the Letter **Pp**..36
Understanding the Story: Character 37

Letter Qq: *Quinn and the Quilt*
Practice the Letter **Qq**..38
Understanding the Story: Events 39

Letter Rr: *Rex and the Rake*
Practice the Letter **Rr**..40
Understanding the Story: Character 41

Letter Ss: *Sam in the Sun*
Practice the Letter **Ss**..42
Understanding the Story: Setting 43

Letter Tt: *Tere and the Tomato*
Practice the Letter **Tt**..44
Understanding the Story: Character 45

Letter Uu: *Umberto and the Umbrella*
Practice the Letter **Uu**..46
Understanding the Story: Events 47

Letter Vv: *Vic, Val, and the Vacuum*
Practice the Letter **Vv**..48
Understanding the Story: Character 49

Letter Ww: *Wes and the Watermelon*
Practice the Letter **Ww**..50
Understanding the Story: Setting 51

Letter Xx: *Xavier Gets an X-ray*
Practice the Letter **Xx**..52
Understanding the Story: Setting 53

Letter Yy: *Yolanda and the Yo-Yo*
Practice the Letter **Yy**..54
Understanding the Story: Events 55

Letter Zz: *Zack and His Zipper*
Practice the Letter **Zz**..56
Understanding the Story: Character 57

Letter Check 1 58

Letter Check 2 60

Letter Check 3 62

Letter Review..64

LEARNING
Without Tears®

8001 MacArthur Blvd.
Cabin John, MD 20818
LWTears.com | 888.983.8409

Art Director: Shannon Rutledge
Graphic Designer: Sammie Simon
Curriculum Designers: Adam Berkin, Nicole Iorio, Cari Meister, Casey Schultz

Copyright © 2022 Learning Without Tears
First Edition
ISBN: 978-1-954728-42-4
23456789RRD232221
Printed in Dongguan, China

The contents of this consumable workbook are protected by US copyright law. If a workbook has been purchased for a child, the author and Learning Without Tears give limited permission to copy pages for additional practice or homework for that child. No copied pages from this book can be given to another person without written permission from Learning Without Tears.

A-Z for Mat Man® and Me

Practice for Developing Readers

LEARNING Without Tears®